Community Care

Policy and Practice

Robin Means

and

Randall Smith

MACMILLAN

First published 1994 by
THE MACMILLAN PRESS LTD
Houndmills, Basingstoke, Hampshire RG21 2XS
and London
Companies and representatives
throughout the world

ISBN 0–333–54931–7 hardcover
ISBN 0–333–54932–5 paperback

A catalogue record for this book is available
from the British Library.

Printed in Hong Kong

Public Policy and Politics

Series Editors: Colin Fudge and Robin Hambleton

Public policy-making in Western democracies is confronted by new pressures. Central values relating to the role of the state, the role of markets and the role of citizenship are now all contested and the consensus built up around the Keynesian welfare state is under challenge. New social movements are entering the political arena; electronic technologies are transforming the nature of employment; changes in demographic structure are creating heightened demands for public services; unforeseen social and health problems are emerging; and, most disturbing, social and economic inequalities are increasing in many countries.

How governments – at international, national and local levels – respond to this developing agenda is the central focus of the *Public Policy and Politics* series. Aimed at a student, professional, practitioner and academic readership, it aims to provide up-to-date, comprehensive and authoritative analyses of public policy-making in practice.

The series is international and interdisciplinary in scope and bridges theory and practice by relating the substance of policy to the politics of the policy-making process.

Public Policy and Politics

Series Editors: Colin Fudge and Robin Hambleton

PUBLISHED

FORTHCOMING

To Joanna and Kate

Contents

List of Tables and Figures

Tables

Figures

Acknowledgements

Like most authors, our ability to produce a book has been dependent upon the support, advice, stimulation and criticism of a wide range of people. We have been particularly fortunate to work in an organisation, the School for Advanced Urban Studies (SAUS) at the University of Bristol, which is involved in research, consultancy and teaching not only in community care, but also in health, housing and public service management. More specifically, we would like to thank our colleagues Lyn Harrison, Lesley Hoyes, Rachel Lart, Philip Leather and Sheila Mackintosh for comments on earlier drafts. This has been backed up by detailed feedback on the first full draft from our academic editors (Colin Fudge and Robin Hambleton), from Steven Kennedy of the publishers from Keith Povey, Editorial Services Consultant, and from an anonymous reviewer. We found all their comments to be of enormous help, including the more critical ones.

The authors have been fortunate in being able to draw upon ongoing community care research at SAUS, and in this respect we would like to thank the Joseph Rowntree Foundation for its funding of research on community care reform implementation and the Gatsby Charitable Foundation for its support of a study on collaborative working in community care.

Even in such a positive environment, the production of a book is a long and arduous business. In this respect, we would like to thank family and friends for not only offering encouragement, but also for putting up with bouts of weekend and evening working. Finally, our ability to pull the book together owes much to secretarial staff at SAUS and, in particular, Lorraine Cantle and Jackie Carreyett.

The authors and publishers wish to thank the following who have kindly given permission for the use of copyright material: The Office of Population Censuses and Surveys for two tables from J. Martin, H. Meltzer and D. Elliot, *The Prevalence of Disability Among Adults*, 1988; School for Advanced Urban Studies for a table from M. Taylor, L. Hoyes, R. Lart and R. Means, *User Empowerment in Community Care: Unravelling the Issues*, 1992, and for an illustration from P. Hoggett, 'The Politics of Empowerment' in *Going Local*, no. 19, 1992; Oxford University Press for a table from P. Cambridge, 'Case Management in

Community Services: Organisational Responses' in *British Journal of Social Work*, vol. 22, no. 5, 1992; the Audit Commission for an illustration from *Community Care: Managing the Cascade of change*, 1992; Personal Social Services Research Unit for a table from M. Knapp, G. Wistow, J. Forder and B. Hardy, *Markets for Social Care: Opportunities, Barriers and Implications*, 1993: Basil Blackwell Ltd for a table from G. Wistow, M. Knapp, B. Hardy and C. Allen, 'From Providing to Enabling: Local Authorities and the Mixed Economy of Social Care' in *Public Administration*, vol. 70, no. 1, 1992, and for a table from J. Higgins, 'Defining Community Care: Realities and Myths' in *Social Policy and Administration*, vol. 23, no. 1, 1989; The Joseph Rowntree Foundation for a table from L. Watson and R. Cooper, *Housing with Care*, 1992; Professor Alan Walker and the Commission of the European Communities for a table from Eurobarometer Survey, *Age and Attitudes: Main Results from a Eurobarometer Survey*, 1993; St Helens Metropolitan Borough Council for a table from its *1992–93 Community Care Plan*, 1992.

Guide to Reading the Book

The aim of this book is to provide a context for and an overview of recent developments in community care in England and Wales. The examination of changes and continuities at national level is linked to specific local studies and to particular concerns about the role of the service user and carer in a mixed economy of welfare. Social services authorities have been officially designated as the lead agency for community care under the National Health Service and Community Care Act 1990, though it is arguable whether adequate resources have been made available to carry out their responsibilities effectively. It is also the case that a range of agencies is involved in the delivery of community care and the restructuring of the welfare system has widened that range. Collaboration between agencies such as health and local authorities has never been easy, and their increasing number has made working together even more difficult.

These are among the themes of this book, which is aimed at students on courses for the caring professions, social policy students and the reflective practitioner. The story is still unfolding, but the authors argue that the continuities may be as important for understanding what is happening as the changes brought about by the reforms in the policy and practice of community care in the early 1990s.

Chapter 1 introduces the notion of community care and locates it in the politics of health and social care and in the legislative framework. The extent of need for community-based services is examined and the chapter ends with a scrutiny of the key issues addressed in the book. Chapter 2 offers a perspective of community care over time and suggests that there has been a long history of neglect in the development of non-institutional services. Differing explanations for this neglect are outlined. Chapter 3 places community care in the contemporary context of the restructuring of welfare in the UK, starting in the mid-1980s with the run-up to the 1988 Griffiths Report, which offered an agenda for action, and following developments through the 1989 White Paper and the 1990 legislation and its associated policy guidance. The notions of post-Fordism and quasi-markets are introduced as plausible explanations for the direction in which policy change has gone. These notions also underlie the theme of Chapter 4, which reflects on whether the reforms are likely to lead to increased involvement and participation on the part of the consumers of services – users and carers. The first part of the chapter examines ideas about normalisation and ordinary living and also focuses on the contribution to the empowerment debate of the disability movement. The second half outlines various strategies of empowerment, covering 'exit', 'voice', consultation and rights.

Chapter 5 looks at the problems faced by the local authority social services department as lead agency in implementing the community care reforms. The uncertain political and financial climate provides a backcloth to a commentary on care management, the implications of a mixed economy of welfare, the concept of the purchaser–provider split and the emergence of a new funding regime for community care. Chapter 6 wrestles with the decades-old problem of collaboration between care agencies, particularly health and social care. It summarises theoretical approaches to collaborative working and the arguments about the differences between health and social care. The policy decision to close the long-stay institutions is examined for its impact on working together, including collaboration at the levels of planning and commissioning services. Chapter 7 looks at the part to be played by housing in the community care context, both supported and mainstream housing. In relation to the latter, issues of availability, affordability, repair and adaptations are examined in some detail, as this has traditionally been a neglected aspect of community care. The chapter ends with a comment on the prospects for an integrated service.

Chapter 8 outlines some of the community care issues faced by some other member states of the European Community, particularly Greece, Germany, Italy and Denmark. A number of themes are pursued, including the role of the family in caring, the part played by institutional care, working together, user empowerment and the salience of the mixed economy of welfare arguments. In the second part of the chapter, the institutions of the European Community are described briefly, together with an outline of the EC policy process. The impact of particular EC policies on community care are followed through in relation to older and disabled people and in terms of the agencies, such as local authorities, which are providers of community care. Finally Chapter 9 takes an overview on achievements so far, problems to be faced and the likelihood of policy failure. It ends with a summary of future challenges and future prospects.

1 Introducing Community Care

Over the past thirty years community care has come to be almost universally espoused as a desirable objective for service providers and users and a central pillar of policy for governments and politicians of all persuasions. This chapter provides the reader with an initial introduction to community care in terms of definitions, key issues, the legislative framework and the main agencies which are involved in policy making and implementation. The obvious starting point for a book about the policy and practice of community care is to offer a clear statement on what it understands by the term 'community care'. Which groups will be covered? Will the book cover unpaid care as well as paid care? Does it include institutional care as well as domiciliary services? Which health care services are included? What does 'community' mean in the context of the term 'community care'? These are simple questions but do not necessarily have simple answers. 'Community care' has long been a contested term used by different people in different ways at different points in time.

It is very difficult to pin down the exact source of the term 'community care'. In a 1961 lecture delivered to the National Association of Mental Health, Titmuss (1968) claimed he had tried and failed to discover in any precise form its social origins, but went on to reflect that:

> Institutional policies, both before and since the Mental Health Act of 1959, have, on the other hand and without a doubt, assumed that someone knows what it means. More and more people suffering from schizophrenia, depressive illnesses and other mental handicaps have been discharged from hospitals, not cured but symptom-treated and labelled 'relieved'. More and more of the mentally subnormal have been placed under statutory supervision in the community. (p. 105)

Titmuss' concern was that the reduced reliance on hospitals would not be balanced by a major expansion of community-based services. In the following year, the then Minister of Health, Enoch Powell, took the policy of community care one stage further with his 1962 Hospital Plan

1

which launched an official closure programme for large mental health and mental handicap hospitals and their replacement by a network of services to be provided in the community by local health and welfare services.

Although the origins of the term are obscure, it is clear that it was initially used to refer to a policy shift away from hospitals and towards community-based provision for mentally handicapped people and for people with mental health problems. However, the term soon began to be used in reference to the provision of services for elderly people and for people with physical disabilities. For example, the Chief Welfare officer at the Ministry of Health was claiming in 1964 that with regard to older people:

> the true centre of the picture so far as geriatric services are concerned, really has shifted, or is rapidly shifting to care in the community supported by domiciliary services, and the important thing is to remember that residential homes are in fact a vital and most important part of community service. (Aves, 1964, p. 12)

The context of this quotation was government concern about the cost of long-term hospital care for frail elderly people. The Chief Welfare Officer was justifying a move to a cheaper form of institutional care (local authority residential care) by referring to it as a community service.

The Chief Welfare Officer had included the residential home in her definition of community care. But this was increasingly challenged in the 1970s. Residential care was seen by many as an expensive form of provision which consumed resources which needed to be used to fund genuine community services such as home care, day care and sheltered housing (Bosanquet, 1978). By this definition, community care policies are about keeping people out of expensive hospital *and* residential home provision. But how was this to be achieved? *A Happier Old Age* was published by the then Labour Government as a discussion document (Department of Health and Social Security, 1978) and it asked whether a combination of suitable ordinary housing, high quality domiciliary services and more support for informal carers could keep the majority of frail elderly people out of expensive local authority residential care.

In the 1980s the definition of community care seemed to have been tightened by central government yet again. The White Paper response, *Growing Older*, to the discussion document was produced by a Conservative rather than Labour Government. It argued that:

Whatever level of public expenditure proves practicable and however it is distributed, the primary sources of support and care for elderly people are informal and voluntary ... It is the role of public authorities to sustain and, where necessary, develop – but never to displace – such support and care. Care in the community must increasingly mean by the community. (Department of Health and Social Security, 1981b, p. 3)

The overall message was that community care (that is, informal care) needed to be maximised, partly because it was cheaper than care based on the provision of state-provided domiciliary services. By this definition, community care becomes what Abrams (1977, p. 151) called 'the provision of help, support and protection to others by lay members of societies acting in everyday domestic and occupational settings'.

In the past, therefore, the term 'community care' has been used to argue for changes in service emphasis. The positive virtues of community care have been juxtaposed against expensive, rigid and bureaucratic alternatives, such as hospitals, residential care, and sometimes even domiciliary services. However, any legitimacy this approach might have had seems to have evaporated in recent years. The Wagner Committee (1988) review of residential care found it very difficult to distinguish between residential care services and care in the community services because of the growth of sheltered housing schemes, resettlement hostels and 'core and cluster' schemes. Equally, the boundaries between informal care and paid care have become blurred with the emergence of a variety of payment for caring schemes through tax allowances, social security benefits and social services payments, which are designed to increase the willingness of relatives, neighbours and volunteers to perform caring roles (Ungerson, 1992).

Increasingly, 'community care' is used to refer to the full spectrum of care and services received by certain groups. This is the approach adopted by the 1989 White Paper on community care, *Caring for People*, which states that:

Community care means providing the right level of intervention and support to enable people to achieve maximum independence and control over their own lives. For this aim to become a reality, the development of a wide range of services provided in a variety of settings is essential. These services form part of a spectrum of care, ranging from domiciliary support provided to people in their own homes, strengthened by the availability of respite care and day care for those with more intensive care needs, through sheltered housing, group homes and hostels where increasing levels of care are available, to residential care and nursing homes and long-stay hospital care for those for whom other forms of care are no longer enough. (Department of Health, 1989a, p. 9)

The White Paper explains that its focus is mainly upon the role of the statutory and independent sectors but that 'the reality is that most care is provided by family, friends and neighbours' (ibid.). The statutory and independent sectors are seen as responsible for providing social care (including housing), health care and appropriate social security benefits. This book takes a similarly broad view of what is meant by the term 'community care'. It thus considers not only informal support by unpaid carers but also the provision of the full spectrum of institutional and non-institutional services by the public, private and voluntary sectors.

The politics of community care

The last section provided a broad definition of community care for the purposes of this book but did not address the loaded power of the word 'community' within the term 'community care'. In a lecture delivered in 1961 Titmuss described community care as 'the everlasting cottage-garden trailer' and went on to remark:

Does it not conjure up a sense of warmth and human kindness, essentially personal and comforting, as loving as the wild flowers so enchantingly described by Lawrence in 'Lady Chatterley's Lover'? (1968, p. 104)

Over thirty years later, in more prosaic language, Baron and Haldane (1992) complained that 'today we are in a period of striking certainties about the value of community care, still strangely combined with silences and absences about the details of what care in the community means, and how it is to operate for the benefit of those with special needs' (p. 3).

But where does the positive power of the term 'community care' come from? Baron and Haldane argue that it flows from the fact that 'community' is what Raymond Williams (1976) calls a keyword in the development of culture and society. From the ninth century BC through to the present time, Williams is able to trace the use of the term 'community' to lament the recent passing of a series of mythical Golden Ages. Each generation perceives the past as organic and whole compared to the present. As Baron and Haldane point out, the term 'community' thus enables 'the continuous construction of an idyllic past of plenty and social harmony which acts as an immanent critique of contemporary social relations' (p. 4). Thus the call by politicians and policy makers to replace present systems of provision with community care feeds into this myth by implying that it is possible to recreate what many believe were the harmonious, caring and integrated communities of the past.

This perspective helps to explain the popularity of terms such as community care, community schools and community policing with politicians and policy makers. However, a key objective of our book is to delve beyond the rhetoric of community care and caring communities. For example, several authors have pointed out that individuals and not communities carry out caring work, and that unpaid care is primarily carried out by female relatives (see Chapters 2 and 4). Equally, most people, including the users of community care services, have a highly complex notion of community. For some it is a small number of local streets, and for others their sense of community may come from work or leisure networks which are not geographically based. The provision of community care services based on local authority boundaries rarely reflects how service users perceive community. A day centre may not seem like a community service to a user who has to travel there three miles by specialist bus.

The book does refer repeatedly to community care and the community care reforms, despite the above comments. The term 'community care' is now almost universally used and has legislative credence through the NHS and Community Care Act 1990. To have placed inverted commas around the term community care each time it was used would have made an important point but at the likely cost of severe irritation for the reader. The word 'reform' is used extensively with regard to the 1990 Act because the legislation ushers in major changes, but this does not imply that the authors believe these changes will necessarily prove beneficial for service users.

Throughout this book we use the terms 'older people' or 'frail older people' rather than phrases such as 'the elderly'. This emphasises the 'people status' rather than the 'thing status' of older people (Fennell,

Phillipson and Evers, 1988). We also use phrases such as 'physically disabled people', 'people with mental health problems' and 'people with learning disabilities' to make the same point. The last phrase reflects the growing rejection of the term 'mental handicap' as stigmatising to people with a learning disability. Finally, the term 'carer' is used to refer to people who carry out what are mainly unpaid caring or personal assistance tasks for others.

The range of needs to which community care services are intended to respond are constantly being expanded. The community care changes associated with the 1990 Act emphasise that local authorities now have major responsibilities for people with HIV/AIDS and for people with alcohol and drug abuse problems. *Community Care: Policy and Practice* does not attempt to address the needs of these 'newer' groups in detail, although much of the general discussion is highly relevant to those involved in providing services for these groups. Indeed, a major difficulty faced by the authors was the mushrooming literature associated with all the main care groups, most of which now have an academic journal devoted to exploring different aspects of disability in relation to them. We hope, however, that we have done justice to the key insights provided by these specialist literatures.

How many users? How many carers?

So far, Chapter 1 has offered definitional guidance on various aspects of community care. However, this leaves open the question of how many people are either receiving services or who have disabilities which relate to the care group definitions. It also fails to address how many relatives and friends are providing personal assistance and caring roles on behalf of such people.

In the mid-1980s, the Office of Population Censuses and Surveys (OPCS) was commissioned by the DHSS to carry out a series of surveys of the prevalence, range and severity of disability in Great Britain. The survey distinguished thirteen different types of disability based on the international classification of impairments, disabilities and handicaps used by the World Health Organisation (see Table 1.1). The survey team also developed a classification system for severity of disability which could be used to classify people with different numbers and types of disabilities. The severity of disability in each of the thirteen areas was established for each individual and the three highest scores were then

Table 1.1   *Estimate of numbers of disabled adults in Great Britain with different types of disability (thousands)*

Type of disability	In private households	In establishments	Total population
Locomotion	4 005	327	4 332
Reaching and stretching	1 083	147	1 230
Dexterity	1 572	165	1 737
Seeing	1 384	284	1 668
Hearing	2 365	223	2 588
Personal care	2 129	354	2 483
Continence	957	185	1 142
Communication	989	213	1 202
Behaviour	1 172	175	1 347
Intellectual functioning	1 182	293	1 475
Consciousness	188	41	229
Eating, drinking, digesting	210	66	276
Disfigurement	391	*	*

* data not provided.
Source: Martin, Meltzer and Elliot (1988) p. 25.

combined so that people could be allocated to an overall severity category. Category one was for the least severe, and category ten was for the most severe. Two pen pictures of 'typical' examples from severity categories 2 and 9 are provided in Table 1.2.

With regard to adults, it was estimated that six million people in Great Britain have one or more disabilities, of whom 400000 are living in some kind of communal establishment. One million adults are assigned to the lowest severity category. Smaller numbers are identified in each successive category, with 200000 in category ten. Elderly people dominated the two highest degrees of severity:

The rate of disability at this level of severity did not rise steeply until age 70, and rose very steeply after 80. Altogether 64% of adults with this degree of severity were aged 70 or over; 41% were aged 80 or over. (Martin, Meltzer and Elliot, 1988, p. xii)

With regard to types of disability, problems of locomotion were found to dominate (over four million adults) followed by difficulties with hearing and personal care (see Table 1.1). A separate report was published on

Table 1.2   *'Pen pictures' of typical cases*

Severity category 2

Case: Man aged 75
Overall severity score 4.25

Intellectual functioning score 3.5
Often forgets what was supposed to be doing in the middle of something
Often loses track of what's being said in the middle of a conversation
Often forgets to turn things off, such as fires, cookers or taps

Behaviour score 1.5
Sometimes sits for hours doing nothing
Finds it difficult to stir himself to do things

Hearing score 0.5
Has difficulty following a conversation against background noise

Severity category 9

Case: Man aged 30
Mentally retarded
Overall severity score 17.55

Dexterity score 10.5
Cannot pick up and hold a mug of coffee with either hand
Cannot squeeze out water from a sponge with either hand
Has difficulty serving food from a pan using a spoon or ladle
Cannot pick up and carry a 5lb bag of potatoes with either hand

Behaviour score 10.5
Gets so upset that hits other people or injures himself
Gets so upset that breaks or rips things up
Feels the need to have someone present all the time
Finds relationships with members of the family very difficult

Consciousness score 7.0
Has fits once a year but less than 4 times a year
Loses consciousness during a fit

Locomotion score 6.5
Cannot walk up and down a flight of 12 stairs

Communication score 5.5
Finds it quite difficult to understand people who know him well

Continence score 4.0
Loses control of bowels occasionally

Source: Adapted from Martin, Meltzer and Elliot (1988) pp. 13–15.

disability amongst children (Bone and Meltzer, 1989) and this concluded that 360000 children in Great Britain have some degree of disability, of which 2 per cent live in some kind of communal establishment. The most common disabilities are to do with behaviour, followed by disabilities in the areas of communication, locomotion and continence.

However, great care needs to be taken with this type of approach to defining disability, for a number of reasons. First, the overall figures are open to challenge as over- or under-estimates because they are very dependent on the assumptions made by the researchers. For example, the Mental Health Foundation (1993) has estimated that three million Britons have severe mental health problems and twelve million adults approach general practitioners every year with a mental health problem, but only seven million are correctly diagnosed as needing help. Second, the OPCS approach is driven by medical rather than social assessments of the meaning and implications of disability. Hence, the focus is on personal inadequacy or functional limitation, rather than on the disabling impact of many physical and social environments (Abberley, 1991). For example, many people defined as having major locomotion difficulties in the OPCS survey may be suffering from a societal failure to build housing to mobility or wheelchair standard rather than from their own 'limitations'. The OPCS approach can also be criticised for trying to draw strict lines on the types and severity of disabilities experienced by individuals where the situation is in reality much more blurred and perhaps constantly changing. The episodic nature of some mental health problems is but one example of this.

A rather different issue is that a national profile of disabled people is not the same as a profile of community care service users. The OPCS surveys did identify that general practitioners were playing a key role in terms of contact with disabled people, since 82 per cent of those in private households had seen their GP in connection with their disability in the last twelve months (Martin, White and Meltzer, 1989). The survey also found that the 30 per cent of disabled adults who lived alone were more likely than others to receive services from their local authority. Thus, 75 per cent of the most severely disabled received home care compared with just under 20 per cent of those who lived with others. However, the next section underlines the wide range of services and entitlements which exist and how this relates to the patchwork quilt nature of British legislation.

The OPCS surveys also confirmed the extent to which disabled people receive help and support from informal carers. The 1985 General

Household Survey indicated that there were 3.5 million female carers and 2.5 million male carers, but that women were far more likely than men to be full-time carers. Only 6 per cent of those carers were in contact with social workers while only 23 per cent were receiving back-up from the home help service and 7 per cent from meals-on-wheels services (Green, 1988). The research on caring is now extensive and Finch (1989) has argued that this indicates a 'hierarchy of obligations', based around four principles:

1. The marriage relationship takes primacy, so that one's spouse becomes the first support for married people.
2. The parent–child relationship is the second source of obligation, with children being a major source of support for elderly parents and parents being the principal supporters of adult handicapped children.
3. People who are members of a household are major providers of care, so that a child who shares a home with his/her parents is much more likely to be giving them personal care than any siblings living away from the family home.
4. Gender is a crucial factor, so that women are much more likely to become the carers when there is an apparent choice between male and female relatives.

For feminist social scientists, the gendered nature of this caring activity is a major issue within their more general critique of the impact of the welfare state on women (Wilson, 1977; Land, 1978). Their central complaint is that women are carrying out unpaid domestic labour to the advantage of both central government and of men. The consequence of this for women is stress, poverty and a financial reliance on men and the state (Finch and Groves, 1983; Dalley, 1988).

The legislative framework

It is now necessary to ground our book on the policy and practice of community care within the realities of the legal and administrative framework in which it operates. If our concern was child care, it would be possible to focus down upon a single Act, namely the Children Act 1989. Prior to this, child care law was fragmented across the statute book in numerous different Acts, some of which dated back to the

1930s. However, the NHS and Community Care Act 1990 made no such effort to draw all the relevant legislation together and so a very complex patchwork of community care law remains (Fishwick, 1992) which makes it very difficult for local authorities and health authorities, let alone service users and their carers, to be absolutely clear about all their duties, powers and responsibilities. The National Assistance Act 1948 remains the pivotal piece of legislation with regard to residential provision and the legislative situation with regard to the provision of domiciliary services is even more complex. For example, the Chronically Sick and Disabled Persons Act 1970 made local authorities responsible for finding out the numbers of disabled people within their area and required them to offer a range of services to those persons. The Disabled Persons (Services, Consultation and Representation) Act 1986 increased the rights of disabled people to be assessed for such services.

The situation with regard to people with mental health problems is rather different since the bulk of powers affecting them are contained within the Mental Health Act 1983 and the accompanying code of practice. These place an emphasis on providing community services to meet individual need, and also stress that admission to hospital for treatment should be voluntary where possible. However, the Act and the code also outline the compulsory admission powers of the state through the approved social worker system. The Act also specifies a system of guardianship (initially for up to six months) for those receiving treatment and services in the community who are deemed to need either direction or protection.

It is now necessary to say something about the policy and organisational context which is responsible for generating this legislation and for ensuring its implementation. The mapping exercise carried out by Hunter and Wistow (1987) illustrated the enormous complexity of these systems at national and local level, and hence it would be easy to overwhelm the reader with detail. However, since our central concern is the community care reforms which have allocated a lead agency role to social services, our mapping focus will be on social services departments and the various local actors and organisations which influence their attempts to fund, co-ordinate and deliver community care provision.

Our starting point is to stress the need to grasp the complexity and variety of the 116 social services departments (SSDs) in England and Wales, and the twelve social work departments in Scotland. Challis (1990, p. 2) has argued that 'the claim which SSDs can make to being something special in the world of organisations does not rest on any one unique feature but upon the dazzling array of problematic characteristics which they exhibit'. These include the accountability of officers to members, the wide range of responsibilities, the variety of employed staff and high media interest. One consequence of this situation, and in particular the location of social services in local government, has been a history of organisational variation. Individual departments can split their activities by such categories as client age (for example, child care services and adult services), geography (for example, north and south of the authority) and function (for example, field services and residential care services) and these dimensions can be combined in a variety of complex ways.

Variation in organisational form is matched by variations in the range and depth of services provided by different social services authorities. A mid-1980s study by the Audit Commission (1985) on services for elderly people in seven different authorities found wide differences, both in terms of residential places per 1000 elderly people and in terms of expenditure on domiciliary services. This was particularly marked with certain services such as day care. The Audit Commission found that none of their authorities had a clear statement about the objectives of providing day care. Facilities varied considerably, while attendance frequency differed from a norm of one day per week to four or more times per week.

Such organisational and service variation is partly a reflection of the fact that social services are part of local government, where councillors from different political parties have differing views about what kinds of services should be provided and how best they should be delivered. Clough (1990) provides one of the few detailed considerations of social services departments as a part of local government. He describes both the formal policy-making system of the full social services committee and also the more informal meetings and contacts which ensure that most decisions have been made prior to full committee meetings. In deciding on priorities for future service developments, local authorities vary in the extent to which they are officer- or councillor-driven. Tensions between the two are common, partly because of the external pressures they face (see Figure 1.1). Many of them are top-down pressures from central government. These flow from such factors as the strengths and weaknesses of the legislation, Treasury-driven financial restrictions as well as the guidance issued by the Department of Health on good practice. Against this, councillors are struggling with a range of professional opinions from social services managers, health managers and others about the

Figure 1.1 *Pressures upon social services committees*

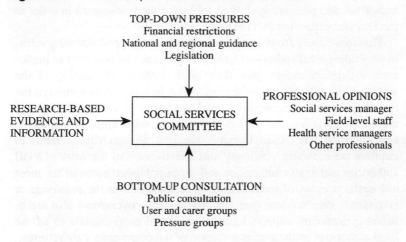

direction that community care policy should take in their authority. Both the local professionals and those responsible for central government guidance also make reference to research-based evidence to justify their views. Finally, members see themselves as the conduit for the views of local people in terms of public consultation. However, professional staff are also increasingly taking responsibility for organising consultation meetings with specific groups of service users and carers, so as to increase their ability to influence service developments, and the disability movement is calling for a fundamental change to the way professionals engage with the consumers of their services.

Working out these conflicting pressures in respect of the community care reforms is a central focus of this book. This section concludes by examining the top-down pressures from central government. What are the mechanisms by which guidance is issued by central government to local authorities on how they should develop services? In terms of the legislation, much of it is permissive and discretionary in nature rather than mandatory and authoritative. In the past, various attempts have been made by central government to establish service norms for provision such as residential care and the home help service, and these have usually been expressed as the number of places required per one thousand of the care group (Hambleton, 1986). However, more recently such norms have been seen as idiosyncratic in that the origins and justification for the norms are difficult to pin down. Equally, they are seen by central government as problematic because they can be used by local authorities and pressure groups to lobby for more resources in order to fund service expansion to meet those norms.

This move away from service norms has not stopped central government sending local authorities a mass of guidance on how best to implement legislation and on how they might improve the quality of the services they deliver or commission. Much of this is issued through the Social Services Inspectorate of the Department of Health. Social services authorities are also subjected to various other kinds of inspection and guidance. The Audit Commission is a quango with a remit to improve the economy, efficiency and effectiveness of the work of local authorities and health authorities and it has published some of the most influential reviews of local authority performance in the provision of community care services (see Chapter 3). The government also established a temporary support force of seconded professionals to advise local authorities on the implementation of the community care reforms.

Key issues in community care

Many of the key issues and dilemmas in community care which form the central concerns of this book have already been touched upon in this chapter, which concludes by drawing out five of the most important debates. The first debate concerns the most appropriate role, if any, for institutions such as hospitals, residential homes and nursing homes in the provision of health and social care to the main community care groups. The next two chapters examine in some detail the emergence of institutions as the main form of provision and subsequent attempts to shift service delivery towards approaches which enable people to remain within their own homes. Later chapters consider whether the implementation of the community care reforms has led to an obsession with the new funding'regime for residential and nursing homes to the detriment of attempts to switch resources to the development of innovative and non-institutional services. In addition, policies of institutional closure will not lead to the improved well-being of service users unless good quality care services are backed up by housing policies which deliver affordable and appropriate housing to those with personal assistance and care needs, an issue which is explored in Chapter 7.

The second key issue concerns the respective roles and responsibilities of the individual, the family and the state. Again this is a debate which our book will trace back into the late Victorian period. A continuity in emphasis upon the responsibilities of female relatives is found, although in the context of the state showing an increased willingness to support such carers through the provision of publicly funded services. A key question is whether the community care reforms represent an incremental development of such an approach, or a more radical change of policy, signalling the beginning of a state withdrawal from this arena apart from the provision of service funding for the least well off and those most 'at risk'.

The third key issue is more clear-cut in that central government has been unambiguous about its desire to stimulate a mixed economy of social care in which the primary role of local authorities as the lead agency will be as enablers rather than as service providers. But this raises fundamental questions about the willingness and ability of local authorities to stimulate and then manage such markets, and it also makes essential an analysis of the likely impact of such a mixed economy upon users and carers. What are the main dangers in strengthening the role of markets in community care and what can the experience of other countries tell us about this? The reforms are very much about developing markets, but this does not resolve the need to establish effective systems of collaboration and co-ordination between a wide range of different agencies at both strategic and field levels. The challenge of effective working together is thus our fourth key issue. The whole history of community care provision in this country is characterised by disputes about the respective roles of social services, health and housing agencies. Have the community care reforms proved helpful in reducing such tensions, or do major areas of argument still remain?

One final key issue, and the most important one in the opinion of the authors, concerns user and carer empowerment. The justification for the community care reforms came from the critique of past practice which argued that community care systems were being driven by the interests of the producers (the professionals) rather than the consumers (the clients and carers). As a result, service users and carers are offered little service choice or flexibility, and in general they lack power compared to the professionals. A key test of the community care reforms will be whether or not they have a positive or negative impact upon the empowerment of service users.

In addressing such fundamental issues about an important and rapidly changing area of public policy, the tendency is to focus down upon the main changes and their likely impact without any detailed consideration of the earlier development of provision and the emergence of the reform debate. There is also a temptation to become so fascinated by the change elements that the continued relevance of certain basic assumptions and ongoing debates becomes forgotten. Chapter 2 will therefore consider, outline and discuss the long history of neglect of service provision for elderly disabled people and other 'cinderella' groups.

2 From Institutions to Care in the Community: The History of Neglect

This chapter discusses the historical development of social care and health provision for elderly people and for people with physical disabilities, learning disabilities and mental health problems. The response to the perceived needs of all these groups was overwhelmingly institutional in the nineteenth and early twentieth century. Current services for these groups carry this institutional legacy and present community care policies are, at least in part, an attempt to shake off that legacy. Thus the inclusion of this chapter is based on the strong belief that a knowledge and understanding of community care history is of practical value to busy social care managers, field level staff and students as well as of interest to the community care academic. Those struggling with contemporary policy issues can be supported through a grasp of the way the current situation came about. Undertaking contemporary social history certainly has its own intellectual justification, but it also offers to the practitioner a perspective on the basis of which she or he can understand the dilemmas and the problems of today's agenda. As Parker (1988, p. 3) has argued in the context of residential care, no informed conclusions about the future can be reached without an understanding of key external factors and 'that, in turn, cannot be done satisfactorily without some understanding and appreciation of those forces that have shaped its history'.

The history of community care services is highly complex. Therefore tackling this theme in one chapter of a textbook risks the danger of over-simplifying events and issues. No attempt will be made to provide a detailed history for all services since such accounts exist elsewhere for most of the main care groups. Rather the focus will be on the extent of service neglect in terms of priority for resources and in terms of the quality of what has been provided from the resources made available. In the 1950s and 1960s, critics of this neglect often referred to the 'Cinderella services' or the 'Cinderella groups'. In terms of priority for resources, they were always waiting for a fairy godmother to arrive and get them to the ball. The second half of the chapter goes on to explore the main explanations which have been put forward to account for this situation.

The long history of neglect – services for elderly people and physically disabled people

Through much of the Victorian period, there was little recognition of a social group, definable as elderly people, who needed special provision because of their age. Elderly people, and especially elderly men, were expected to work until they died. Those elderly people who were unable to support themselves in the community through the labour market or with the help of relatives were often forced to enter the workhouse, where no distinction was made between them and other paupers. The stereotype of the workhouse is one of brutality, although research suggests regimes were often more neglectful in terms of boredom and regimentation rather than anything else (Crowther, 1981) and that there was also considerable local variation in practice (Digby, 1978).

However, a variety of pressures began to change the role of the poor law in meeting the needs of older people from the late Victorian period onwards. Technological changes were seen as forcing older workers out of the labour market through no fault of their own and into dependence upon poor law indoor and outdoor relief. Social researchers such as Booth were chronicling the extent of poverty in old age and calling for the establishment of a national system of old age pensions (M. Martin, 1990). Major pension legislation was passed in 1908, 1925, 1940 and 1948. However, it would be wrong to believe that this was solely a reflection of societal concern about older people. Increasingly, pension developments were driven by concerns about younger workers. As Roebuck (1979) explains:

> In the 1920s the demand for the reduction of the pension age was supported less by a concern for old age poverty than for the working age poverty caused by unemployment. After a brief post-war boom, England entered a period of chronic depression and unemployment and there was a growing feeling that the pension age should be reduced, partly in the interests of the elderly, but mainly in the interest of unemployed younger people. All political parties made the

lowering of the pension age a major election issue in the mid-1920s in the hope that this lowering of the pension age would reduce unemployment. (p. 423)

The complex system of contributory and non-contributory pension arrangements which emerged resulted in the gradual removal of older people from the labour market and the social construction of the concept of retirement (Phillipson, 1982). Nevertheless, large numbers of elderly people continued to enter the workhouse, where they became an increasingly dominant group (M. Martin, 1990). Meanwhile, workhouse provision for older people was itself undergoing change with separate medical provision for the 'chronic sick' gradually emerging as well as a more general segregation of older people from other inmates in some institutions. Major organisational change of the poor law system was introduced by the Local Government Act 1929, through which the best poor law hospitals were retitled public health hospitals and became the responsibility of local authority health committees, and hence no longer part of the poor law system. However, these hospitals were almost entirely focused on the acute sick, rather than medical provision for older people, who were usually seen as chronic cases.

The remaining medical provision together with other workhouse provision also ceased to be the responsibility of the 62 poor law boards, and was transferred to 145 counties and county boroughs, each of which was required to establish a public assistance committee. The workhouse was retitled the public assistance institution (PAI). However, the 1929 Act made little attempt to abolish the taint of pauperism. For example, entry to a PAI meant that the new elderly 'inmate' was disqualified from receiving a pension unless he or she was admitted specifically for medical treatment and even then pension rights were lost after three months. Equally, the principle of family responsibility for destitute people was maintained. The Poor Law Act 1930 stated that:

It should be the duty of the father, grandfather, mother, grandmother, husband or child, of a poor, old, blind, lame or impotent person, or other poor person, not able to work, if possessed of sufficient means, to relieve and maintain that person not able to work.

In other words, an application for relief involved an assessment of the means of near relatives, who were also expected to make a contribution to those in institutional care.

Restrictive regulations remained in force about different elements of the institutional regime such as clothing, the retention of personal possessions, visiting rights and the ability to take days out. As Roberts (1970, p. 26) put it, most elderly inmates continued to sleep 'in large dormitories, sat on hard chairs, looked out on cabbage patches diversified by concrete, were separated by sex and, except on one day a week, could not pass the gates without permission'. Disquiet about this situation was beginning to develop in the late 1930s. For example, Matthews (undated) called for more colour to be brought into the lives of elderly people in institutions 'through contact with visitors from the outside world, by providing occupations as well as entertainments and by introducing more variety into their food, clothing and surroundings' (p. 13). A campaign emerged calling for the introduction of pocket money for inmates. Some public assistance committees developed small homes with more liberal regimes, although they were usually reserved for 'women of the more gentle type' or men of 'the merit class' (quoted in Means and Smith, 1985, p. 22).

A more detailed picture of life in the medical and non-medical parts of public assistance institutions emerged during and just after the Second World War. It was a portrait of extensive neglect (Means and Smith, 1985, Chapters 2 and 3; Titmuss, 1976). With regard to the so-called 'elderly chronic sick', there seems to have been a shortage of both beds and high quality care. Writing in the late 1940s, McEwan and Laverty (1949) argued that the 1929 Act had a disastrous impact upon people with long-term health care needs since 'many of the new and aspiring municipal hospitals got rid of their undesirable chronic sick ... sending them to Public Assistance Institutions to upgrade their own medical services' (p. 9). This placed added pressure upon the medical wards of public assistance institutions, many of which could not cope with the increased demand for beds, and so elderly patients often had to be 'housed' elsewhere in the institutions. For example, in Bradford:

In the Public Assistance Hospitals (The Park and Thornton View) ... patients are discharged or returned from the chronic sick wards to the ambulant or 'house' section ... In The Park, where the chronic sick wards were overcrowded, the most fit (but often frail) patients had to be sent to the ambulant wards to make room for admissions to the hospital section. There was, in consequence, a proportion of sick or disabled people in the ambulant section, where they had to remain, often confined to bed, there being no room for them in hospital. (p. 8)

The overall situation was further worsened by the creation of a 300 000 bed Emergency Medical Service at the outbreak of the Second World War since this involved the discharge of 140 000 patients in just two days. Many of the reserved beds were in PAIs and one commentator of the time claimed that:

> the people who fared worst of all were the chronically sick, the bed-ridden, the paralysed, the aged, people suffering from advanced cancer or from tuberculosis who were discharged in their hundreds from public institutions to their own homes, where they could get little, if any, care, where in all too many cases they were regarded as an intolerable burden on their relatives, and even to houses from which all their relatives had been evacuated to the country. (Morris, 1940, p. 189)

As the war progressed, further problems appeared. Many elderly patients who remained in PAI hospitals were in danger from bombing raids but there was government reluctance to move them. The ability to manage outside the hospital was undermined by the disruptions of war and so 'thousands who had formerly been nursed at home were clamouring for admission to hospitals when families were split up, when homes were damaged or destroyed, and when the nightly trek to the shelter became a part of normal life for Londoners' (Titmuss, 1976, p. 448). Some of these problems eased, but the extent to which such hospitals continued to fail to offer effective treatment to their 'chronic sick' patients was underlined by the government hospital surveys of the 1940s. Ten survey teams were appointed in 1941, some by the Minister of Health and some in conjunction with the Nuffield Provincial Hospitals Trust to cover both voluntary and public hospitals. The aim of the surveys was to gather information about existing hospital facilities as a basis for future planning for a possible National Health Service. The findings were drawn together in *The Domesday Book of the Hospital Services* which stressed how the surveys outlined the haphazard growth and lack of planning within existing hospital services. The Domesday Book showed how care for the 'chronic sick' received the bitterest comments from the investigators:

> All are agreed that 'the reproach of the masses of undiagnosed and untreated cases of chronic type which litter our Public Assistance Institutions must be removed'. Without proper classification and

investigation, at present young children and senile dements are 'banded together' in these institutions, along with many elderly patients whom earlier diagnosis and treatment might have enabled to return to their homes ... 'The great essential is that every patient should be thoroughly examined and treated with a view to restoration to a maximum degree of activity. Only if treatment is unsuccessful or is clearly useless, should he be regarded as chronically sick', and 'even then (he) should be subject to periodic review'. (Nuffield Provincial Hospitals Trust, 1946, p. 16)

All the investigators called for hospital services and accommodation to be completely divorced from public assistance institutions.

The subsequent establishment of the National Health Service in 1946 did bring the PAI hospitals under the same administrative system as other types of hospital provision. The Domesday Book did generate government awareness of the cost of blocked hospital beds from the failure both to tackle the acute illness of elderly patients and to provide them with appropriate rehabilitation services. Elements of the medical profession also began to argue the need to develop geriatric medicine so as to transform the quality of medical care available to elderly patients (Anderson Report, 1947; Amulree, 1951). There is not the space in this chapter to trace the development of hospital-based geriatric medicine after the Second World War. However, it remained a low status route for medical graduates and a low priority for health care expenditure. Some impressive initatives did emerge but many elderly people were classified as non-curable and placed in long stay annexes and supervised by visiting GPs. Martin (1992) has argued that these annexes were little better than the over-crowded chronic wards of the inter-war years.

The Second World War also had a negative impact upon the ability of elderly people to remain in their own homes even when they had no major health problems. Support from children was reduced. Others were made homeless as a result of bombing raids. One consequence was that 'respectable' elderly people were being pushed towards PAIs, as were many elderly people definable as war victims or casualties. Many felt that regimes of PAIs and their continued association with pauperism were inappropriate for such people. A campaign around these issues emerged in Spring 1943 as a result of a letter which appeared in the *Manchester Guardian*. The letter was entitled 'A Workhouse Visit' and spoke of 'a frail, sensitive, refined old woman' of 84 who was forced to live in the regime described in the following extract:

But down each side of the ward were ten beds, facing one another. Between each bed and its neighbour was a small locker and a straight-backed, wooden uncushioned chair. On each chair sat an old woman in workhouse dress, upright, unoccupied. No library books or wireless. Central heating, but no open fire. No easy chairs. No pictures on the walls ... There were three exceptions to the upright old women. None was allowed to lie on her bed at any time throughout the day, although breakfast is at 7 a.m., but these three, unable any longer to endure their physical and mental weariness, had crashed forward, face downwards, on to their immaculate bedspreads and were asleep. (Quoted in Samson, 1944, p. 47)

The subsequent Nuffield survey committee on the problems of ageing and the care of old people which was chaired by Seebohm Rowntree indicated that poor conditions and restrictive regimes were not unusual:

Day-rooms in such institutions are usually large and cheerless with wooden Windsor armchairs placed around the walls. Floors are mainly bare boards with brick floors in lavatories, bathrooms, kitchens and corridors. In large urban areas such institutions may accommodate as many as 1,500 residents of various types, including more than a thousand aged persons. (Rowntree, 1980, p. 64)

The survey committee confirmed that rules in these large institutions were often harsh or harshly administered, while apathy was widespread among the residents.

The National Assistance Act 1948 was presented to Parliament as the solution to these problems. Section 21 of the Act stated that 'it should be the duty of every local authority ... to provide residential accommodation for persons who are by reasons of age, infirmity or any other circumstances in need of care and attention which is not otherwise available to them'. Townsend (1964) argued in *The Last Refuge* that changing the names of PAIs to residential homes and transferring responsibility for running them from public assistance committees to health/welfare committees had achieved little. This is perhaps a little unfair. The old system of family responsibility for maintenance was abolished and users were now perceived as residents who contributed to their keep through their pension, although they were allowed to retain five shillings for pocket money (Means and Smith, 1985). However, in many respects, the tradition of neglect continued. For example,

Townsend (1964) reported that ex-PAIs 'accounted for just over half the accommodation used by county and county borough councils, for just under half the residents and for probably over three-fifths of the old people actually admitted in the course of a year' (p. 190). With regard to the thirty-nine former PAIs visited by Townsend, 57 per cent of the accommodation was in rooms with at least ten beds. Basic amenities such as hand-basins, toilets and baths were not only insufficient, but were often difficult to reach, badly distributed and of poor quality. With regard to staff, Townsend found that many were middle-aged and elderly persons who had given 'a lifetime's service under the old Poor Law as well as the new administration' (p. 39). Townsend felt:

> ... it would be idle to pretend that many of them were imbued with the more progressive standards of personal care encouraged by the Ministry of Health, geriatricians, social workers and others since the war...Some were unsuitable, by any standards, for the tasks they performed, men and women with authoritarian attitudes inherited from Poor Law days who provoked resentment and even terror among infirm people. (p. 39)

In conclusion, Townsend argued that the main shortcoming was not the failure to improve the quality of residential buildings and staff, but rather the failure to develop community-based services so as to reduce the need for people to enter institutional care.

The legislative power to provide social care services in the community was very slow to develop and is a further indication of neglect, especially towards elderly people. Section 29 of the National Assistance Act 1948 did empower local authorities 'to promote the welfare of persons who are blind, deaf or dumb and others, who are substantially and permanently handicapped by illness, injury or congenital deformity'. Nevertheless, it remained *ultra vires* for local authorities to develop preventive services for most frail elderly people, with the exception of home care, where legal empowerment was provided through the National Health Service Act 1946. Under the 1948 Act, local authorities could not develop their own meals-on-wheels services, chiropody facilities, laundry services, visiting schemes or counselling services for elderly people, a situation which led Parker (1965) to remark:

> The concern to maintain and foster family life evident in the Children Act was completely lacking in the National Assistance Act. The latter

made no attempt to provide any sort of substitute family life for old people who could no longer be supported by their own relatives. Institutional provision was accepted without question. (p. 106)

The belief of the legislators behind the 1948 Act was that domiciliary services were an 'extra frill' and so could be left to voluntary organisations, such as old people's welfare committees (now Age Concern), the W(R)VS and the Red Cross to develop. A complex patchwork of visiting services, day centres, meals services and chiropody did emerge but much of this provision was not easily available or was unevenly spread geographically, despite attempts by central government to develop the planning role of local authorities (Sumner and Smith, 1969). For example, Harris (1961) carried out a survey of 453 meals-on-wheels schemes and found that 40 per cent had difficulties finding enough volunteers, 40 per cent of recipients received a meal on only one day a week and 162 schemes closed completely for part of the year.

However, legislative change to empower local authorities occurred very slowly despite growing research evidence of the paucity of services being provided through the voluntary sector (Means and Smith, 1985, Chapter 6). The National Assistance (Amendment) Act 1962 allowed local authorities to provide meals services directly for the first time, whereas before they could only provide a grant to enable a voluntary organisation to do so. The Health Services and Public Health Act 1968 gave local authorities the general power to promote the welfare of elderly people, while the National Health Service Act 1977 made home care a mandatory responsibility rather than a discretionary power as previously. The implementation of this 1968 Act was delayed until April 1971 to coincide with the creation of unified social services departments. These new departments were soon dominated by child care concerns, especially after the death of Maria Colwell in January 1973 (Parton, 1983). Research studies confirmed that social services departments maintained client group hierarchies with elderly people at the bottom so that elderly clients were usually allocated to unqualified staff on the grounds that intervention was perceived as likely to be routine and unglamorous (Bowl, 1986). Hopes of a major expansion of domiciliary services were further hit by the first tremors on the public expenditure front in the mid-1970s with the oil crisis. Increasingly, debate shifted away from the need for overall increases in social care expenditure towards arguments about the need for a shift of priorities between domiciliary and residential provision (DHSS, 1978).

It could be argued that Section 29 of the 1948 Act shows that people with physical, visual and sensory impairments were not neglected in the postwar period especially when compared to frail elderly people, since this section gave local authorities the power to develop domiciliary services for these groups. However, this was largely illusory, for reasons pointed out by Eyden (1965):

> It is clear ... that if local authorities implement to the full this legisla-tion in close co-operation with voluntary organizations, all groups of the handicapped or their families should have a comprehensive service to which they can turn to meet any of their specialized needs. Unfortunately, this has not been the case. The duty of providing services was continued under the National Assistance Act only for the blind. Guidance to local authorities on the provision of welfare services for other classes of handicapped persons was issued by the Ministry of Health in Circular 32/51 in August 1951, and local authorities were invited to submit schemes and their subsequent implementation was not made compulsory until 1960 ... As a result, the development of services for the deaf and other categories of handicapped persons over the past sixteen years has been patchy and inadequate. (p. 171)

Even the 1960 deadline had little meaning since local authorities were able to offer minimal provision yet still meet the requirements of the act. This situation meant that the main community-based service available to physically disabled people and their families was the home care service (Topliss, 1979).

These inadequacies of provision led Alf Morris, MP, to introduce a private member's bill designed to compel local authorities to develop comprehensive welfare and support services for disabled people and this subsequently became the Chronically Sick and Disabled Persons Act 1970. This Act imposed duties but did not link this to the allocation of sufficient extra resources to local authorities. Topliss claims that 'this has meant that the claims of the disabled have had to compete with the claims on the local authority budget of all other sections of the community' and that 'the sort of massive reallocation of expenditure needed to implement the ... Act fully, in the absence of special ear-marked funds, has apparently proved politically impossible for local authorities' (p. 114).

With regard to residential care for physically disabled people, research by Miller and Gwynne (1972) discovered some of the same inadequacies found by Townsend (1964) for elderly people. The National Assistance Act 1948 did make reference to the specific needs of younger physically disabled people as being different from those of frail elderly people. However, most local authorities continued to place physically disabled people in residential homes for older people. Only a minority of local authorities developed separate homes in the 1950s and 1960s, despite the growing awareness that the overall number of younger disabled people had increased because of a number of factors including the war, the 1950s polio epidemic and increased life expectancy from medical advances. Detailed figures in the balance of provision are difficult to come by, although Leat (1988, p. 206) shows that in 1972 'there were 8000 younger people in homes also housing elderly people although more than half of these younger people were in their early sixties'. She also draws upon the survey by Harrison (1986) to show that by the mid-1980s only 54 of the 115 local authorities in England and Wales had set up homes catering specifically for younger physically disabled people, but she points out that many of the others may have been making use of specialist voluntary and private homes. By far the most influential of these independent sector providers of residential care was Cheshire Homes, which was founded in 1948 and developed the concept of a 'family home' which claimed to meet the needs of younger physically disabled people.

Services for people with mental health problems and learning disabilities

Having looked at the development of provision for elderly and physically disabled people, it is now appropriate to consider the growth of services for people with mental health problems and learning disabilities. Does the same pattern of neglect emerge? Several authors have charted the growth of asylums for 'lunatics' (people with mental health problems) and 'idiots' (people with learning disabilities) from a community care perspective (see for example Murphy, 1991; Malin *et al.*, 1980; Ryan and Thomas, 1980) while others have studied asylums from a more general sociological interest in madness (Scull, 1979). Murphy (1991) has argued that asylum growth from the late 1840s onwards was initially a development to be welcomed, since previous workhouse provision was failing to cope. She argues that the social reformers had a vision of a therapeutic community in which 'insanity ... might be healed by a gentle system of rewards and punishments, amusements, occupation and kindly but firm discipline' (p. 34) although she accepts that the reality proved far inferior to the vision. Others have been far less sanguine. Scull (1979) saw the asylums as a mechanism by which the community and individual families could shed their responsibilities for troublesome and unwanted people. Certainly the legislative framework was draconian up to 1930, since admission depended on certification as 'a lunatic, an idiot or a person of unsound mind', which involved an order to be detained by a judicial authority. As Parker (1988, p. 12) points out:

> Such a requirement imposed a stigma additional to any that was associated with being in an asylum. Not only was admission dependent upon certification, but the order for commitment carried with it the prospect of its irrevocability. De-certification and release were not easily obtained.

The majority of such inmates were also certified as paupers unless they or their relatives could pay privately for their detention.

The numbers of people with mental health problems detained in asylums (renamed mental health hospitals in 1930) grew spectacularly. Gibbins (1988, p. 161) talks of a situation where:

> By 1890 there were sixty-six county and borough asylums in England and Wales with an average 802 inmates and 86 067 officially certified cases of insanity in England and Wales, more than four times as many as forty-five years earlier. By 1930 there were nearly 120 000 patients in public asylums and by 1954 at the peak in numbers, there were over 148 000.

Gibbins sums up this situation as being one in which there were 'ever larger numbers of chronic cases in institutions of increasing size, with ever fewer therapeutic pretensions' (p. 160).

Murphy (1991) provides a glimpse of life in the typical Victorian asylum. She claims that:

> Life ... was governed by a rigid timetabled regime of sleep, work, eat. Whitewashed walls; plain brick, stone or wooden floors; deal benches and tables; and two WCs for thirty or forty patients provided a fairly cheerless though roomy environment. Windows were

generally barred and many wards were locked, although the better asylums gave considerable internal freedom to the inmates. (p. 38)

Such asylums had few trained doctors, perhaps three or four for every thousand patients. Hence, much of the day-to-day work was performed by low-paid nursing attendants who often worked a 90-hour week.

In many respects, the situation was even more alarming for people with learning disabilities in the prewar period. The term 'neglect' is probably misleading since services for this group have often been influenced by moral panics about the need to protect the genetic stock of the country by discouraging those of 'low' intelligence from 'breeding'. Ryan and Thomas (1980) indicate that the Victorian period was often a period of optimism about the potential for training and educating people with learning disabilities, even if this was often in the context of their removal to an institution under the Idiots Act 1886. However, they also point out that the growth of such institutionalised provision reflected pressures upon families as a result of the industrial revolution which undermined the capacity of families to care for those with long-term dependency needs.

In any case, optimism about the potential of institutions to help those with learning disabilities was undermined by the new science of genetics with its tendency to perceive 'mental defectives' as less than human. Most geneticists believed that intelligence was innate. They were alarmed by high birth rates amongst the poorest, and by implication the least intelligent members of society, since such a trend could undermine the overall genetic stock of the nation and hence the capacity to remain a dominant colonial power. Mental defects were seen as genetically inherited and hence the segregation of 'mental defectives' from the rest of society was essential.

Several authors have charted how this led to calls for the establishment of farm and industrial colonies, together with the prohibition of marriages involving those labelled as 'moral defectives' who were seen as often on the borderlines of 'mental defectiveness' (Abbott and Sapsford, 1987; Malin *et al.*, 1980, Chapter 4). Such views had a major impact upon the thinking of the 1908 Royal Commission on the Care and Control of the Feeble-minded and on the legislative details of the Mental Deficiency Act 1913. This Act made reference to idiots, imbeciles and the feeble-minded, categories based on the extent of the learning disability, while the term 'moral imbecile' was introduced to cover what was seen as a more generalised social problem group whose low intelligence made them prone to 'loose morals'. Section 2 of the Act specified the circumstances under which a 'defective' from these groups might be dealt with by being sent to an institution or placed under guardianship:

(a)   at the insistence of his parent or guardian;
(b)   if in addition to being a defective he was a person (i) who was found neglected, abandoned, or without visible means of support, or cruelly treated or ... in need of care or training which could not be provided in his home; or (ii) who was found guilty of any criminal offence, or who was ordered to be sent to an approved school; or (iii) who was undergoing imprisonment, or was in an approved school; or (iv) who was an habitual drunkard; or (v) who had been found incapable of receiving education at school, or that by reason of a disability of mind require supervision after leaving school. (Quoted in Malin *et al.*, 1980, p. 41)

Once a person had been admitted to an institution on these grounds, the Board of Control was in a position to block the discharge of anyone they considered unfit to live in the community. Certain safeguards were built into this draconian system. Parents and guardians needed two medical certificates, one of which had to be approved for such purposes by the local health authority or the Minister of Health. Section 2(b), quoted above, used the term 'in addition to being a defective'. However, in practice, it was relatively easy to place any person with learning disability in an institution using this act while others experiencing social difficulties such as homelessness were equally vulnerable irrespective of their mental abilities. Once they were committed, the term "certification' had a permanence about it, probably enhanced by the prevailing views of invariance of intellectual abilities and certainly compounded by the essentially subjective nature of the definitions of the Act' (Malin *et al.*, 1980, p. 42).

Ryan and Thomas (1980, p. 107) summed up the overall situation in the following way:

This Act established the basis of a separate and unified service, which would exclude mental defective people from other welfare and social agencies as well as from the general education system.

The total number of 'defectives' under the care and control of the mental deficiency legislation rose rapidly. Figures supplied by Tredgold

(1952) and quoted by Malin *et al.* (1980, p. 43) show that numbers rose from 12 000 in 1920 to 90 000 by 1939. Most of them were placed in large isolated 'colonies', whose regime was outlined in the Report of the Mental Deficiency Committee (1929):

> The modern institution is generally a large one, preferably built on a colony plan, takes defectives of all grades of defect and all ages. All, of course, are probably classified according to their mental capacity and age. The Local Mental Deficiency Authority has to provide for all grades of defect, all types of case and all ages, and an institution that cannot, or will not, take this case for one reason and that case for another is of no use to the Authority. An institution which takes all types and ages is economical because the high-grade patients do the work and make everything necessary, not only for themselves, but also for the lower grade. In an institution taking only lower grades, the whole of the work has to be done by paid staff; in one taking only high grades the output of work is greater than is required for the institution itself and there is difficulty in disposing of it. In the all-grade institution, on the other hand, the high-grade patients are the skilled workmen of the colony, those who do all the higher processes of manufacture, those on whom there is a considerable measure of responsibility; the medium grade patients are the labourers, who do the more simple routine work in the training shops and about the institution; the rest of the lower-grade patients fetch and carry or do the very simple work. (Quoted in Malin *et al.*, 1980, p. 43)

How was the situation changed for people with learning disabilities and mental health problems by the creation of a National Health Service and other related reforms? The National Health Service saw provision for those with mental health problems and learning disabilities brought more into mainstream health care provision. Asylums were redesignated as hospitals and became the responsibility of regional hospital boards. Local authorities became responsible for the following range of services under Section 28 of the National Health Service Act 1946:

(a) The initial care and removal to hospital of persons dealt with under the Lunacy and Mental Treatment Acts.

(b) The ascertainment and (where necessary) removal to institutions of mental defectives, and the supervision, guardianship training and occupation of those in the community, under the Mental Deficiency Acts.

(c)   The prevention, care and after-care of all types of patients, so far as this was not otherwise provided for.

However, the first two were statutory responsibilities, while the third represented a permissive power. Local authorities showed little enthusiasm for using their permissive powers and in 1958/59 overall local authority expenditure on people with mental health problems was only £4.1 million (Goodwin, 1990, p. 68).

Expenditure on hospital-based provision was not much more impressive. Drawing upon a number of sources, Goodwin (1990, p. 67) found that in the early 1950s, mental and mental deficiency hospitals contained 40 per cent of in-patient beds in the NHS but received only 20 per cent of the hospital budget. He also pointed out that the average cost of treating a mentally distressed in-patient was £3 15s 11d in 1950/51 compared to £4 13s 11d in 1959/60 (at 1950/51 prices) but that far more dramatic price rises had occurred for other groups in the same period. For example, the cost of in-patient maternity care rose from £6 9s 5d to £16 11s 3d. Goodwin claims 'these figures clearly underline why the mental health services have earned the tag of a "Cinderella" service' (p. 67).

At first glance, the Cinderella tag appears to have been removed as a result of the Royal Commission on Mental Illness and Mental Deficiency which sat from 1954 to 1957, and the subsequent Mental Health Act 1959. The latter reformed the legislative framework of constraint and envisaged a major reduction in hospital provision for people with mental health problems and learning disabilities which would be balanced by the development of a complex infrastructure of local authority-provided services such as hostels, day care, social work support and sheltered employment schemes. Such services failed to materialise. As a result, Murphy (1991, p. 60) describes 1962–1990 as 'the disaster years' for people with mental health problems. She points out that 'by 1974 there were 60 000 fewer residents in large mental hospitals than there had been in 1954, but very few services at all existed in the community'. In a similar vein, Atkinson (1988) notes the failure of local authorities to develop services for children and adults with learning difficulties. She indicates that 'a few residential homes, or hostels, appeared here and there' while 'local authorities developed some training facilities in the community and appointed Mental Welfare Officers to make routine visits to the family homes' (p. 128). Provision remained based on hospitals.

Institutional and treatment regimes remained controversial. For people with mental health problems, the emphasis was now on treatment not custody. However, the introduction of anti-psychotic drugs and new treatments such as ECT were seen to raise major issues about civil liberties. There were also numerous exposes of physical and mental cruelty by staff over patients. Such practices with regard to psychogeriatric patients were outlined by Robb (1967) in *Sans Everything: A Case to Answer* while Morris (1969) in *Put Away* provided evidence of the generally poor conditions in many long-stay mental handicap hospitals. Against this, Jones (1972) lamented how the popular press of the late 1960s began to exaggerate such stories and to imply that the worst abuses were the norm rather than the exception.

It is impossible to be certain about the overall standard of provision and how this varied in the forty-year period from the establishment of the National Health Service in 1946 to the publication of *Making a Reality of Community Care* by the Audit Commission in 1986. However, Frank Thomas' diary of everyday life in the ward of a large mental handicap hospital in the late 1970s perhaps captures how 'patients' become treated as less than fully human through mundane everyday actions rather than through spectacular examples of abuse. Here are two examples:

1. Tea mixed with milk and sugar to save time, mess and trouble. How many lumps, say when with the milk? You must be joking. (Thomas, 1980, p. 35)
2. Bad habit I picked up from the other nurses. Fitting out someone for his trip to the workshop and muttering 'That'll do', as if the guy's appearance meant nothing to him, just a neat reproduction of my own preferences or lack of them. Not asking the guy if he was all right, whether it'll do. If a person is not allowed a say in what he looks like, then what is the point?

Haircuts en masse – short back and sides, no one is allowed to refuse. Choice of raincoat from a communal pile, communal underwear and socks. Communal combs and brushes. One tube of toothpaste and a couple of tooth mugs for twenty-five patients. (p. 43)

Throughout this section on the long history of neglect of community care services for all the main care groups, one cannot but be struck by the continuity of the images of institutional regimes over the last one hundred years, and the persistent failure to develop alternative community-based systems of provision.

Explanations of neglect

How can we explain the long history of neglect of services for these 'Cinderella' groups? This chapter makes no pretence that there is a single simple answer to this question, but rather identifies a number of strands. Some of these are mutually exclusive and some are more appropriate for some groups than for others. However, several of the explanations overlap and support each other, a point increasingly recognised by such writers as Fennell, Phillipson and Evers (1988) and Oliver (1990) who are trying to understand how old age and disability are socially constructed rather than medically given.

Five different explanations will be addressed. First, we will look at the political economy approach which explains social policy developments (or lack of them) by reference to the changing needs of the capitalist mode of production. Second, the complex role of institutions in social control will be considered, and third, we will outline the central concern of governments to encourage informal care and the knock-on consequences of this for the neglect of community-based services. The fourth explanation looks at cultural stereotypes about ageing and disability while the final explanation considers the issue of policy implementation failure which can lead to a major gap between the rhetoric of policy and the reality of practice.

The political economy perspective

The main tenets of the political economy approach to disability have been clearly summarised by Oliver (1990):

> Changes in the organisation of work from a rural based, co-operative system where individuals contributed what they could to the production process, to an urban, factory-based one organised around the individual waged labourer, had profound consequences ... As a result of this, disabled people came to be regarded as a social and educational problem and more and more were segregated in institutions of

all kinds including workhouses, asylums, colonies and special schools, and out of the mainstream of social life. (p. 28)

Oliver stresses this is a major simplification of some highly complex processes but stresses that the key insight is the need to search for linkages between changes in public policy and changes in the sphere of production.

Perhaps the clearest example of this relationship concerns the emergence of a system of retirement pensions in the early twentieth century as part of a process of removing elderly people from the labour market during a period of high unemployment (Phillipson, 1982; Macnicol and Blaikie, 1989). The effect of such initiatives has been to minimise opportunities for elderly and disabled people in the labour market and this has ensured their 'structured dependency' on the state (Townsend, 1981). At the same time, elderly people form a reserve army of labour which can be drawn back into work during periods of labour shortage. Several authors have provided graphic illustrations of the way retirement from work was painted as encouraging physical decline and death in the labour market shortage years of the 1950s so as to draw older people back into employment (Phillipson, 1982; Harper and Thane, 1989). Against this, in the recession years of the 1980s, older workers have been encouraged to make way for younger workers by retiring as early as possible.

Structured dependency has taken a number of forms. First, it has involved dependence on state benefits which keep many elderly and disabled people trapped within poverty (Walker, 1986; Morris, 1990b). Second, it has encouraged an outlook in which health and community care services for disabled people are seen as a low resource priority, compared with service developments for children, since the latter have a clear future rôle in production and reproduction. During the Second World War there was early support for the evacuation of children and mothers from areas under threat from bombing raids but a great reluctance to extend this provision to frail elderly people because they were not, in the government jargon of the day, 'potential effectives' (Means and Smith, 1985, Chapter 2). Equally, the overall cost of providing health and social care services for elderly and disabled people can be seen as a public expenditure burden which inhibits economic growth. Such concerns have appeared in official reports. For example, *The Rising Tide* from the Health Advisory Service (1983) explained that the number of people with dementia would rise rapidly because of the growth of the very old and that 'the flood is likely to overwhelm the entire health care system' (p. 1).

There are several criticisms which can be levelled at the political economy approach, although, in fairness to most of its proponents, they recognise that its value lies in providing a very broad grasp of the link between changes in the means of production and changes in public policy. In Chapter 1, it was shown how some people misuse history to manufacture a fictitious golden past based on mythical values. Prior to the industrial revolution, all frail elderly people were not supported in the 'bosom' of their extended families, local villages did not 'support' every person with a learning disability, and appropriate work was not found for all those with physical disabilities and mental health problems. However, this is recognised by Oliver (1990, p. 28) who indicates that the industrial revolution had a major impact on disabled people but that it is impossible 'to assess whether these changes affected the quality of the experience of disability negatively or positively, largely because history is silent on the experience of disability'.

Another linked criticism is the argument that the emergence of state benefits represented a major 'gain' for elderly and disabled people compared with their previous reliance on the workhouse, poor law relief, the family and low-paid employment. Paul Johnson (1987) points out that pensions are provided as a right. They protect elderly people from the vagaries of the labour market and hence provide many of them with the option of a fairly comfortable retirement which they are likely to prefer to continued employment in unattractive work. However, Johnson's views can be challenged on the grounds that they deflect attention away from the extent of benefit-based poverty amongst elderly and disabled people. Also, his perspective does little to explain the slow development of health and social care services for the so called 'Cinderella' groups.

A third criticism is that the concept of structured dependency can easily drift into an acceptance of structural determinism which treats elderly and disabled people as 'cultural dopes' who lack any autonomy or capacity for self-determination. It is crucial to recognise the frequent imbalance of power between elderly and disabled people and the providers of state services. However, the consequent 'dependency' should not be perceived as a static, determined phenomenon, but rather recognised as a component of social processes in which elderly and disabled people continue to struggle to influence the form of their lives even in situations where they have only limited power (Dant *et al.*, 1987). However, authors such as Oliver (1990) and Fennell, Phillipson and Evers

(1988) are increasingly careful to outline the existence of structural constraints without implying the existence of structural determinism. In
other words, elderly and disabled people who apply for help from a
social services department may have less power than the social workers
or care managers but they can still attempt to influence and shape the
outcome of any assessment.

Institutions and service neglect

There is a rich and complex literature on institutions and their rôle in
social control. A frequent theme in the literature on institutions is that
many were designed to impose stigma upon residents, and that one
function of the institution was to provide a warning to others. Here are
two quotations reflecting this perspective:

> ... residential homes for the elderly serve functions for the wider
> society and not only for their inmates. While accommodating only a
> tiny percentage of the elderly population, they symbolise the depend-
> ence of the elderly and legitimate their lack of access to equality of
> status. (Townsend, 1986, p. 32)

> ... the workhouse represented the ultimate sanction. The fact that
> comparatively few people came to be admitted did not detract from
> the power of its negative image, an image that was sustained by the
> accounts that circulated about the harsh treatment and separation of
> families that admission entailed. The success of 'less eligibility' in
> deterring the able bodied and others from seeking relief relied heavily
> on the currency of such images. (Parker, 1988, p. 9)

From this perspective, neglect within institutions can be understood in
terms of the need to generate a negative image to those outside their
walls. This negative image, in turn, helps to persuade people into accept-
ing the lack of sufficient public expenditure on benefits, health care
services and social care services which would enable people to remain in
the community with comfort. Instead, the choice is between discomfort
in the community, and discomfort and stigma in the institution.

Not everyone has been satisfied with this approach to understanding
institutions. Jones and Fowles (1984) argue that the classic literature on
'total institutions', 'institutional neurosis' and 'carceral power' associated with Goffman (1968), Barton (1959), Foucault (1967) and others

contained 'sweeping statements, massive generalisations, and some fairly shoddy reasoning; but also disturbing insight, sound scholarship and lively argument' (p. 1). Not all institutional regimes are totally oppressive, and this was true of workhouses (Digby, 1978) let alone more recent institutions. Not all institutions have a negative impact upon potential users. Nevertheless, the literature on institutions does provide insights into the neglect of health and social care services for elderly and disabled people.

Finally, it is quite clear that the growing cost of institutional provision has been a factor in the growing emphasis of governments in this and other countries in arguing for a need to switch resources from institutional provision to the development of domiciliary services in the community (Scull, 1977; Maclean, 1989; Goodwin, 1990). What had started as a low-cost form of provision had become an increasingly expensive response to the needs of disabled people. However, to understand the slow government response to the growing criticisms of institutions on grounds of both cost and quality of care, it is necessary to consider the politics of informal care.

Informal care and service neglect

Most disabled people have always lived in the community rather than in institutions, and the majority of them have received enormous support from their families and relatives, and in particular from female kin. There is an extensive literature which argues that the reluctance of government to fund the development of domiciliary services springs from a fear that such services will undermine the willingness of families (that is, female kin) to continue their caring rôle. This would have the effect of both increasing public expenditure and undermining the family as an institution (Means, 1986). This is a line of argument that has been particularly powerful in respect of services for elderly people and physically disabled people. Governments have been reluctant to respond to the needs of these groups in contrast to policies for people with mental health problems and disabilities where the emphasis has more often been on the desirability of removing them from their families.

Detailed information about the extent of informal care and the pressures that this places upon carers has been available for a long time. For example, Sheldon (1948) studied 600 elderly people from Wolverhampton and found that the management of illness was carried out by wives and daughters so that 'whereas the wives do most of the nursing of the men, the strain when the mother is ill is yet to fall on the daughter, who may have to stay at home as much to run the household as to nurse her mother' (p. 164). Sheldon felt the burden upon such women needed to be shared with the rest of the community through the establishment of a national home help service. Sheldon's findings were subsequently backed up by a number of other studies, which emphasised not only the willingness of families to care but also the costs this imposed upon them (Townsend, 1963; Lowther and Williamson, 1966; Shanas *et al.*, 1968).

However, such evidence was being generated at a time of concern that the welfare state reforms of the 1940s might undermine the willingness of families to carry out their traditional obligations, one of which was to provide care and support for disabled members. Thompson (1949) was involved in the surveys of chronic sick patients after the NHS reforms and he argued that:

> The power of the group-maintaining instincts will suffer if the provision of a home, the training of children, and the care of disabled members are no longer the ambition of a family but the duty of a local or central authority. (p. 250)

Ten years later, a consultant physician from a geriatric unit was putting forward a similar argument:

> The feeling that the State ought to solve every inconvenient domestic situation is merely another factor in producing a snowball expansion on demands in the National Health (and Welfare) Service. Close observation on domestic strains makes one thing very clear. This is that where an old person has a family who have a sound feeling of moral responsibility, serious problems do not arise, however much difficulty may be met. (Rudd, 1958, p. 348)

From such a perspective, it was essential for the state to avoid the development of domiciliary services if families were not, in turn, to avoid their domestic responsibilities towards elderly and disabled people. The failure to expand home care services and the heavy reliance upon the voluntary sector for the provision of other domiciliary services is a consequence of this point of view.

Such views were heavily challenged by those involved in research on caring:

The health and welfare services for the aged, as presently developing, are a necessary concomitant of social organisation, and therefore, possibly of economic growth. The services do not undermine self-help, because they are concentrated overwhelmingly among those who have neither the capacities nor the resources to undertake the relevant functions alone. Nor, broadly, do the services conflict with the interest of the family as a social institution, because they tend to reach people who lack a family or whose family resources are slender, or they provide specialised services the family is not equipped or qualified to undertake. (Townsend in Shanas *et al.*, 1968, p. 129)

Rather than being restricted from a fear of undermining the family, domiciliary services needed to be rapidly expanded to support families and help the isolated.

This argument was gradually accepted by central government. However, this was achieved by emphasising the capacity of domiciliary services to persuade family members to continue to care for disabled relatives rather than their capacity to offer such members real choices about whether or not to continue such care. Moroney (1976) put the argument for more services quite bluntly:

By not offering support, existing social policy might actually force many families to give up this function prematurely, given the evidence of the severe strain many families are experiencing. If this were to happen, the family and the state would not be sharing the responsibility through an interdependent relationship and it is conceivable that eventually the social welfare system would be pressured with demands to provide even greater amounts of care, to become the family for more and more elderly persons (p. 59).

Cultural stereotypes about ageing and disability

Most western societies support negative stereotypes about old age and about disability. Wilson (1991) has argued that most western views of the life course are pyramidal, in which 'ageing is seen as an inevitable or irreversible slide downwards into dependency' (p. 43). Or as Malcolm Johnson (1990) has put it:

Dependency is one of the words closely associated in the public mind with old age. The image of older people becoming like children –

dependent on able-bodied adults – and the loss of mental faculties, are other stereotypes which have wide currency. Even my children, long schooled in the rejection of ageism, like to remind me of the epigram 'old professors never die, they only lose their faculties'. (p. 209)

Similarly negative images and stereotypes are often associated with the term 'disability'. Lonsdale (1990), for example, talks of the oppression of disabled people by the able-bodied:

> Oppression here is taken to refer to a situation in which one group of people systematically undermines another group materially and psychologically, thus invalidating the experiences of the oppressed group ... Much of the rejection experienced is not overtly hostile (although it can and does sometimes become so) but comprises a consistently low and patronising expectation of the person with the disability. (p. 2)

Morris (1990a, p. 22) puts the situation even more bluntly by claiming 'just as the issue for black people is racism rather than being black so the issue for disabled people is the fear and hostility that our physical difference and limitations raise for non-disabled people'.

Such everyday cultural attitudes to elderly and disabled people will be part of the assumptive worlds of many of those who develop community care policies and by many of those who deliver community care services. Certainly, Rowlings (1981) has argued that this helps to explain the oft remarked reluctance of social workers to develop their careers in community care rather than child care:

> ... old age confronts us not just with death (which is inevitable) but with decline (which is probable, at least to some degree) ... It is the prospect of loss in old age – impairment in mental and/or physical function, loss of spouse and family and loss of independence – which is more frightening to contemplate than loss of life itself ... Social workers may well be faced with clients whose experience of and response to ageing represent those very aspects of old age which they, the social workers, fear most for their future selves. (pp. 25–6)

Although this quotation is from a book on *Social Work with Elderly People*, similar comments could be made about the fear of many professionals about working with younger physically disabled people, and people with learning disabilities and mental health problems.

Such fear may provide a partial explanation of service neglect, especially if combined with an appreciation of the low status of work with these groups rather than in child care (for social workers) or acute medicine (for doctors), and the extent of pessimism about what can be achieved in terms of improving lives through health and social care intervention. This pessimism has deep roots. Haber (1983), for example, found in her study of medical models of growing old in the late nineteenth and early twentieth century that:

> Most European clinicians seemed to imply that illness and old age were inseparably intertwined, if not quite synonymous. At best the division between the two was extremely subjective. A large proportion of the diseases of old age are attributed to natural intractable changes in the organism. (p. 62)

The term 'chronic sick' sums up this attitude of mind within the medical profession; illness in old age was chronic, inevitable and barely treatable since 'the organic difficulties that increased with age made the hope of corrective treatment illusory' (p. 72).

However, such arguments do have their limitations. To say that older people and disabled people are oppressed by the negative stereotypes generated by the young and able-bodied does little to help us understand how such stereotypes emerge from a complex interplay of cultural, political, economic and social factors. For example, how do such stereotypes relate to the process of removal from the labour force associated with the industrial revolution? Are these stereotypes and their implications the same for disabled men as for disabled women (Morris, 1990a; Lloyd, 1992)? And are negative attitudes to frail elderly people connected not just to issues of age but also to the fact that the majority of them are women rather than men (Peace, 1986; Arber and Ginn, 1991)?

The politics of implementation

The final approach to explaining service neglect focuses down upon issues of policy implementation. Although it is possible to characterise the history of services as one of policy neglect, it is also true that health and social care provision for elderly and disabled people have often proved highly resistant to policy change and policy reform. An excellent example of this is that, even when central governments have been persuaded of the need to switch the policy emphasis away from institutional care and towards community-based services, progress has often been painfully slow. The next chapter considers this issue in some detail with regard to the slowness of the rundown of large mental health and mental handicap hospitals in the 1980s. In earlier decades progress was equally slow in developing non-residential provision for elderly and physically disabled people, a fact which has been explained by reference to the resistance of those with a vested interest in residential care (Townsend, 1981), continued debates about the cost effectiveness of care at home for the very frail or dependent (Sumner and Smith, 1969; Means, 1986) or the vested interests of those voluntary sector providers of domiciliary services who wished to discourage increased local authority involvement (Means, 1992).

However, it is important to stand back from the details of the history of community care provision and to recognise the existence of a wider literature on policy implementation which stresses the frequency of a major gap between the stated objectives of legislative change and what continues to happen on the ground across all policy areas. The seminal book on implementation deficit was a study of a job creation scheme in Oakland, USA by Pressman and Wildavsky (1973). The authors argued that such schemes could only be successful if numerous organisations linked up to create a successful implementation chain. Relatively small failures of co-operation between the different organisations can easily multiply to create a major implementation deficit, which is what occurred in the Oakland scheme.

Two main approaches to theorising implementation deficit subsequently emerged, namely the top-down perspective and the bottom-up perspective (Ham and Hill, 1993). The top-down approach tends to offer advice to policy makers on how to minimise the discretion of actors lower down the implementation chain so as to ensure that implementation is consistent with policy objectives. The bottom-up approach emphasises that implementation is the inevitable product of negotiation and compromise between the formal policy makers and those with the task of interpreting how to turn these into practice. As Barrett and Hill (1984) argue:

(a) many policies represent compromises between conflicting values;

(b) many policies involve compromises within key interests within the implementation structure;

(c)   many policies involve compromises with key interests upon
       whom implementation will have an impact;
(d)   many policies are framed without attention being given to the
       way in which underlying forces (particularly economic ones)
       will undermine them. (p. 222)

Such tensions mean that some decisions on goals and objectives are left
to what is normally seen as the implementation stage. Top-down
theorists tend to see this as regrettable and undesirable. Bottom-up
theorists see this as inevitable and some would perceive it as desirable
on the grounds that field-level implementors are in the best position to
assess the local situation and set appropriate objectives. Even where the
discretion to make policy is not formally given by the 'policy maker',
lower-level implementors will still perceive themselves as important
'stakeholders' with the right to pursue their own agendas. Smith and
Cantley (1985) in their study of a psychiatric day hospital illustrated
how this complicates assessment of 'success' or 'failure' for any given
policy initiative. The key stakeholders (administrators, doctors, nurses,
relatives and patients) may all try to influence the policy and its implementation, and all will have different views about what represents
success and failure. At the very least, stakeholders may have the power
to block or disrupt innovation in policy areas such as community care.

The gap between policy change towards user-centred services at the
top and the continuance of institutional and professionally dominated
services on the ground can be explained by reference to the capacity of
vested professional and provider interests to disrupt and undermine
well-meaning reforms. However, the level of commitment of central
government to these policy changes can also be queried since the implementation literature also refers to symbolic policies (Edelman, 1971)
which are designed to reassure the public about good intentions but
which are never intended to be appropriately resourced in relation to
their far-reaching objectives.

Concluding comments

The focus of this chapter has been upon the neglect of services for
elderly and disabled people and the different ways in which this can be
explained. However, as we warned at the outset, there is a real danger
that a compressed chapter on the complex history of services will serve

to over-simplify policy developments. More specifically, the thematic focus on neglect risks obscuring the fact that social care and health provision for these groups has achieved a high visibility on political and policy agendas from time to time.

At least three main strands to such periodic increased interest can be identified. First, wars can generate concern about the quality of health and welfare provision for members of the armed forces and/or civilians. For example, the emergence of blind welfare legislation in 1920 was a response to the perceived needs of blind and partially sighted ex-servicemen from the First World War. With regard to civilians, this chapter has illustrated the lack of priority allocated to older people in terms of evacuation places and with regard to access to health care services. However, the second half of the Second World War saw the debate on reconstruction driven by the Beveridge Report (1942) . This period saw elderly citizens being increasingly defined as war victims and deserving of state support. This helps to explain the *Manchester Guardian* campaign about workhouse conditions in the 1940s (see earlier discussion) as well as the emergence of home care and meals-on-wheels services for older people in the same period.

Second, the ideology of family and family care means that there are great sensitivities about the 'abandonment' of elderly and disabled people to the state, especially if this is low-quality provision where staff abuse inmates. The history of institutional provision is one of periodic scandals, taken up by pressure groups and the media, and then responded to with campaigning energy by politicians. However, such energy rarely lasts and the Cinderella groups return to being the concern of the committed few at the margins of political and policy influence. Despite this periodic determination to improve and humanise institutional regimes, one is struck by the continuity of the institutional descriptions in this chapter from the Victorian period to the present day. One of our SAUS colleagues has remarked that the workhouse regime description in the *Manchester Guardian* article of Spring 1943 could have been a description of the geriatric ward she worked on in the early 1980s. This tradition of scandals about individuals in institutions may be in the process of being transformed into media stories of people being abandoned in the community with inadequate support services.

Third, policy makers raise the visibility of community care debates when they become concerned about the cost of existing, usually institutional, provision because of demographic and other trends. This became the case in the mid-1980s when concern grew about both the projected growth in the old old (those over 75 years), the mushrooming cost of social security payments to residential and nursing homes, and the failure to run down expensive mental health and mental handicap hospitals. The development of disquiet about this situation and how this eventually fed into *Caring for People*, the 1989 White Paper on community care, is the initial focus of the next chapter. A central concern of the rest of the book is whether or not the Cinderella tag has become outdated.

3 Community Care and the Restructuring of Welfare

The focus of the last chapter was upon the neglect of service provision for elderly people and for people with physical disabilities, mental health problems and learning disabilities. However, it was pointed out that this neglect has never been absolute. At various times, concern about demographic change or the abuse of inmates in institutions has raised the political profile of these services and led to expressions of a commitment to improve or change the overall situation. This chapter begins by describing how the pressure for reform began to build up in the 1980s and ultimately led to the Griffiths Report (1988) on *Community Care: An Agenda for Action* which in turn fed into the White Paper on community care (Department of Health, 1989a) and the National Health Service and Community Care Act 1990. The second half of the chapter argues that it is a mistake to see these changes either as peculiar to community care or as the product of a temporary phenomenon known as Thatcherism. The community care reforms reflect broader debates about how best to manage large organisations in the private and public sectors and provide an illustration of a growing trend to introduce markets into public services.

The run-up to the Griffiths Report

Chapter 2 traced the growing disillusion with hospitals as the main form of provision for people with learning disabilities and mental health problems. This was to lead to the development of a care in the community initiative designed to close most of the larger hospitals after their replacement by a network of community-based services, to be run jointly by social services authorities and health authorities. Patients in hospitals were to be returned to the community as residents.

The origins of this policy shift are complex. There has been a long-standing concern within central government about the high costs of hospital provision (Guillebaud Report, 1956). In the 1970s pressure groups such as Mind and Mencap began to argue the need for a major rethink about the emphasis upon hospital-based provision and they found increasing support from key practitioners and academics. For example, *An Ordinary Life* (King's Fund Centre, 1980) provided a detailed argument for and outline of 'comprehensive locally-based residential services for mentally handicapped people'. The report was based on three fundamental principles:

1. Mentally handicapped people have the same human value as anyone else and so the same human rights.
2. Living like others within the community is both a right and a need.
3. Services must recognise the individuality of the mentally handicapped.

However, the main starting point of the care in the community initiative was growing concern about basic standards of care in hospitals for people with learning disabilities and with mental health problems. Chapter 2 showed how the issue of standards was raised initially by Robb (1967) in a book on hospital provision for elderly mentally infirm people in which allegations of ill-treatment were made. Two years later came the official report on Ely Hospital, Cardiff, which confirmed staff cruelty to patients at this mental handicap hospital. The level of media publicity generated by these incidents became so high that a policy response became inevitable.

Action taken took three main forms. Special money was set aside, a Hospital Advisory Service (now Health Advisory Service) was established to visit such hospitals, and a major policy review was announced. The White Papers, *Better Services for the Mentally Handicapped* (DHSS, 1971) and *Better Services for the Mentally Ill* (DHSS, 1975) argued strongly for the abandonment of hospitals as the mainstay provision for these two groups. Both papers set targets for the rundown of long-stay hospitals and for the build-up of community-based services to replace them. But how could the DHSS encourage health and local authorities to set about this task? The NHS Reorganisation Act 1973 established new machinery for joint planning between the two authorities, through member-based Joint Consultative Committees, and these new mechanisms were intended to drive forward the de-institutionalisation policies. They were followed in 1976 by the introduction of joint finance arrangements, partly as an incentive to joint planning, which was failing to make progress. Joint finance was a mechanism by which social services departments could obtain health authority money for a time limited period to fund community care initiatives, which would either make a contribution to the hospital rundown programme or provide support for people to remain in the community rather than to seek hospital entry.

The next major policy development was the production of the consultative document *Care in the Community* (DHSS, 1981a) which contained a wide-ranging analysis of available options for speeding up the transfer of patients into the community, including some quite radical proposals for transferring and managing funds. However, the subsequent circular, *Care in the Community and Joint Finance* (DHSS, 1983) was a disappointment to those frustrated by the slow progress. The circular discarded the more radical proposals in the discussion document and adopted a fairly unimaginative and incremental approach. With regard to joint finance, the main provisions of the circular were a modest increase in money available, longer periods of funding and an extension to include housing and education projects. Voluntary sector representation on Joint Consultative Committees was announced and resource transfer arrangements between health authorities and local authorities were encouraged. A pilot project programme, financed by special DHSS funds, was initiated.

The conservatism of the 1983 circular suggested that community care still had only limited political salience. However, the pressure for radical change intensified rather than lessened in the mid-1980s. Again, it is difficult to be precise about the reason. There was government frustration at the lack of progress achieved by the 1983 circular. There was growing concern about the implications of demographic change, especially because of the projected growth in numbers over 75 (the old old) who are known to be high consumers of health and social care services (DHSS, 1981b). But a new factor had also arrived. The mid-1980s saw the rapid growth of the private residential and nursing home sectors (Parker, 1990). In the early 1980s, the DHSS amended the supplementary benefit regulations to make it easier for the low-income residents of private and voluntary homes to claim their fees from the social security system. Public subsidy was based on an assessment of financial entitlement only and not on the need for such care. This encouraged a mushrooming of new homes in the private sector. Places rose from 46 900 in 1982 to 161 200 in 1991 (Laing and Buisson, 1992, p. 156). Although the bulk of new provision was for elderly people, some health authorities used the private sector as a source of alternative accommodation for patients from mental handicap hospitals (Hoyes and Harrison, 1987).

There was growing unease within central government about the public expenditure implications of the growth of the private sector, despite various attempts to restrict the level of charges. In 1979, such expenditure was only £10 million, but it had reached £459 million per annum by early 1986, the main reason being the rise of those in receipt of social security payments, from 12 000 to 90 000. A joint working party from the DHSS and the local authority associations was set up to review the situation and concluded that the social security system was providing a major incentive to the development of residential care at a time when central government wished to place the emphasis upon the development of domiciliary services. However, such expenditure on private institutional care continued to rise and had reached a staggering £1872 million per annum by May 1991 (Laing and Buisson, 1992).

The mid-1980s saw several other official reports which were highly critical of the failure to develop coherent community care policies. For example, the House of Commons Select Committee report on community care focused on adults with mental health problems and learning disabilities (Social Services Committee, 1985), concluding that:

1. There was a bias in policy towards getting people out of hospitals. This bias was reflected in the joint finance rules and in the selection of pilot projects.
2. Most people with special needs were already being cared for in the community (mainly by their families, that is women). This fact needed to be recognised in policies.
3. There was a lack of agreed philosophy and no consensus on what constitutes 'good' community care. The committee argued that community care should be based on ordinary housing.
4. The pace of running down hospitals was far outrunning the provision of alternative community-based services. It described this as 'the cart and the horse' phenomenon.
5. There was a lack of appropriate financial mechanisms. The mental disability service was under-financed and under-staffed. Joint finance was 'virtually played out' as a means of transferring responsibilities from health to local authorities. It argued that a real increase in total resources was required and that a Central Bridging Fund should be set up for the transitional period.

6. Joint planning arrangements needed strengthening and, in particular, the consumer's voice should be listened to in the design of services.

The government's response in November 1985 was brief and disappointing. It said that authorities were already aware of and paid attention to the needs of people in the community. It argued that financial arrangements should encourage the best models of care, but rejected the Committee's proposals for more resources and for additional bridging finance. It did, however, concede that a good community-based service was likely to be more expensive than a bad hospital service.

Progress in Partnership (Working Group on Joint Planning, 1985) reflected the growing concerns of the Local Authority Associations, the National Association of Health Authorities and the Department of Health and Social Security about the existing systems of joint planning. The report made five main points:

1. There was a need for what they described as an 'engine to drive joint planning' rather than relying on the commitment of individuals. The Working Group envisaged Joint Consultative Committees (JCCs) performing this function.
2. It argued for full joint plans for all client groups covering all agencies. These should be at both strategic and operational levels and encompass all agencies, including Family Practitioner Committees and voluntary organisations.
3. Plans should be based on the total resources available to all agencies for the particular client group, including staff and finance, both capital and revenue.
4. It called for the improved use of joint finance by:
   (a) linking its allocation to jointly produced strategies, and
   (b) not penalising local authorities for expenditure incurred under joint finance arrangements.
5. Small, genuinely joint planning teams should be established at local level for each client group and senior officers should be identified as having specific responsibility for joint planning.

Finally, the Audit Commission (1986a) report on *Making a Reality of Community Care* focused on the movement of people with mental health problems, people with learning disabilities and elderly people from hospitals into community-based provision. The report concluded that progress towards community care had been slow, especially for people with mental health problems. It had been geographically uneven and too many residents had been moved from one institution (the hospital) to another institution (private residential or nursing homes) rather than into genuine community-based provision. Five underlying problems were identified:

1. *Mismatch of resources.* Funds for community care came from numerous sources and they were not co-ordinated. The way in which resources were determined and allocated to regions did not make any provision for the shift of services and responsibility for funding them from the NHS to local authority social services departments. The system for distributing rate support grant was a deterrent to the expansion of community-based services in many local authorities, since such an expansion in many local authorities could lead to rate-capping.
2. *Bridging fund.* As argued in previous reports, this was needed to fund the transition from a hospital to a community-based service.
3. *Perverse effects of social security policy.* The present system had the effect of encouraging health and local authorities to place people in private residential and nursing homes rather than 'ordinary' housing with community care back-up. Access to benefit was not based on any assessment of need.
4. *Organisational fragmentation and confusion.* Large numbers of agencies were involved in community care. The structure of local community-based services was confused, with responsibility fragmented between different tiers of the NHS and within local government.
5. *Inadequate staffing.* Sound staff planning and effective training were largely absent even though large numbers of hospital staff wished to transfer to community-based work.

On a more optimistic note, the report focused on the characteristics of good community care schemes, which were seen as developing despite, rather than because of, existing arrangements. They tended to have five features:

1. Strong and committed local 'champions' of change.
2. A focus on action, not on bureaucratic machinery.
3. Locally integrated services, cutting across agency boundaries.

4. Focus on the local neighbourhood.
5. A multidisciplinary team approach.

But the report did not believe such 'good practice' could become the norm through incremental tinkering with the present system. Strategic change was required, including clarification of which agencies should have responsibility for which care groups. One possibility was to create joint boards which would be separate from the NHS and from local authorities, but which would draw their budgets from these agencies. The Audit Commission called upon central government to set up a high-level review to come to clear decisions on these issues.

The Griffiths Report

It did not take long for the government to respond to the Audit Commission's recommendation for a high-level review. In December 1986, the then Secretary of State for Social Services asked Sir Roy Griffiths 'to review the way in which public funds are used to support community care policy and to advise me on the options for action that would improve the use of these funds as a contribution to more effective community care'. The review was to be brief and geared to action. Sir Roy did not take formal evidence but did appoint eight advisers.

Sir Roy produced an eight-page letter to the Secretary of State and a thirty-page main report. Throughout his letter and the main report, certain themes dominated, which reflected the conclusions of earlier reports. These themes were:

1. That central government for thirty years had failed to develop any link between the objectives of community care policy and the resources made available to meet those objectives.
2. That responsibilities at the local level were unclear between health authorities, social services authorities, housing authorities, the voluntary sector and the private sector, and co-ordination was not well developed.
3. That choice and efficiency should be stimulated through a mixed economy approach in which the public, private and voluntary sectors compete to provide services on an equal footing.
4. That the system of subsidising private and voluntary sector residential and nursing home places through the social security system was

wasteful because of the lack of assessment of need for residential care.

To the surprise of many, Sir Roy rejected the Audit Commission's idea of a joint board to manage community care provision. He argued that 'major restructuring can be disruptive and time-consuming and before it is contemplated it has to be shown that the existing authorities are incapable of delivering' (p. 16). Instead, he came up with the following package of proposals.

Central government should appoint a Minister of Community Care who would be responsible for defining the values and objectives of community care as a guide to service development. The minister would be responsible for ensuring the maintenance of a link between objectives and resources as well as monitoring progress towards the achievement of objectives. A system of earmarked funds should be available to social service authorities to ensure the speedier development of community care services on the ground. The payment of such funds by central government would be dependent upon approval of submitted plans. Where possible the community care plan of a health authority should be approved at the same time as that of its corresponding social services authority. The details of this grant system were not specified but it would be about 40–50 per cent of the money to be spent by social services departments on community care.

Social services departments should play the lead role for all community care groups in terms of the identification of need, the creation of packages of care and the co-ordination of services. They should regulate private and voluntary residential and nursing homes. Griffiths stressed this was not a remit for local authorities to become a monopoly supplier, but a remit to organise or regulate a mixed economy system. Community care services needed to be responsive to local need. Social services departments were grounded in the community and were accountable to democratically elected councillors. Hence, Griffiths argued that they should have the lead role.

Housing authorities should be responsible for providing only the 'bricks and mortar' component of community care. In other words, they should provide sheltered housing but not employ wardens or organise meals-on-wheels services.

Health authorities would continue to be responsible for medically required community health services, including any necessary input into assessing needs and delivering packages of care. They would be responsible for health care, narrowly defined.

General medical practitioners should be responsible for ensuring that their local social services department is systematically informed about the needs of their patients for non-health care.

Residential and nursing home residents in the public, private and voluntary sectors should receive public financial support only following separate assessments of the financial means of the applicant and of the need for care. These assessments should be managed through social services departments. The process should start with an assessment of whether residential care is the most appropriate way of meeting care needs. The social security system should then contribute a financial assessment but the resultant benefit (the residential allowance) would be set in the light of the average total of income support and housing benefit to which someone living other than in residential care would be entitled. This system would 'leave the social services authority to pay the balance of the costs' (p. 19).

Individuals in the future would be expected to plan well ahead to meet more of their community care needs in old age. This would include making use of private pension plans and the equity tied up in owner-occupied property. Public subsidy would in the future be aimed at those on low incomes.

Reactions to the Griffiths Report

Academic commentators criticised the Griffiths Report on several grounds. It made assumptions about the ability of people to provide for their own social care needs which were not supported by available information on income and resources (Bosanquet and Propper, 1991; Oldman, 1991). The report praised the rôle of informal carers, but failed to address how burdensome that care can often be (Baldwin and Parker, 1989). It marginalised the importance of the housing dimension of community care (Oldman, 1988) and it treated the further development of a major service delivery role for the private sector as unproblematic (Walker, 1989).

However, many felt that the Griffiths Report had much to recommend it, despite these ambiguities and weaknesses. It avoided massive organisational disruption and showed a commitment to local government. It specified the responsibilities of central government, including the need for a Minister of Community Care, so that the relationship of resources to objectives could be addressed for the first time. Earmarked funds seemed to offer the guarantee of service development at the local level. A clear way forward was offered in terms of local leadership for social care and in terms of how best publicly to fund private residential care. There was a recognition of the need to foster local energy and innovation in response to local needs rather than to insist upon a national blueprint. Writing in 1988, one of us commented that:

> All these are major gains and they are worth striving to get implemented especially when we remember the range of reports over the last few years that have continued to identify the same problems. However, the spirit of implementation at both the national and local levels will be crucial. (Means and Harrison, 1988, p. 18)

Unfortunately, a key theme of the rest of this book is the lack of a positive spirit of implementation, especially at central government level.

Social services authorities welcomed the Griffiths Report with some enthusiasm. They had feared their rôle was to be marginalised, whereas the Griffiths Report had offered them the lead agency rôle for all the main community care groups, even if this involved a reduction of their rôle in direct service provision over time. Others were less convinced. Health professionals and the independent residential and nursing home sectors were unhappy with the main recommendations. Health professionals had lost in the 'battle' for the lead agency rôle (Clay, 1989). The independent sector feared the report was hostile to institutional care, and were concerned that the new funding regime would undermine the viability of individual homes.

Central government was silent on its views, but many commentators felt it was surprised and dismayed by the report (Baldwin and Parker, 1989; Means and Harrison, 1988). The Treasury were seen as hostile to the concept of earmarked funds for community care since this would make explicit the level of commitment of central government, and identify clearly when cutbacks in such services were being made. Several members of the Cabinet were said to be horrified at the idea of extending the powers of local authorities in community care; they had expected the Griffiths Report to criticise local authorities and to demand a dramatic reduction in their role (Hencke, 1989).

The White Paper on community care

The Griffiths Report was published in March 1988 and yet the White Paper on community care did not appear until November 1989. During that period, central government examined several alternatives to the proposals in the Griffiths Report, but in the end decided that none of them was implementable. The White Paper therefore followed the main recommendations of the Griffiths Report, but with some notable exceptions, and stated that all these changes were to be implemented on 1 April 1991.

Social services authorities retained their lead agency role and it was stressed that 'the Government also endorses Sir Roy's vision of authorities as arrangers and purchasers of care services rather than as monopolistic providers' (Department of Health, 1989a, p. 17). The White Paper went on to list the main responsibilities of this lead agency role:

* carrying out an appropriate assessment of an individual's need for social care (including residential and nursing home care), in collaboration as necessary with medical, nursing and other caring agencies, before deciding what services should be provided;
* designing packages of services tailored to meet the assessed needs of individuals and their carers. The appointment of a 'case manager' may facilitate this;
* securing the delivery of services, not simply by acting as direct providers, but by developing their purchasing and contracting role to become 'enabling authorities' (p. 17).

Thus, at the operational level, social services authorities were to develop case management (later called care management) as a way to deliver needs-led rather than service-led systems of assessment and care delivery. At the strategic level, social services were to be responsible for producing community care plans consistent with the plans of health authorities and other relevant agencies, and these plans were to be submitted on an annual basis to the Social Services Inspectorate of the Department of Health. These plans were intended to show how services were to make maximum use of the independent sector.

Three other important changes were announced in the White Paper. First, a new system of complaints was to be introduced. Second, a new system of inspection was to be developed for residential care in all sectors. The inspection units were to be 'at arm's length' from the management of services and were to be accountable to the Director of Social Services. Third, a new funding structure for those seeking public support for residential and nursing home care was proposed with local authorities taking over responsibility for financial support of people in private and voluntary homes, over and above their entitlement to general social security benefits. This was to be funded through a transfer of money from the social security budget to local authorities. However, local authorities would have discretion to use some of this money to fund domiciliary services which might reduce the need for so many people to enter residential care.

Most of these proposals were very close to those of the Griffiths Report. However, the White Paper did not propose a Minister of Community Care and it did not offer a new system of earmarked funds for social care along the lines advocated by Griffiths. Apart from a limited scheme to fund community services for those with severe mental health problems and another to fund alcohol and drug services, extra funds to meet the increased social care responsibilities of local authorities were to be channelled through the revenue support grant system. Most of this extra finance was to come from a transfer of money away from the social security budget where it was used as payment for residents with low incomes and resources in private and voluntary residential care. In future, local authorities were to have discretion about how much of this money should be used to develop community services rather than to fund residential provision.

The White Paper followed the Griffiths Report in encouraging local authorities to focus their energies on meeting the needs of consumers. This was to be achieved at an individual level by care managers who were to be responsible for client assessment and then for delivering flexible packages of care. At an aggregate level, this would be supported by the new system of local authority community care plans based on an assessment of need within the whole community. These plans were to be the basis for developing a wide spectrum of services, many of them contracted out, which could be drawn on as appropriate by care managers for their individual clients. The White Paper was quite clear that such packages should 'make use wherever possible of services from voluntary, 'not for profit' and private providers insofar as this represents a cost effective care choice' (p. 22). In other words, social services authorities were expected 'to take all reasonable steps to secure diversity of provision' (p. 22) and 'in particular, they should consider how they will encourage diversification into the non-residential care sector' (p. 23).

However, the White Paper did not recommend compulsory competitive tendering as the best way to achieve such a mixed economy of care. Rather it indicated that 'the government ... favours giving local authorities an opportunity to make greater use of service specifications, agency agreements and contracts in an evolutionary way'. The White Paper suggested that this required local authorities to separate their purchaser functions from their provider functions. Through this mechanism, purchasing staff within social services could be encouraged to assess objectively the contribution of 'in house' service providers, such as the home care service, against what the independent sector might be able to provide.

The NHS and Community Care Act was passed by Parliament in summer 1990, only for the government to announce major delays in the implementation timetable. Proposals on the inspection of residential homes, the new complaints procedure and the earmarked mental health grant would proceed on 1 April 1991, but community care plans would not become a statutory requirement until twelve months later and the 'takeover' of social security payments for residents would not begin until April 1993. There were several possible explanations for these delays. Were they a sensible reaction to the failure of local authorities to prepare adequately for the changes? Social services authorities may have complained about the delay but many senior managers accepted that they needed much longer preparation time (Hoyes and Means, 1991). Were the delays an attempt to control local government expenditure because of sensitivities about the then poll tax-based system of local government finance? Or did the Conservatives wish to abandon local authorities as the lead agents in community care, if and when they won the next general election?

These issues are picked up again in Chapter 5. In the rest of this chapter the focus is on responses to the more general thrust of the White Paper. If the verdict on the Griffiths Report was one of 'cautious optimism' (Baldwin and Parker, 1989, p. 151), then reactions to the White Paper were far less favourable. Some have expressed relief that the lead agency rôle for local authorities has been preserved but others have stressed the deficiencies of the White Paper compared with the Griffiths Report (Means, 1991).

There have also been several commentators who have attacked the whole basis of the White Paper. Hudson (1990, p. 33) claimed 'the primary imperative for the Government has been to find the least bad option for capping social security payments to private residential care', and hence the White Paper owed 'more to political expediency than to a commitment to a vision of "caring for people"'. Langan (1990) has attacked the White Paper as being part of a Thatcherite strategy of marketisation of public services, a view she justifies by reference to the emphasis upon the contracting out of social care services to the independent sector and the failure to guarantee adequate public resources. She concludes that these 'market-led proposals for community care' will 'guarantee only greater hardship to that section of society that is least capable of bearing it' (p. 69). Biggs (1990/91) is equally critical of the marketisation of community care, which he believes is built upon both a deep hostility to local government and a misplaced faith in the capacity of the market to generate choice for consumers. More specifically, he attacks the emergence of care management and 'arms-length' inspection systems as part of a process of professionals distancing themselves from users. Both involve a shift from client care-giving to negotiation and networking with other bodies and Biggs expresses the fear that:

> ... they also include a tendency to replace client feedback from consumers as an indicator of effectiveness, with administrative or technical issues to do with the internal 'efficiency' of the organisation and in so doing obscure judgments of a political and ethical nature. (p. 24)

He laments that 'a decade of hostility to local government welfare has severely weakened confidence amongst existing providers, so much so, that radical proposals to replace public with private welfare and change the balance of client care-giving in favour of management systems have not, as yet, been significantly resisted' (p. 35).

Quasi-markets and the restructuring of welfare in Britain

The strength of the critiques by Hudson, Langan and Biggs is that they locate the community care reforms within broader debates about the restructuring of welfare in Britain. Their weakness is that they fail to address fully the extent of the growing criticism of welfare states across the political spectrum.

In the nineteenth century, Marx argued that developed capitalist economies could produce a vast range of goods but not distribute them according to any concept of need. Increasing unemployment and poverty was the inevitable consequence of capitalism for large sections of the working class. A just society could only be achieved through the socialisation of the means of production. The speeding up of welfare reforms in Britain during the 1940s seemed to offer an alternative approach and one capable of attracting a consensus across the political spectrum. The 1942 Beveridge Report notion of insurance against the hazards of the market economy represented the social component of what was frequently called 'the welfare state'; increasingly, both Labour and Conservative governments believed that social policies should offer a universal minimum standard of housing, income, education and health for all. However, Mishra (1984) has argued that the ideas developed by Keynes were equally influential because they provided the economic component. Reduced to bare essentials, Keynesian economics argued that governments could and should intervene to manage demand in the market economy. In particular, public spending during a recession could be used to avoid the mass unemployment of the 1930s.

The attraction of such policies was hardly surprising. The Second World War caused enormous social and economic disruption and encouraged widespread concern to develop policies which would foster social integration and citizenship for all. Such policies represented a stimulus to the war effort and a practical programme for economic recovery after the war had been won. Alternatives to the compromise of welfare statism between capital and labour seemed less than appealing. For the right, there was the fear of labour unrest and, for the left, an appreciation of the exhaustion of the working class from the war, combined with growing gloom about trends in Eastern Europe and especially Stalinist Russia. Commentators on the left, including most mainstream social policy writers such as Titmuss (Abel-Smith and Titmuss, 1987) saw the welfare state as undermining capitalism by bringing out the essential 'goodness' and altruism in human beings. The welfare state might become a peaceful stepping-stone into socialism, the completion of which required a series of Labour Party victories in general elections. For the right, there was the reassurance of a recovering world economy after the Second World War.

Such policy developments are not a purely British phenomenon. Both Mishra (1984) and Deakin (1987) emphasise that similar trends in welfare provision can be traced in all developed countries. Equally, both these authors illustrate how the legitimacy of large-scale state provision came under challenge from the late 1970s onwards in nearly all these countries. Writing in the early 1980s, Mishra listed the following reasons why welfare states in the industrialised west were in disarray. These were:

> First, the onset of 'stagflation' and the end of economic growth – not only has the resource base for social expenditure ceased to grow but, more ominously, the welfare state is being seen as a barrier to economic recovery. Second, the end of full employment in some countries. Third, the 'fiscal crisis' of the state: partly as a result of the economic recession, governments in many countries face a yawning gap between the resources necessary to finance public expenditure and the revenue actually raised. Fourth, a decline in the resources available to the social services followed, recently, by a deliberate policy of cutback in services in a number of countries. Fifth, a general loss of confidence in the social system of the Welfare State. (p. xiii)

New Right theorists argue that the social policies associated with Beveridge and the economic policies associated with Keynes undermine economic growth and wealth creation. Entrepreneurial energy is undermined by excessive taxation and excessive regulation. Jobs are not taken up because the unemployed are happy to live off social security benefits rather than take low-paid employment. Government had spread its tentacles too far and too deeply; many of the resultant complex and expensive interventions, such as higher education, housing and urban regeneration, had been a failure, with little evidence of tangible results. Finally, the welfare state had become a vast vested interest, largely run for the benefit of those who worked for it (civil servants, welfare professionals). Such individuals were always keen to support new demands from new pressure groups if they seemed likely to generate yet more jobs and career opportunities within the welfare state itself.

The post-1979 Thatcher governments in Britain supported the New Right critique of the welfare state and this was reflected in many of their social and economic policies. Flynn (1989), in reviewing general public expenditure trends, together with specific policies in social security, education, housing, the personal social services and health care, concluded that policies were being driven by an ideology with four main elements:

1. Market mechanisms should be used wherever possible, even if there cannot be a fully free market for the services. In almost all the examples there are elements of the market mechanism at work, as opposed to planning, rationing and allocation.
2. Competition should be established between providers, and consumers should be allowed to opt out of state provision to sharpen competition, with the private and voluntary sectors where possible, but also between different public providers. Competition is seen as a spur to efficiency and customer orientation.
3. Individualism and individual choice take precedence over collective choices and planned provision.
4. State provision should be kept to a minimum, to encourage those who can afford it to supplement state provision or opt out. If possible, individuals should manage without help from institutions of any sort, except their own families.

However, it has been argued that, up to 1987, this support took the form of rhetoric rather than action so that few major welfare changes had been carried through (see Hills, 1990). This changed in 1988 and 1989, 'years that in retrospect will be seen as critical in the history of British social policy' (Le Grand, 1990, p. 1). Major reforms and reviews included the 1988 Education Reform Act; the NHS White Paper, *Working for Patients* (Department of Health, 1989b); the Griffiths Report (1988) on community care and White Paper (Department of Health, 1989a) on community care; and two major housing acts.

Le Grand argues that all these reforms have a common strand, namely:

> … the introduction of what might be termed 'quasi markets' into the delivery of welfare services. In each case, the intention is for the state to stop being both the funder and the provider of services. Instead, it is to become primarily a funder, with services being provided by a variety of private, voluntary and public suppliers, all operating in competition with one another. (p. 2)

Le Grand refers to these developments as quasi-markets rather than simply markets because he believes that they differ from conventional markets in a number of ways on both the supply and demand side. In terms of supply, there may be a development of multiple independent providers but:

> ... in contrast to conventional markets, these organisations are not necessarily out to maximise their profits, nor are they necessarily privately owned. (p. 5)

On the demand side, quasi-markets differ from conventional markets in that purchase is normally achieved not through money but through a voucher or earmarked budget, which are confined to the purchase of a specific service. Not only this, but 'the immediate consumer is not the one who exercises the choices concerning purchasing decisions; instead those choices are delegated to a third party (a care manager, a GP, or a health authority)', (p. 5). For Le Grand, the challenge is to assess these quasi-market reforms in terms of whether they increase or decrease efficiency, equity and choice.

Post-Fordism and the community care reforms

It could be argued that this major restructuring of welfare was driven by the energy and dynamism of a particular prime minister with a vision of an enterprise culture. However, Margaret Thatcher resigned in November 1990 and, without Thatcher, there may turn out to be no Thatcherism. Many of the quasi-market reforms are experiencing difficulties of varying degrees of severity (Le Grand and Bartlett, 1993). The premiership of John Major may see a gradual return to a belief in the provision of services on a near monopoly basis by public bureaucracies such as local government.

This seems an extremely unlikely scenario. The depth of the crisis of welfare states in a number of countries was underlined by the earlier Mishra quotation. The need to revolutionise welfare is recognised by commentators of the centre and left as well as New Right theorists (Clode *et al.*, 1987; Coote, 1992; Hadley and Hatch, 1981; Hoggett and Hambleton, 1987). In other words, dissatisfaction with the welfare state of the 1950s, 1960s and 1970s goes much deeper than the New Right. Hadley and Hatch (1981) produced *Social Welfare and the Failure of the State: Centralised Social Services and Participatory Alternatives* in the early 1980s. As suggested by the title, their central thesis was that the centralised social services of the 1940s onwards had been a failure, the reason given being that they had developed into ossified bureaucracies which alienate and despise consumers, the very people such services had been set up to serve in the first place. As a way forward, they proposed an alternative structure of social services based on four main elements:

1. Plural provision. A greater proportion of all forms of social service should be provided by voluntary organisations, the one major exception being social security.
2. Decentralisation and community orientation of statutory services. The predominant mode of statutory provision should be the community-oriented one, implying flatter structures, a different interpretation of professionalism and reinforcement as opposed to replacement of informal sources of care.
3. Contractual rather than hierarchical accountability. In return for funding and the contracting out of more services to voluntary organisations, government, both local and central, should exercise a stronger monitoring and inspection role than at present.
4. Participation and representation. The counterpart of greater monitoring and inspection should be the participation of consumers and providers in statutory decision-making.

This type of approach came increasingly to be referred to as welfare pluralism (N. Johnson, 1987). It differed from the New Right policy agenda because of its emphasis upon public subsidy rather than self-provisioning and its suspicion of the private sector as a possible service provider.

Similar themes have emerged in the body of work associated with those calling for a radical decentralisation of local government services. After their 1979 election victory, an early focus of the new Conservative Government was the deficiencies of local government in general and Labour-run authorities in particular. At the same time, many socialists saw local government as a possible base from which to undermine the recent ascendancy of the right. At the very least, there was a need to defend public services against cutbacks, but for some the task was also 'to explore the socialist potential of local government and local political space' (Boddy and Fudge, 1984, p. 2). Such islands of successful socialism could be used to wean the general population away from its apparent growing scepticism about large scale state intervention. These more radical Labour authorities were developing a range of new initiatives, relating in particular to employment, women, race and the decentralisation of services. It is the emphasis on decentralisation which most concerns us here.

A feature of the early defence campaigns was that service users, especially council house residents, seemed remarkably reluctant to identify with councillors and activists in this struggle. This became a pivotal factor in encouraging a reconsideration of the relationship of service consumers to service providers in Labour-run local authorities. The emerging critique was very similar to that of Hadley and Hatch (1981). The culprit was 'centralised, state run, functionally managed, public service provision' (Hambleton and Hoggett, 1984) which was generating growing dissatisfaction:

> This dissatisfaction rolls together concern about the remoteness of centralised decision-making structures, irritation with the insensitivity and lack of accountability of officers employed by the state, and discontent with the sectional and blinkered approach to problem solving and service provision often associated with departmental (or functional) organisational structures. (p. 4)

One response to such dissatisfaction was to decentralise services into neighbourhood offices in which rigid departmental boundaries could be broken down. Such initiatives usually included at least the aspiration to involve local residents more fully in the running of services. Initiatives developed in authorities such as Walsall, Hackney, Islington and Birmingham (Hoggett and Hambleton, 1987).

This critique of central bureaucracies had much in common with aspects of the argument put forward by those calling for privatisation or welfare pluralism. However, the proposed solution differed in that the concern was not to turn away from state provision but rather to change the way in which public services were provided: 'it involves shifting attention from the quantity of service provision to questions of quality and seeks to change the relationship between public servants and the public they serve' (Hambleton and Hoggett, 1984, p. 5). The aim was not only to improve the distribution, accountability and quality of public services, but also to raise political awareness. This was to be achieved primarily via the empowerment of the consumers and local residents through giving them more direct control over local services.

But where have the fresh organisational ideas of the New Right, the centre and the left come from, and why do all of them seem to stress devolved management, devolved budgets, cost centres, control by contracts and the need for more individually tailored services? In observing this phenomenon, Hoggett (1990, 1991) has argued that the public sector reflects the private sector in its dominant forms of organisation. In the 1950s and 1960s, industry was dominated by the large-scale production of standard necessities (sometimes called Fordism). It is interesting to note that the newly created social services departments were often disparagingly called 'Seebohm factories' in the early 1970s. The recommendations of the Seebohm Report (1968) on local authority and allied personal services had led to large numbers of smaller welfare departments being consolidated into a single larger authority. A common concern was that this would lead to more rigid managerial and bureaucratic control over the discretion of field-level staff to agitate on behalf of their low-income clients (Bailey and Brake, 1975). In other words, social services staff were becoming workers in large social work factories.

However, Hoggett points out that the technological base of bureaucracy in the private sector was undermined during the 1970s by the emergence of flexible automation and information technologies. The result was that 'the emerging market conditions of the late 1970s and 1980s heralded a shift towards a much greater degree of market segmentation built around more highly differentiated products with a much shorter lifespan' (1990, p. 11) than that associated with Fordist systems of production. In terms of private sector organisation, this saw the development of what Peters and Waterman (1982) called 'tight/loose' systems of organisation in which the centre loosens its grip over many aspects of production so that it can more effectively control the essentials of values, culture and strategy. Contracting out, decentralised production units and localised cost centres have been made possible by the emergence of computerised management and financial systems. Fierce arguments exist over the extent of these changes and whether the term 'post-Fordism' manages to capture their thrust and/or diversity. Hoggett (1991) expresses the view that 'perhaps one of the few advantages of the term … is its agnosticism about the future, i.e. it suggests that we're more clear about where we're coming from than where we're going to' (p. 243). The search is on for what Hoggett calls post-bureaucratic systems of organisational control.

It is these core–periphery models that have now come to the British public sector. But this does not mean that there are no alternatives to present Conservative Party policies in areas such as community care. Hoggett argues that:

> ... whilst contemporary processes of modernisation may be tech-
> nologically driven, they are not technologically determined. A variety
> of social choices are possible within the frame provided by a given
> techno-managerial paradigm. It follows that a variety of different
> forms of the post-bureaucratic welfare state will be constructed in
> different nations – even within the UK today the ultimate form that
> the welfare state will assume is by no means a closed book. (1990,
> p. 15)

Indeed, Hoggett believes that the opportunities created by the new para-
digm could be used to develop internal decentralisation within local
authorities, backed up by a strong commitment to democratic accountability and community involvement. However, what cannot happen is a
return to the old system of delivering inflexible community care services
through bureaucratic social services departments and health authorities.

What is occurring is a move from 'control by hierarchies' (the
bureaucratic or Fordist organisational form) to 'freedom within boundaries' (the post-bureaucratic or post-Fordist organisational form) based
on radically devolved forms of operational management. The slimmed
down centre is then left with three main tasks, namely establishing the
vision or mission around which the new regime can be constructed;
the establishment of potential objectives and performance targets; and
the maintenance of monitoring, evaluation and inspection. However,
within these broad trends, there is enormous scope for variation. The
values driving the system may vary widely. The extent of delegated
powers to the periphery can equally vary, requiring the following
questions to be asked.

1. Has the devolved unit its own budget?
2. Has the unit any control or influence over the size of this budget?
3. What control does the unit have over the way this budget can be
   used?
4. Has the unit any control over what services it provides, how they
   are provided, and to whom? (Hoggett and Bramley, 1989)

There are choices to be made, therefore, over the degree of delegation,
choices which reflect the political assumptions of the organisation and

the extent to which it prioritises issues of efficiency, equity and responsiveness. Finally, there are choices to be made over whether such delegation should be based on developing provider cost centres inside or outside the strategic core organisation. Hoggett argues that 'the radical left and the radical right may differ in terms of their preference for internal or external decentralisation (the right preferring to contract out, the left preferring to maintain a public monopoly of service provision) but whatever the preference, a much greater degree of administrative and spatial segregation of strategic and operational matters is likely in the future' (1991, p. 254).

There can be no simple drift back to the old-style social services department or 'Seebohm factory'. In the short and medium term, many social services departments seem likely to aspire to 'tight/loose' systems of management without having the sophisticated information technology (IT) systems to back this up (Hoyes, Means and Le Grand, 1992). But IT does create enormous possibilities for information and budgetary control which will develop despite the inadequacy of IT provision within social services in the early 1990s. Also the term 'post-Fordism' implies enormous organisational change but it does not specify the details of change. New Right theorists as well as other advocates of quasi-markets believe that competition between providers is essential for the efficient allocation of scarce public resources. It is the absence of such competition which undermined innovation, efficiency and concern for the consumer in traditional bureaucracies. Decentralisation enthusiasts are less convinced that competition is the main missing ingredient which explains previous poor performance. For them, consumer empowerment comes from having a strong voice or even direct control over services; work motivation comes from the right to innovate.

Conclusion

This chapter began by describing the run-up to the White Paper on community care in terms of some very specific concerns about the mushrooming costs of institutional care and the failure to run down large mental handicap and mental health hospitals. However, it has been argued that the resultant reforms need to be understood in terms of the major restructuring of the British welfare state in the late 1980s. The springboard for this was not the radicalism of the then prime minister but rather the impact of much broader international trends. These included not only growing doubts across the political spectrum about the efficiency and effectiveness of large-scale public bureaucracies, but also the emergence of radical organisational alternatives, drawn from the private sector and made possible by technological advances in information and budgetary systems.

However, the approach to community care reform chosen by the Conservative Government does reflect their distrust of the public sector, their dislike of public expenditure and their belief in the efficiency of markets. The next chapter considers how local authorities have set about developing their lead agency rôle in the co-ordination of health and social care provision for elderly people and for people with physical disabilities, learning disabilities and mental health problems, within the radical framework set down by the White Paper and the 1990 Act.

4 Towards User and Carer Empowerment?

The key theme of the last chapter was to place the community care reforms within the context of the broad criticism of welfare state institutions being run in the interests of staff rather than consumers. Increasingly, commentators talk in terms of the need to encourage user empowerment. Some have called this a theme for the 1990s (Clarke and Stewart, 1992). Certainly, it is a theme which was addressed by central government when considering the community care reforms. The White Paper claims that 'promoting choice and independence underlies all the government's proposals' (Department of Health, 1989a, p. 4) while subsequent practitioner guidance stressed that 'the rationale for this reorganisation is the empowerment of users and carers' (Department of Health/Social Services Inspectorate, 1991a, p. 7). The focus of this chapter is on the likelihood of such empowerment occurring.

The starting point is to consider what is meant by the term 'empowerment' and the contribution made to the debate by advocates of normalisation and ordinary life approaches and by the disability movement. Key issues are identified, such as whether or not all service users have common interests and whether or not the interests of users and carers are likely to be in conflict. The second half of the chapter looks at three different strategies for achieving empowerment, namely exit, voice and rights strategies. Each of these is linked to the assumptions of the community care reforms.

What is empowerment?

There is no simple answer as to what does and what does not represent user empowerment, since it is a contested concept. However, most would agree that it involves users taking or being given more power over decisions affecting their welfare and hence it probably involves taking at least some power away from service providers. Any discussion of empowerment, therefore, has to consider the concept of power. Lukes (1974), in his illuminating analysis of this concept, outlines three main

71

perspectives. The one-dimensional concept of power focuses on observable conflict and seeks to study whose preferences prevail. The two-dimensional view is more subtle in that it takes into account the way in which the powerful mobilise bias so as to ensure that the rules of the game operate in their favour so that they can keep some sources of conflict or potential conflict off the political agenda. However, Lukes argues the need to develop this perspective one stage further into a three-dimensional view of power which:

> ... allows for consideration of the many ways in which potential issues are kept out of politics ... What one may have here is a latent conflict, which consists in a contradiction between the interests of those exercising power and the real interests of those they exclude. These latter may not express or even be conscious of their interests. (p. 25)

In other words, the victims of non-decision making may not always be aware that they are victims because they do not always appreciate their real interests. This perspective, if accepted, has major implications for the empowerment debate in community care. It suggests that creating opportunities for greater participation, dialogue and control over services will not be enough, since many services users and potential service users will not be fully aware of their real interests. It suggests that empowerment requires a general raising of awareness about how society discriminates against and oppresses older people and disabled people. Professional evangelists in the ordinary life and/or normalisation movement and user groups in the independent living and/or disability movement have always been centrally interested in the more subtle forms of power. They have been concerned to identify the real interests of disabled people and then to fight for services which have the capacity to foster those interests. Each of these movements will be considered in turn.

Normalisation and ordinary living

The campaign for normalisation and ordinary life principles is primarily associated with professionals attempting to act in the interests of people with learning disabilities. There are several useful outlines available showing how the concept of normalisation originated in Scandinavia, was further developed in North America and subsequently transported to Britain (Emerson, 1992; Race, 1987). Normalisation was initially a straightforward concept which emphasised that services should attempt to deliver a high quality of life for users and that this required them to reproduce the life style experienced by non-disabled citizens through such characteristics as the rhythm of the day, progression through the life course, the development of sexual relationships, self-determination and economic standards. In other words, normalisation was 'a statement about how services can reflect the basic rights of people with learning difficulties in an egalitarian society' (Emerson, 1992, p. 3).

However, Northern American theorists, such as Wolfensberger, introduced a more sociological perspective to normalisation theory by arguing that it should be much more concerned both with the way people with learning disabilities are portrayed and perceived by the public and with the need to develop socially valued rôles for such people (Wolfensberger and Thomas, 1983). The emphasis switched to the way people with learning disabilities are labelled and have rôles forced on them. The way forward was to improve both the social image of service users and their personal competence. Proponents of normalisation see this approach as having the capacity to empower people with learning disabilities through offering them self-determination. Others have been less sure. Even if normalisation theorists attempt to empower, the driving force for achieving this is the professional. As Chappell (1992) argues:

> Normalisation offers a theory of how to improve services. As services are controlled by professionals, normalisation has enabled professionals to retain a key role in the debate about quality. It does not challenge the legitimacy of the professional role in the lives of people with learning difficulties. It has enabled professionals to adapt to de-institutionalisation by developing new models of practice. It therefore continues to legitimise their authority. (p. 40)

This is a rather harsh view, given the overall beneficial impact of ordinary life and normalisation theory upon the quality of services provided for people with learning disabilities. It should be recalled that normalisation theory was a major factor in persuading policy makers and professionals to reject hospital-based services in the UK (King's Fund Centre, 1980). However, many in user groups would agree with Chappell, especially when she argues that real empowerment would require tackling the material poverty of people with learning disabilities rather than just marginally improving the services which provide shelter at night and 'recreation' during the day.

Empowerment and the disability movement

It can be argued that many professionals have become concerned about issues of empowerment only because they are under growing pressure from users and their organisations. Oliver (1990) and Morris (1991) provide useful accounts of the development of the disability movement in Britain. They chart the growth of traditional voluntary organisations such as the Royal National Institute for the Blind and the formation of single-issue pressure groups such as the Disablement Income Group. Both tended to be ineffective in terms of improving the situation of disabled people, who began to appreciate the need to establish their own organisations. More specifically, 1981 was the International Year of Disabled People and saw the establishment in Britain of the British Council of Organisations of Disabled People, which by the early 1990s comprised over 80 independent organisations. Equally important was the subsequent formation of Disabled People International. This organisation of disabled people was formed after Rehabilitation International rejected a resolution at its 1980 conference that at least 50 per cent of the members of each national delegation should be disabled people. Morris (1991) sees this as a crucial moment of fighting back which required a struggle for power between organisations of disabled people and organisations for disabled people: 'disabled people had to assert their autonomy and attempt to take power away from the professionals who controlled not only the disability organisations but also the individual lives of disabled people' (p. 175).

The disability movement rejects the medical model of disability which places responsibility for disablement within the individual 'patient' and then gives control over their lives to professionals who are given the power to decide what they are and what they are not capable of (see Chapter 2). The movement supports a social model of disability in which the emphasis is upon how people with impairments are disabled by society both through the prejudices of its non-disabled members and the complete failure to develop the kind of public policies which would ensure the rights of disabled people to participate fully in society.

Common needs? Common interests?

The disability movement argues that the way forward is for disabled people to organise together and hence to act as capable agents rather than passive victims. Such an approach leads to an emphasis upon the common experiences, common needs and common interests of people with a wide range of disabilities. User groups such as Survivors Speak Out (mental health) and People First (learning disabilities) need to feed into a broad disability movement which in turn can join other oppressed and marginalised groups in challenging the existing political system.

Not all agree with this view. For example, some 'survivors' may feel discussions in the disability movement continue to place too much emphasis upon physical access, unless, of course, they have a physical impairment themselves. This debate has similarities to the racial dualism discourse in which some argue that a simple black – white dichotomy has served to marginalise the Asian experience of Britain (Modood, 1991). However, there is a danger of caricaturing the common interests perspective. A political position which emphasises the commonality of oppression does not preclude the recognition that different groups have specific needs, both in terms of services required and in terms of the processes which may be required to empower them at an individual and strategic level. But to what extent does such variation reflect the different disabilities of the conventional community care groupings of elderly people, people with physical and sensory impairments, people with learning disabilities and people with mental health problems?

The answer to this is: only to a limited extent. Certainly, empowerment requires a challenging of professional stereotypes about old age, mental health, learning disabilities and physical disability and these need to be replaced by a much deeper understanding of the problems faced by older people and people with disabilities. It is also clear that the stage of development of user groups is not evenly spread. People with physical impairments seem to have the strongest profile, though mental health self-advocacy groups have grown since the formation of Survivors Speak Out in January 1986 (Campbell, 1990). Numerous self-help groups campaign on behalf of people with learning disabilities, but many are composed of parents/carers rather than the users themselves. Social services managers sometimes complain about 'decibel planning' by which such groups, composed of articulate middle-class parents, attract resources to the detriment of others, such as those with mental health problems, who are seen as poorly organised and transient to the locality. Older people seem to be another badly organised group; voluntary organisations such as Age Concern claim to speak on their behalf but genuine user groups are far less common and tend to focus on broad preventive health issues (Meade and Carter, 1990).

Some types of service users find it harder than others to express dissatisfaction with the quality and appropriateness of what is provided. Older people are especially reluctant to be critical. Consumer surveys generate very positive responses about services being received, although a much less clear-cut picture emerges when the interviewer explores levels of satisfaction through a more in-depth discussion with the user (Means and Harrison, 1990). But is this also true of younger adults with physical disabilities or are they much more likely to complain direct to the service provider? In a recent study, a Crossroads scheme organiser claimed her organisation had been asked to work with younger disabled people because home help organisers from the local authority were too used to working with passive older people (Hoyes and Means, 1991). It is hard to be sure whether such views are well grounded or reflections of societal stereotypes (passive older women and aggressive young males in wheelchairs).

In general, conventionally defined care groups exhibit a very wide range of situations and requirements. The capacity of an 85-year-old with a broken hip to express an opinion about services required is very different from that of an 85-year-old person in advanced stages of senile dementia. Many individuals have a complex combination of impairments and illnesses. For example, people with learning disabilities grow older and this means they will have to cope with the same range of illnesses and physical disabilities faced by other older people. Perhaps most striking is the importance of the level of impairment or the stage of impairment. Severe learning disability or the advanced stages of senile dementia can limit communication between user and professional, especially over planning rather than individual care management issues.

The biggest weakness of a narrow focus upon the nature of the impairment is that it encourages a denial of other sources of disadvantage and discrimination, such as gender, class and race, and the implications of this for user empowerment. Some service users can afford to pay for nursing services, personal assistance and cleaning services, but the vast majority cannot. Most elderly people are female and this has important consequences for likely income levels, and for the way they are treated by health and social care professionals (Peace, 1985; Arber and Ginn, 1991).

There is a more limited literature on race and ethnicity than for gender for all the main care groups. However, studies are beginning to emerge, such as the work of Baxter *et al.* (1990) on issues and services for people with learning disabilities from black and ethnic minority communities. Their starting point is to argue that:

> only now are the white cultural assumptions underpinning current community care policies being recognised, their limitations understood and their relevance to services for people with learning difficulties from black and ethnic communities challenged. (p. 2)

Certainly for all groups, the colour-blind nature of much previous provision means that many potential recipients of services may have failed to come forward to express their needs. This, in turn, may have helped to perpetuate complacency about previous services and to encourage sweeping assumptions about the capacity and desire of black families to care for all members without support from publicly funded services (Bowling, 1990). Such a situation may mean present service recipients are skewed to certain types of user, and a real danger exists that a simplistic approach to user empowerment may fail to recognise the unmet needs of many potential users from minority ethnic groups. The avoidance of this requires key agencies to involve black and minority ethnic communities in service planning (Baxter *et al.*, 1990; Atkin, 1991).

Users versus carers?

The last section raised some important issues about whether or not the needs of all service users are the same. However, there are equally fundamental issues about the relationship of empowerment of users to the empowerment of carers. One extreme position would be to argue that this is one and the same thing, but another extreme view would be to claim that users and carers always have conflicting interests.

To grapple with this issue, it is important to start by returning to the critique which has emerged regarding the assumptions made by central government about the rôles and responsibilities of carers, and especially female relatives who provide caring functions. The White Paper stressed that:

> The Government acknowledges that the great bulk of community care is provided by friends, family and neighbours. The decision to take on a caring role is never an easy one. However, many people make that choice and it is right that they should be able to play their part in looking after those close to them. But it must be recognised that carers need help and support if they are to continue to carry out their role: and many people will not have carers readily available who can meet all their needs. (Department of Health, 1989a, p. 4)

Chapter 2 illustrated how one explanation of the neglect of community care services in the years after the Second World War was that government believed that such provision undermined the willingness of families to maintain caring rôles and so vast numbers of disabled and frail elderly people would be abandoned to the state at enormous cost. Such views changed only when research indicated that either services went to those without informal carers or their effect was to persuade carers that it was feasible for them to continue their caring activities longer than would otherwise be the case.

Chapter 1 outlined the extent to which caring roles are performed by women and how feminists have argued that community care policies represent an intensification of the exploitation of women, since they involve a shift of responsibility from paid staff in institutions to unpaid care by largely female relatives in the community. Such a perspective raises the immediate issue of how best to move forward. This has led to calls for both a major expansion of domiciliary services and a more equitable sharing of caring rôles between men and women (Walker, 1982). However, Finch (1984) in her very influential article on non-sexist alternatives to community care argued that 'on balance ... the residential route is the only one which ultimately will offer us a way out of the impasse of caring' (p. 16). In other words, the exploitation of women carers could only be overcome by persuading frail elderly and disabled people to accept high-quality institutional alternatives to living in their previous homes (see also Dalley, 1988).

This type of argument can be criticised on a number of fronts. First, many commentators believe that it is impossible to make residential care an acceptable alternative to independent living (Baldwin and

Twigg, 1991). Second, the feminist literature on caring tends to concentrate upon certain types of care situation to the exclusion of others and, in particular, too little attention has been given to the co-resident carer (usually a spouse or long-term partner) where the sense of exploitation and lost labour market opportunities may be far less (Arber and Ginn, 1991). Connected to this is the evidence cited by Morris (1991) that the extent of the female imbalance in the caring role has been exaggerated, since the 1985 General Household Survey suggested there were 2.5 million male carers and 3.5 million female carers, although the women were more likely to be involved in such activity on a full-time basis. Morris also points out that the strict dichotomy between carer and cared for is misleading in that many people with disabilities are involved in active caring roles. Third, it has been pointed out that care receivers have a gender too: for example, most frail elderly people are women, who have themselves experienced a lifetime of discrimination and exploitation, and feminists should be as much concerned about their needs as about the needs of their female carers (Peace, 1985).

Morris is quite clear about what service users perceive as the best way forward, despite the feminist critique of caring:

> Disabled and older people experience daily the inadequacies of 'community care' and would agree with everything that feminists such as Finch and Dalley say about the isolation, poverty and sheer hard work which too often characterises both their lives and that of their carers. However, disabled and older people as individuals and through their organisations have almost without exception put their energies into achieving a better quality of life *within* the community (taking this to mean outside residential care) and have thus maintained a (critical) support of community care policies – whilst recognising that the Conservative government may have some questionable motivations for promoting such policies. (p. 153)

Morris goes on to argue that feminists should be fighting alongside disabled people and their organisations for the full spectrum of support services which would enable people to remain outside or leave residential care. Such services would enable partners who care about a disabled person to make a positive choice as to whether or not they also wish to assist that person physically. This does not have to result in the bolstering of the dependency of female carers in the nuclear family, if access to extensive support services is a right for the disabled person irrespective of their family circumstances. The interests of users and carers do not inevitably have to conflict, so long as both are offered real alternatives. However, the present community care situation is very far indeed from this state of affairs. It is 'where the choice is between unsupported (or minimally supported) "family care" and residential care' that 'the physical and emotional suffering incurred by both parties to a caring relationship is often enormous' (p. 164). There are real tensions between users and carers over whose voice is being listened to by the statutory agencies, both in terms of individual care packaging and more strategic decision making about priorities for service developments.

It is also important to recognise that tensions between users and carers can flow from a number of other factors and not just from resource shortages. Values and aspirations may be in conflict and, even where a sense of reciprocity exists between carer and disabled person, this may become undermined in due course by the impact of ageing upon one or both. It is again important to recognise that users and carers may require different approaches to participation, especially in the area of learning disability. There has been a tendency to bias consultation at both the individual and strategic level towards the carer rather than towards the person with the disability, as occurred in the All-Wales strategy for people with learning disabilities (McGrath and Grant, 1992). Even where great effort has been made to ensure strong user and carer representation, the tendency is for those with the better communication skills to dominate the consultation proceedings (Wertheimer, 1990).

The heterogeneity of carers and caring situations also needs to be recognised. Carers differ by age, gender, ethnicity and in terms of their relationship with the disabled person and this has implications for the support services that they need. It is essential to recognise that 'caring situations vary widely in the extent and types of responsibilities, in the stage of life at which such responsibilities were taken on and in the constant or periodic nature of the need for caring' (Taylor *et al.*, 1992, p. 21). Hence, personal care may be the main feature of caring for a person with a physical impairment, but this is less likely to be the case in situations of mental ill-health. The parents of children with a learning disability and the partner of people with dementia are at very different stages in the life course. Yet both these roles tend to involve constant responsibilities, in contrast with the periodic caring required of a person

supporting someone with a recurrent physical impairment or mental
health problem (Perring *et al.*, 1990).

Strategies of empowerment

It is important to consider the degrees of empowerment which might be
achieved by users and carers and the different strategies or broad
approaches which might be adopted for ensuring that such empowerment occurs. Table 4.1 illustrates the enormous variation in the degree
or extent of power that can be conferred on users or taken by them.
There are very different views about how best to achieve progress up
this ladder and not all would agree about the importance of all the steps.
For example, Ramon (1991) argues that the term 'empowerment'
should be reserved for situations where real power and control are taken
by users. She complains of 'the use of the concept of empowerment by
politicians, who are constantly cutting back on services and benefits
available to people with disabilities' since they confuse 'buying power
with empowerment' (p. 17). This underlines the need to look at the three
main approaches to achieving empowerment and the different assumptions that they make. These are:

1. Empowerment through 'Exit';
2. Empowerment through 'Voice';
3. Empowerment through 'Rights'.

The assumptions behind each of these approaches are considered in turn
and their implications for the community care reforms are drawn out.

Table 4.1   *Degrees of empowerment*

HIGH	Users have the authority to take decisions
↑	Users have authority to take some decisions
	Users have an opportunity to influence decisions
	User views are sought before making decisions
	Decisions are publicised and explained before implementation
LOW	Information is given about decisions made

Source: Taylor *et al.* (1992) p. 3.

Empowerment through 'exit'

Several authors have drawn upon the work of Hirschman (1970) to distinguish between 'voice' and 'exit' models of user empowerment and consumer control (Hoyes *et al.*, 1993; Taylor *et al.*, 1992). The 'voice' approach is critical where consumers want to remain with an existing provider but wish to change the nature of the relationship, while 'exit' emphasises the importance of being able to switch services and move to alternative providers if empowerment is to occur. There is a considerable overlap in debates about the strengths and weaknesses of exit versus voice and debates about market and democratic approaches to empowerment:

* The *market* approach seeks to empower consumers by giving them choice between alternatives and the option of 'exit' from a (ie finding another) service and/or provider, if dissatisfied. Here the total pattern of provision is dictated by the sum of consumer choices – those services which are not chosen will go to the wall.
* The *democratic* approach would keep more services in the public sector but seeks to empower users by giving them a voice in services and thereby the chance to change (ie transform) their existing service or service organisation. All citizens have a say in the total pattern of services, in theory at least, through the democratic process. (Taylor *et al.*, p. 8)

However, 'exit' is not fully synonymous with the market approach, nor is 'voice' fully synonymous with the democratic approach. It is possible for users to be given the choice between a range of publicly provided services and hence the option of 'exit'. Service providers from the voluntary and private sectors may place as high an emphasis upon representation or 'voice' for their services as public sector providers. Community care planning represents a 'voice' mechanism for user and carer groups even in those local authorities committed to contracting out the vast majority of their services.

Hoggett (1992) has underlined how debates about 'exit' versus 'voice' and markets versus democracy fit into the broader debates about the restructuring of welfare which were outlined in Chapter 3:

Two distinctive strategies for reforming the public services ... began to emerge in the UK. The 'new right' set the agenda of central government whereas the 'new left' tended to set the agenda for reform at local level. Each group perceived the need to shift the balance of power between the providers and users of services in favour of the latter, but the strategies they offered differed radically. (p. 18)

For central government and the 'New Right', the preferred system of exit was through self-provisioning. Their vision of an enterprise culture was based on low taxation and minimal state intervention and provision of services. Those who gained most from the wealth generated from this enterprise culture had two obligations. As citizens, they should be willing to make charitable donations to help those struggling to take advantage of the new opportunities. As individuals, they should develop a strategy through private pensions and insurance, both to ensure they could maintain a reasonable income after retirement, and to help them meet their future health and social care needs. Publicly funded services would be a residualised service for the less well off. These views and values were quite explicit in the Griffiths Report (1988):

> In looking at future options for the funding of community care, planning needs to take account of the possibilities of individuals beginning to plan to meet their own care needs at an earlier stage in life ... Encouraging those who can afford to plan ahead to do so should help to ensure that public resources are concentrated on those in greatest need. I therefore recommend that central government should look in detail at a range of options for encouraging individuals to take responsibility for planning their future needs. (p. 22)

This position was further justified on the grounds that the incomes and savings of elderly people were rising in real terms, and that this trend would continue because of the growth of occupational pension schemes.

How feasible is this purist model of 'exit' in which the elderly person with health and social care needs would, in the future, be able to shop around for a high-quality provider, drawing upon their own resources? Considerable doubts about the viability of the model have been expressed by Oldman (1991), Bosanquet and Propper (1991) and Mackintosh, Means and Leather (1990) among others. These authors indicate that forecasts about the income and wealth of elderly people in the 1990s can be made with a fair degree of certainty because of the dominant influence of past life events in shaping future prospects for those generations now in and entering retirement. Retirement marks a significant drop in income levels for most elderly people. Over half of present retirees depend on social security benefits as their main source of income, and are thus highly reliant on changes in levels of social security. The present practice of indexation to prices means elderly people do not directly share in economic growth as reflected in the wages of earners. Despite the growth in occupational pensions, this source of income will not greatly improve the income situation of elderly people in the near future. The latest data suggest 52 per cent of employees have access to such schemes but many policies are not fully indexed to inflation, while many employees who have recently retired have had disrupted work careers and so have failed to accrue full entitlement. Finally, the interaction between state benefits and the private market means that, for some, occupational pensions act only to replace income that would once have been provided by the state.

The main source of wealth for elderly people is home ownership and the Griffiths Report suggested this could be unlocked to help develop a greater degree of self-provisioning. Bosanquet and Propper (1991, p. 277) draw on data which suggest that housing assets of older people by the year 2000 may be as high as £279 billion and that the amount of equity owned outright by this group is likely to reach £240 billion. However, many elderly owner-occupiers have low incomes. They thus find it difficult to maintain their properties, yet alone self-provide for their health and social care costs through finding ways of releasing the equity stored in their homes (see Chapter 7). The above trends suggest that there will be no dramatic explosion in the income and wealth of most elderly people in Britain during the 1990s.

If this is true of older people, it is even truer of younger disabled people, since disability is associated with poverty in most circumstances. The situation has been summarised by Craig (1992):

> The *incomes* of people with disabilities are substantially below those of the rest of the population, and three-quarters of disabled adults in private households (4.3m claimants) rely on state benefits as their major source of income. Seventy-eight per cent of disabled people live in households where there are no earners; for married disabled non-pensioners with and without children, the relevant proportions were thirty per cent and forty two per cent ... For those disabled people with jobs, earnings are lower than those of non-disabled employees, and drop with increasing severity of disablement.

Working parents of disabled children earn less, on average, than other parents. (p. 27)

Craig goes on to outline the complex web of state benefits which are available to disabled people. He points out that some of these benefits have enabled some disabled people to buy some care services, but that the scope of this for most of them is very limited and at the margins of their care needs.

What are the options available to a central government committed to 'exit' models of empowerment in community care in a situation where the resources of most do not allow self-provisioning? One possibility is to assess the level of need of disabled people, and then to offer a voucher or benefit related to that need (and their existing resources) with which they could buy the services they wanted. The Independent Living Fund (ILF) was based on these principles and it gave disabled people substantial sums of money to buy care services. The ILF was established as an independent trust to provide a weekly payment to those severely disabled adults who lost out from the abolition of additional requirements payments as part of the 1988 supplementary benefit changes. The initial press release of the Department of Social Security stressed that the aim of the ILF was 'to help severely disabled people on low incomes who need to employ personal care or domestic assistance to enable them to live independently in the community' (quoted in Craig, 1992, p. 41). It was initially expected that the ILF would provide a service for about 350 people and require a budget of around £5 million, yet by March 1991 it was helping 7724 people with a budget of £54 million.

Research carried out on the experiences of ILF clients found that they were able to use their ILF money to pull together a care package which met their needs in a way which fostered their sense of independence:

> The findings from this research challenge the assumption that disabled people are incapable of exercising effective choice and control over their own care arrangements. They also show that independent living is a relevant and important concept not only for the *young* disabled, but also for older people with many different kinds of disability, including the most severe. The experience of ILF clients ... shows how, with enough money to have care assistance under their own control, or that of a chosen advocate, many disabled people can greatly improve the quality of their lives as well as stay out of residential care. (Kestenbaum, 1992, p. 78)

As such, the ILF experience can be used by central government and the 'New Right' to justify a commitment to 'exit' models of empowerment.

Nevertheless, central government has moved to phase out this scheme. In April 1993, two new funds took over. Local authorities can provide up to £210 worth of services per week and, if further funding is required, application may be made to the Independent Living Fund for cash up to a total of £300 per week. The government has argued that the ILF was always seen as a temporary response to the 1988 social security changes rather than a national system of cash payments to buy care for disabled people. However, it is hard to avoid the conclusion that the enthusiasm of central government for the ILF (and for other voucher or cash for care schemes) is tempered by a concern that they generate high levels of public expenditure, since it is difficult to deny payment to those who meet the eligibility criteria.

As we saw in Chapter 3, the preferred exit option of central government in community care has been to develop a quasi-market in community care. The emphasis of the community care changes embodied in the 1990 Act is that social services need to stimulate a market in social care in which the voluntary, private and local authority sectors will compete to provide services. Assessment of individuals and the brokering in of appropriate care packages will be the responsibility of the care manager who will act as an intermediary between the user and the service provider. Enthusiasts argue that this will offer choice for the user and care manager at the point of pulling a package together as well as the prospect of replacing those parts of the package with which the user is subseqently dissatisfied.

Drawing on the theory of markets, Le Grand and Bartlett (1993) have identified five conditions for success:

1. *Market structure*: for a conventional market to be efficient and offer genuine choice, there must be competition or the potential for competition. That is, there needs to be many providers and many purchasers, or at least the opportunity for new providers to enter and existing providers to exit from the market relatively costlessly.
2. *Information*: both sides of a market must have access to cheap and accurate information about the costs and quality of the service provided. Monitoring of quality is an essential part of any quasi-market system.
3. *Transaction costs*: these are the costs involved in drafting, negotiating and safeguarding packages and contracts. These costs need to be

less than the efficiency gains achieved through developing quasi-markets in social care.

4. *Motivation*: for markets to work appropriately, providers need to be motivated at least in part by profit making, whilst purchasers must be motivated to maximise the welfare of users.

5. *Cream skimming*: in order to achieve equity, markets must restrict opportunities for discrimination by either purchasers or providers in favour of the cheaper or less troublesome users (the cream): the relatively healthy, the less needy, the more self-sufficient.

It has become increasingly evident that the division between purchaser and user in the quasi-markets operating in public services like community care poses a number of problems (Le Grand, 1992; Hoyes *et al.*, 1993). Competition in the market may be reduced by the existence of monopoly or near-monopoly purchasers and cosy relationships with dominant providers. Do users have the sanctions to upset these cosy relationships and demand that the authority 'exit' to another contractor? Quality in welfare is notoriously difficult to monitor. If it is defined by purchasers and providers, there is no guarantee it will fulfil user needs. Information flow is constrained by the fact that many choices are made under duress or in crisis. Many welfare providers are not commercially motivated and may find it difficult to make the shift from considering, say, the welfare of their users to the financial state of their provider units. Why should purchasers (indirect consumers) have the direct con-sumers' interests at heart? And how will they know what the consumers' interests are? Finally, welfare services are particularly vulnerable to cream skimming. Chapter 5 takes this argument forward by reviewing the extent to which the implementation of the community care changes is witnessing the emergence of the conditions specified by Le Grand for the successful operation of quasi-markets.

Empowerment through 'voice'

The limitations of 'exit' or market approaches to empowerment in community care are increasingly recognised, even by those who feel they have much to offer service users. One weakness is that the 'exit' literature is most easily applicable to those people who have been assessed as having a need which requires a publicly funded service. It has little to tell us about the processes by which certain groups and not others are defined as a priority for services, and it tells us nothing about how some potential service users will fail to come forward for assessment because of perceptions that care managers and service providers are hostile and prejudiced against certain groups and not others. Such subtle, and not so subtle, mechanisms may disempower large numbers of potential service users in a context where the small number who are receiving a service appear to have great choice, and hence confirm the value of quasi-market approaches. As such, 'exit' approaches appear to have a very unsophisticated view of power when compared to that offered by Lukes, outlined earlier in this chapter.

Second, a quasi-market of social care providers may be helpful to users and potential users at the time of assessment in terms of generating choice. However, once a user begins to receive a service, 'exit' may appear a poor option even where there is dissatisfaction with the quality of service received:

> Exit is a blunt instrument, when the overall service may be what the consumer wants, but there are aspects of it which he/she would like changed, eg the time at which a home help arrives or the range of tasks he or she is able to do. (Hoyes *et al.*, 1993, p. 13)

There are two options in this type of situation. The purchaser can put pressure upon the service provider through the contract if one exists (that is, they can threaten contract withdrawal at a later date unless the service improves). Or the service user can exert an influence upon the service they receive through a user committee or other voice mechanisms. This seems a particularly important issue for those service users for whom 'exit' is not really an option or when 'exit' would impose very high costs. For example, many people receiving a mental health service do not have the right of exit because they are being detained against their will, but it remains crucial that mechanisms are developed by which their voice will be heard. Equally, the majority of elderly people in residential care or nursing home care would not consider moving to a new home as a realistic option.

In fairness to the government, the community care reforms introduced by the 1990 Act included a mixture of 'exit' and 'voice' mechanisms. The whole emphasis of community care planning is that social services as the lead agency are required to seek the views of others before deciding upon the overall strategic direction, and users and carers have been included by the government amongst the key constituencies for consultation. Second, care managers are intermediaries between service users (or applicants) and the developing mixed economy of social care. As such, the user has the potential to influence the professional through a 'voice' mechanism which leads to the putting together and subsequent delivery of an appropriate and flexible care package.

This issue can be further conceptualised by drawing upon the work by Hoggett (1992) who has developed a two axis diagram (see Figure 4.1) based upon four quadrants. The diagram distinguishes both between the degree of control/participation on offer and whether the 'voice' mechanisms are operating at the individual or collective levels. The diagram can be illustrated best by considering what is on offer in terms of 'voice' mechanisms to particular individuals. For example, with regard to a woman with a severe learning disability, the following set of questions would need to be asked:

Figure 4.1   *Dimensions of empowerment through voice*

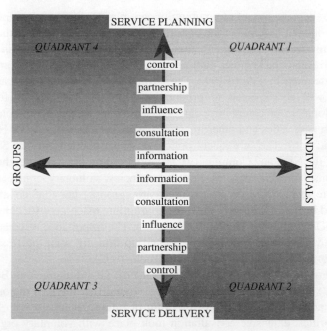

Source: Hoggett (1992) p. 19.

... to what extent does she have influence over the construction of her own care or service plan (Quadrant 1)? As a user to what extent does she have influence over the manner in which these services are then delivered (Quadrant 2)? She may also be part of a group which receives a particular service (for example, they all attend the same day centre). To what extent is this group able to influence the way in which this service is provided (Quadrant 3)? Finally, this woman will be one of many living in her area with similar needs and problems. To what extent is this group involved in the service planning process (Quadrant 4)? (p. 19)

The answers to these questions depend on the extent to which purchasers, providers and, crucially, care managers are willing to share power. They also depend upon the stage within the community care planning and care management process at which this sharing takes place.

User consultation and community care planning

Since the new system of community care planning is such a significant development in terms of the opportunities it creates for local authorities to consult users, this next section examines experiences so far in some detail. All social services authorities had to publish their first community care plans by 1 April 1992. The White Paper stated that 'local authorities will be expected to produce and publish clear plans for the development of community care services, consistent with the plans of health authorities and other interested agencies' (Department of Health, 1989a, p. 6). The subsequent policy guidance pointed out that Section 46 of the NHS and Community Care Act 1990 required local authorities to consult health agencies, housing agencies, voluntary organisations, private agencies, user groups and carer groups, but that no attempt would be made to specify the most appropriate machinery for achieving this (Department of Health, 1990, p. 14). The importance of consulting users widely was subsequently backed up both by some professionals (Osborn, 1991) and by user groups (Took, 1992).

How have local authorities responded? Glendinning and Bewley (1992) studied 99 of these plans. They found that the vast majority of local authorities made use of the joint planning machinery with health authorities, extensive consultation took place with voluntary organisations, but only 16 per cent of plans stated clearly that user groups had been involved in the planning structures and this was usually at working group level only. They concluded that, 'while extensive and creative attempts have been made to publicise the plans, particularly in their draft and final stages, less attention seems to have been directed to ensuring that disabled people, whether as service users or local residents, are actively involved in the actual planning process itself' (p. 25).

These findings have been confirmed by Hoyes and Lart (1992) and Martin and Gaster (1993) in their more detailed case study approach to the evaluation of community care planning. The former looked at four contrasting local authorities, Hammersmith and Fulham, St Helens, Oxfordshire and Devon, in terms of whether or not a central role was given to users and carers in the planning process. Each is outlined in turn, because they give a real flavour of the situation on the ground in terms of the quality of 'voice' mechanisms available to user and carer groups. It should be stressed that the situation described relates to spring 1992 and all four authorities have since had the chance to develop and amend their approach as a result of lessons from producing the first set of plans.

Hammersmith and Fulham is an inner London borough, whose social services department approached community care planning by strengthening the joint planning machinery with the health authority, and by supplementing this with open consultation meetings. The first community care plan was produced in April 1991, a year ahead of the statutory requirement. This document contained detailed information about the borough and its services, and so was able to function as a background resource guide during the production of the second community care plan in April 1992.

Joint planning was strengthened in two ways. First, social services representation on the joint planning teams was at senior officer level. Second, a 'network' of voluntary, community and self-help groups was set up for each of the joint care planning teams so that the voluntary sector representatives on the teams had a forum for support, feedback and discussion. In addition, a small grant was made for servicing these networks while the Hammersmith and Fulham Association of Community Groups had a part-time post funded from joint finance money to work with the joint planning structure and to develop the networks.

Each joint care planning team had a timetable for producing their service planning statement for the community care plan, and these were then edited by social services staff as a key part of producing the initial draft plan. Open meetings on the draft plan were held in early 1992 but these were widely perceived as unsuccessful, mainly because they were publicised at very short notice. An alternative approach to consultation was tried in June 1992 in the form of a 'fair' for the black and ethnic minority communities. The social services department recognised the need to make future consultation exercises more accessible and community-based, and also part of a continuing process rather than a once a year exercise associated with the annual publication of a community care plan.

St Helens is a metropolitan borough council where, since 1986, housing and social services provision has been combined into a single personal services department. The community care plan was drafted by a team of four senior officers from the personal services department. This group drew upon a number of initiatives, including a care management pilot, a multi-agency quality assurance group and a voluntary sector committee on community care which was organised through the local Council of Voluntary Service (CVS). The latter group was composed of members from the CVS, Age Concern, the Spina Bifida Association, the Handicapped Children's Trust and the Crossroads Care Attendant Scheme.

The key initiative in terms of community care planning was a collaborative group of managers from health and social services which was seen as having a very positive impact on working relationships. Not only this, but the published version of the plan was jointly owned and signed by St Helens and Knowsley Health Authority and St Helens and Knowsley Family Health Services Authority. The draft community care plan was circulated very widely for comment in early 1992, while separate presentations were made to the independent residential care sector, among others. The chosen process for community care planning involved only limited direct input from users and carers, although the voluntary sector committee did carry out a small survey of user and carer views and its membership did include the parent of a physically disabled child. This was recognised by the plan itself which stressed that 'in developing future plans particular emphasis will be placed upon ensuring that user groups and individual users of services, particularly those in residential establishments, are consulted'.

Oxfordshire is a large, mainly rural county where, in June 1990, two posts were created by the social services department to oversee the production of a community care plan. The aim was to produce a plan which was joint with key health agencies yet locality-based, with a high involvement of users and carers. Each of the five geographical divisions nominated a community care representative who was responsible for devising a local consultation procedure for the period May to July 1991. Not surprisingly, the chosen procedures and the priority allocated to their implementation varied considerably. In two divisions, large public meetings were used to establish locality planning teams for each care group, and membership included users and carers as well as voluntary organisations and private providers. These groups have now been integrated with the local joint planning machinery. The social services department estimated that over 1000 people were consulted in this period as part of 'an untidy but comprehensive' process.

In addition to the divisional consultation process, a county-wide conference was held in November 1991 on services for people with learning disabilities in which 50 per cent of participants were carers and users, supported by a self-advocacy group. The Oxfordshire Council for Voluntary Action organised two county-wide conferences for voluntary organisations when the initial and final drafts were published. It had been hoped to run separate open conferences in each division, but only six weeks was available for the final consultation stage.

The original intention was to produce a community care plan comprising five divisional sections and a county overview. However, two problems emerged. The resulting draft was lengthy and repetitive, while there was little in the way of actual plans, with even the descriptive sections suffering from inadequate information on activity levels and expenditure. In January 1992, the social services department decided to produce a community care plan without the divisional sections, which were instead to form the basis for the continued development of locality planning and for the publication in September 1992 of local 'commissioning statements' setting out identified needs and bids for budget allocations.

The fourth authority studied was Devon, where the delivery of social services was organised through thirty-two district offices. Devon's approach to community care planning was that the centre should establish strategic aims and values, but the detailed interpretation of these was a district office responsibility in the light of local needs and circumstances. These strategic aims and values were laid out in a document entitled 'Policy Aims and Objectives' which was produced after extensive consultation with the voluntary sector and other key agencies. The draft community care plan was a development of this rather abstract document. Consultation on this plan took four months and involved the distribution of 10 000 copies. Those invited to comment were told a more detailed 'reference file' was available at district offices. Many voluntary organisations and user groups were critical of the lack of detail in the plan and their lack of involvement in its production, although many were complimentary about its wide distribution for comment and recognised that the final version was a major improvement on the draft.

The longer-term aim is to develop district planning statements which will feed into the community care plan of the county. These district plans (or purchasing statements) will be informed by the aggregation of the needs (both met and unmet) of service applicants as well as through a system of district forums which will enable a wide range of local groups and individuals, including users and carers, to engage with the planning process at the local level.

These four case studies confirm the general findings by Glendinning and Bewley (1992) that local authorities are still at the very early stages of thinking through how best to develop a dialogue with users and carers as part of community care planning. This view was forcibly expressed to Hoyes *et al.* (1993) by many of the user and carer groups which they interviewed about their community care planning experiences:

'The current community care plan doesn't reflect the consultations.'

'They have consulted, but are services stitched up already?'

'The drafts aren't readable for most people.'

'It needs a lot of new support to enable users to make decisions. We need money to train people for assertiveness, for example. There is no money in social services for this.'

'People from social services are paid to attend meetings. Carers are doubly exploited, expected to provide care for nothing and attend meetings free of charge.' (Quotations from Chapter 3, Hoyes *et al.*)

The conclusion was that the case study authorities had a genuine desire to improve their dialogue with user and carer groups but that they had an enormously long way to go.

Put another way, the prerequisites to enable user and carer groups to increase their power and influence through such planning mechanisms are not yet in place. Drawing upon the work by Taylor *et al.* (1992), it is possible to identify what some of these need to be (see also Took *et al.*, 1993):

1. *Access* means considering whether users and carers have the facilities to get to key planning meetings, whether the venues are

physically accessible and what the cost implications (including child care and sitting expenses) are of attendance.

2. *Information* is part of access. People cannot make choices if they are not informed about key meetings and they cannot give an informed view without information. Such information must be presented clearly, attractively and in good time – translated into minority ethnic languages where necessary, and into Braille, large print or onto tape. At meetings, British sign language translation, loop systems or lip-reading should be available as appropriate. Interpreters may need to be trained if they are not to reflect existing power structures. Information needs to capture people's attention if it is to be used. Local authorities should use a variety of channels for disseminating information, and publicising its meetings and policies, including broadcasting. The essential foundation for this is a comprehensive map of user and carer groups, backed up by a good, up-to-date mailing list.

3. *Clarity* about the degree of influence on offer is essential since people need to know the scope and limits of the contribution they can make. If people are to contribute effectively, they need to know what it is they are expected to contribute and what the outcome will be.

4. *Support and advocacy* are necessary because many people are not used to being asked for their views. To contribute effectively they may need advocacy, especially if they do not have verbal communication skills or have learning disabilities. This advocacy needs to be independent. Development resources and training are needed if people are to have the confidence and skills they need to speak up, especially in consultation structures.

5. *Timing* must be considered since it is essential to allow sufficient time for people to form views and to feed them back and for material to be translated as appropriate. With consultation structures this is especially important as representatives will need to sound out their constituencies. It is also essential to consult early in the decision-making process, before too many vested interests have been created. Otherwise, the process of consultation is in reality one of ratification.

6. *Results*: social services authorities should commit officers and members at a high level to ensure that consultation can influence decisions. Users should be given an input into the agendas of meeting they attend. Users should be told at the earliest opportunity what has happened as a result of any meeting or consultation exercise.

7. *Commitment and structures*: if users are to have an input to decision making, institutions concerned with planning, purchasing, assessment and delivery will need to transform their decision-making processes accordingly and provide the mechanisms for users to be involved. These should allow for a variety of inputs to reflect the different interests and capacities of users. Experience suggests that unstructured open groups are best for exploring needs and generating ideas; a small structured group is better at translating ideas into well argued implementation strategies.

Rights and empowerment

In his discussion of a 'voice' approach to empowering a woman with a severe learning disability, Hoggett (1992) argued the need not only for options/alternatives and advocacy/representation as preconditions but he also claimed that she needed 'a right/entitlement to a service in the first place' (p. 19). This brings us to the issues of rights and empowerment.

For the New Right, 'rights' are essentially the right of individuals to pursue their own goals and objectives, and to meet their own needs, free from intrusive intervention from the state. This view is taken by de Jasay (1991) who goes on to argue that the alternative approach of the collectivity giving rights to individuals suffers from the fact that a right for one person is an obligation for another, and the temptation is to campaign for rights which one will be the beneficiary of or for which one will not have to pay directly. De Jasay does not believe government has the capacity 'to strike the balance between the advantage of those who get the rights and the burden of those who must assume the obligation' (p. 43).

The opposite perspective is taken by many in the disability movement. They believe an 'exit' approach to empowerment through self-provisioning is meaningless for those on low incomes, while many 'voice' approaches fail to work because they do not address the imbalance of power between the service user and the professional. Hence, service users are treated in patronising and stigmatising ways as they attempt to prove their eligibility for a service which is then delivered in a standardised and uncaring way. For example, Kestenbaum (1992) in her study of ILF clients found that:

the choice and control they valued so highly could not in their experience be provided by statutory authorities. It is not simply a matter of resource levels, though these are very significant. As important are the qualities that any large-scale service-providing organisation would find hard to deliver:- choice of care assistant, flexibility, consistency, control of times and tasks, etc. (p. 77)

Many in the disability movement believe that the way forward from this situation is to argue for a rights-based approach to cash and/or care for disabled people. Hence the concern is to argue for much more than a right to fair treatment and consideration (often called procedural rights) and rather to push the case for legally based rights. They see this as needing to cover not only the right to appropriate services or the cash to buy those services, but also a right to an income which ensures material comfort and an environment which does not disable those with impairments.

A key justification for this view voiced by the disability movement is that, as disabled people, they have a right to participate fully in society and to be full citizens of that society (Oliver,1990; Morris, 1991). As such, their arguments are an important contribution to the broad debate about social rights and citizenship associated with the left wing think-tank, the Institute of Public Policy Research. Coote (1992) has summarised the social rights perspective in the following way:

People do not start out on the proverbial 'level playing field': many have disadvantages, of which some are constructed and avoidable, while others are inherent or insuperable. Welfare policies should therefore aim to minimise the avoidable disadvantages and compensate for the others, in order to equalise the 'life chances' of all. The idea of 'life chances' is closely linked to the idea of individual empowerment as a requirement of citizenship. Citizenship entails being able to participate in society, to enjoy its fruits and fulfil one's own potential, and it follows that each individual citizen must be equally able (or 'empowered') to do so. (p. 4)

The difficulty of this perspective lies in moving away from generalities about social rights to the specification of what these might be. Authors such as Cranston (1976) have long argued that social rights could never be enforceable in the same way as civil rights because they are not universal. For example, the meaning of any right to medical care would vary enormously in content according to which society one was in or what time period one was talking about. Equally, no society could possibly meet every medical need of every single citizen at all times. Social rights are expensive and have to be rationed, even if you believe in high public expenditure, unlike the New Right theorists.

However, it is easy to exaggerate such difficulties, since many of the same issues exist with regard to the enforcement of civil and political rights. Plant (1992) has pointed out that 'there must be a right to the protection of civil and political rights, but there cannot be a right to the services of a policeman, as these are subject to the same problems of scarcity as doctors and teachers' (p. 21). He goes on to argue:

> The idea of rights in the public sector provides a new way forward between the market and democracy as two models of empowerment. This is not to decry either markets or democracy, only to say that there is a case for looking at a new way and seeing how far we can get with it. If these rights can work and be made clear and enforceable, whether they are rights to have certain procedures followed, or actual rights to resources, then this would clearly be a more direct way of empowering the citizen than either the market, or bureaucratic regulation, or greater democratic accountability. (p. 28)

Plant's article is in a collection of essays on developing new social rights, and a subsequent chapter on community care (Doyle and Harding, 1992) specifies how the procedural rights of users could be further developed. The Disability Manifesto Group (1991) has gone further than this by producing detailed proposals on what range of benefits and services need to be available to disabled people if they are 'to move significantly closer to exercising their full rights of citizenship' (p. 1).

However, service users have only limited rights under existing community care legislation. An important exception is the Disabled Persons (Services, Consultation and Representation) Act 1986. Although not fully implemented by 1993, it does address 'rights' in a wide range of different ways:

> ... the right of a disabled person to be represented in dealings with a local authority by a person authorised to speak on his or her behalf; the right of a disabled person to demand full assessment of his or her need for services provided by a local authority; the right to

receive a written statement, following an assessment of what services the local authority intends to provide or why it proposes not to provide services; the right of disabled persons' carers to have their needs taken into account; and the right of disabled people's organisations to be consulted before any person is co-opted to a formal committee to represent disabled people's interests. (Barnes *et al.*, 1990, p. 114)

In addition, we have seen how the NHS and Community Care Act 1990 established a mandatory complaints procedure with which users and carers can challenge the fairness with which they have been treated by their social services authority. It could be argued that the 1986 Act and the new complaints procedure offer no more than procedural justice rather than any prospect of substantive rights. However, some lawyers are beginning to specialise in community care law. They point out that it is difficult for users to know their rights, because the existing law is scattered over numerous Acts (see earlier chapters) and many of the powers and responsibilities of local authorities are allocated through ministerial discretion. The complication of ministerial discretion creates a buffer between the user and the local authorities. Even where the High Court has accepted that a local authority has not met its duties under such Acts as the Chronically Sick and Disabled Persons Act 1970, it has merely referred this back to the Secretary of State to use his default powers under the National Assistance Act 1948 (and now the 1990 Act). Roberts (1992) explains:

A disabled woman with multiple sclerosis claimed damages against a local authority for negligence, and for breach of its statutory duty under section 2 of the Chronically Sick and Disabled Persons Act 1970, claiming that the authority had failed to meet her need for adequate home help services, and for practical assistance in the home. The Court of Appeal dismissed the claim, on the grounds that, where a local authority fails to discharge its functions under the 1970 Act, the *only* proper legal procedure is to request the Secretary of State to exercise the default powers granted to him under section 36 of the 1948 Act. (pp. 16–17)

In Roberts'view, the NHS and Community Care Act 1990 makes only limited changes to this situation. It does strengthen the right of individuals to an assessment since section 47(1) states that:

where it appears to a local authority that any person for whom they may provide or arrange for the provision of community care services may be in need of any such services, the authority (a) shall carry out an assessment of his needs for those services; and (b) having regard to the results of that assessment, shall then decide whether his needs call for the provision by them of any such services.

While Section 47(2) goes on to state:

If at any time during the assessment of the needs of any person under sub-section (1) (a) above it appears to a local authority that he is a disabled person, the authority (a) shall proceed to make such a decision as to the services he requires [under section 2(1) of the Chronically Sick and Disabled Persons Act 1970] without his requesting them to do so, and (b) shall inform him they will be doing so and of his rights under the Disabled Persons (Services, Consultation and Representation) Act 1986.

Roberts interprets this to mean that 'the duty of a local authority in relation to assessment will be strengthened, but the nature and content of the services which can, or must, be provided remain unchanged' (p. 16).

Not all community care lawyers share this gloomy assessment of the 1990 Act. Some believe the wording of Section 47 means that it may be able to establish that a disabled person has a right to a service once assessed by a local authority as having a need. At the time of writing (mid-1993), this situation had not been clarified in law.

This type of welfare rights approach in a hostile political climate does generate tactical dilemmas. The existing government is not going to concede to many, if any, of the demands of the disability movement. Local authorities will continue to face an enormous gap between the limited resources made available for community care and the expansive objectives of the legislation (see next chapter), and we suspect that some gap between need/demand and resources will always exist, irrespective of the attitude of central government to public expenditure. Therefore, in the short term, and possibly in the longer term, community care will be about the language of priorities rather than (or as well as) the language of rights. Local authorities have no alternative but to establish priority groups for a service and to deny services to others. However, we feel local authorities should be honest and clear to users, and their organisations, about these priority processes and show their commitment to user empowerment by funding networks of user advocacy and representation groups. Priority systems need to be fair – between the care groups and to individuals – and decisions need to be open to challenge.

Second, there is a danger that users, in their attempt to escape dependence on social welfare professionals, end up becoming dependent on legal professionals. The same dilemma faced the poverty lobby in the 1960s and early 1970s. Many argued for a legal approach to welfare rights in which the aim was to establish rights for all through establishing a precedent in a single case as a result of a discretionary decision made by a social security office. At one stage, this appeared to be expanding the rights of low-income people on state benefits, but Titmuss (1971) warned that this was leading to excessive legalism which undermined the willingness of officials to make 'one off' humane decisions. It also began to generate an enormously complicated social security system which only legally minded welfare rights experts could cope with. The eventual response of central government was to simplify the system radically. Claimants were given clear rights, but rights to very little. The same dilemma may emerge with regard to community care law.

Conclusion

The first half of this chapter looked at the contribution of the disability movement, and to a lesser extent normalisation theorists, in raising the issue of empowerment for users to the top of the community care agenda in the UK. The second half assessed three markedly different strategies for achieving empowerment, namely exit, voice and rights-based approaches. Despite the obstacles to achieving a rights based approach, we have no doubt that such a perspective is essential for the empowerment of service users and of carers. This is for two main reasons. First, unless disabled people and full-time carers have a right to an adequate income, they will experience poverty and not empowerment (Chappell, 1992; Disability Manifesto Group, 1991). Second, procedural rights may be less preferable than substantive rights, but strong procedural rights can protect users and carers against the arbitrary power of professionals.

However, the community care reforms are more concerned with issues of 'exit' (for example, developing a mixed economy) and 'voice' (such as community care planning) than 'rights'. It is also clear that individual local authorities will vary in their enthusiasm for 'exit' and 'voice' approaches. Hoyes *et al.* (1993) argue that one way of conceptualising this is to think in terms of the following three models of welfare:

1. The *welfare state* model, where the state both finances and provides care.
2. A pure *market* model which makes the consumer or client the purchaser of care from independent providers. The consumer would have a contract directly with the provider, services would need to conform to a British standard and there would be a system of redress in the event of a faulty service.
3. The *quasi-market* model which is embodied in current policy, where the state is the purchaser of care from independent providers, but where the choices of the consumer are mediated through a care manager, with a system of redress related to quality standards set (usually) by the purchaser. The user may have a contract, mediated by the care manager with access to redress via the purchaser, but also with a voice through the democratic system.

Hoyes *et al.* argue that, if the combination of 'exit' and 'voice' that the third model represents is to operate to the best advantage of the user, this requires that authorities, whether they identify more closely with the welfare state or with market aspects of the model should:

1. stimulate a market of diverse providers which offers choice to users and carers;
2. ensure the provision of advice, information and advocacy to help service users and carers through this range of services and to help them assert their claims to a quality service;
3. develop service standards and definitions of quality in conjunction with users and carers;
4. promote and encourage mechanisms which supply service users with the opportunity both to develop their own services and to have a say in existing services (user committees and so on);
5. provide accessible channels for user and carer groups to engage with the community care planning process.

The section in this chapter on community care planning has shown how only limited progress has so far been made with regard to involving users and carers. The next chapter will illustrate how far most local authorities have still to go in terms of stimulating an adequate range of services and introducing user-centred care management systems. It will also suggest that resources to fund advocacy services and to promote a further development of user and carer groups may fail to materialise, both because of overall financial pressures and because of a temptation to restrict service purchase to those activities which can be listed as part of an individual user's care package. Funding for preventative and developmental activities may become badly squeezed.

5 Leaders at Last: The Changing Rôle of Social Services

Chapter 3 looked at Sir Roy Griffiths' recommendation that social services authorities should be given the lead agency rôle for community care and how this proposal was eventually accepted with reluctance by central government. Chapter 4 outlined the limited progress that has so far been made in involving user and carer groups in community care planning. This chapter considers the story of reform implementation by social services and tackles a number of central questions. Have social services been willing and able to stimulate a mixed economy of social care provision? Are social services developing internal purchaser–provider splits? Are systems of care management evolving which are driven by needs rather than the availability of a limited number of traditional services?

The above questions are addressed by drawing upon the emerging literature on the implementation of the community care reforms. In particular, this chapter makes extensive use of a series of research projects with which the authors have been involved in collaboration with colleagues at SAUS (Hoyes and Means, 1991; Hoyes, Means and Le Grand, 1992; Hoyes *et al.*, 1993 and Smith *et al.*, 1993). Much of this material illustrates the limited progress that has so far been made in terms of developing needs-led assessment, involving users in community care planning, stimulating a mixed economy of social care, and so on. However, any judgement about the performance of social services departments as the lead agents in community care needs to be set against an awareness of the difficult climate which has faced social services authorities in their attempts to implement the community care reforms, as well as an appreciation of the size of the task being asked of them, relative to the time that has so far elapsed within which to move forward. Finally, it must be remembered that research on implementation takes time to publish and its results will reflect an earlier situation on which local authorities have had an opportunity to build.

Managing change in a climate of uncertainty

Chapter 2 provided an overview of the history of neglect associated with social care services in England and Wales as a result of which, social services authorities are not only being asked to implement a complex reform package, but they are doing this in a context where existing service provision is often woefully inadequate.

Another important legacy of the past has been professional rivalry over rôles and responsibilities in community care. One objective of the White Paper was to resolve this issue once and for all by allocating the lead agency rôle for all the main care groups to social services authorities. Chapter 6 will outline the long history of professional rivalry, especially between health care and welfare professionals, and go on to illustrate some of the tensions which continue to exist, and which make the successful development of the lead agency rôle by social services a highly complex and difficult task to achieve. However, the emphasis of this section is on the problematic climate faced by social services since the passing of the NHS and Community Care Act 1990 in terms of political uncertainty, financial stringency, change overload and organisational uncertainty.

Political uncertainty flowed in the main from the fact that pushing back the implementation timetable meant that the main funding changes were to take place after the 1992 general election. If a Labour Government had come to power, they would have wanted to reverse the NHS reforms, and they might have wanted to challenge the emphasis within the community care reforms on developing markets through internal purchaser–provider splits and the contracting out of former local authority services. Such a possibility was an encouragement for some Labour-controlled local authorities to delay their thinking on future structures until the outcome of the 1992 general election was known. The suspicion was expressed by several commentators that a further Conservative election victory could mean that the lead agency rôle was to be taken away from local author-ities after all. One study of forty senior managers and members from social services authorities and other key agencies in four different areas in the period March to July 1991 found that the likelihood of 'a General Election within 12 months made strategic long-term thinking .... difficult and unattractive' (Hoyes, Means and Le Grand, 1992, p. 58).

To a large extent, the general election in April 1992 resolved this par-ticular source of uncertainty. A Conservative Government was returned and so far there has been no suggestion of reneging upon the allocation of the lead agency rôle in community care to social services authorities. However, the election result has done nothing to resolve or reduce overall tensions between central government and local government. In Labour authorities, in particular, this has created an immensely stressful climate for senior managers as they attempt to respond to the often conflicting advice, suggestions and instructions from central government and from local politicians.

Closely linked to political uncertainty has been the issue of *financial stringency*, both in terms of local government finance overall and community care funds in particular. In respect of local government finance, reform implementation has been played out against, first, the collapse of the poll tax and the struggle to implement the new council tax. Added to this have been the general attempts by central government to control public expenditure. The result has been that numerous local authorities have been forced to cut services, impose higher charges and freeze posts in order to avoid generating high central government penalties.

The specific funding for community care services is equally problematic. Most money is not earmarked specifically for such services, but has, rather, to be argued for at a local level from the general rate support money disbursed by the Department of the Environment to each local authority. However, built within each block grant are assumptions about what the individual local authority should spend on its main services. These standard spending assessments (or SSAs) include one which defines what the Department of the Environment deems is the amount of money which individual authorities need to spend on their personal social services.

An excellent outline of this highly complex system has been provided by Harding (1992, pp. 8–20). She points out that SSAs are not built up from local need but are, rather, a device for distributing the overall money which ministers and the Treasury have decided can be made available to fund services through local authorities. The social services SSAs were not introduced until 1990/91. They are divided into three blocks, which are children under 18 (35.5 per cent of the total), elderly people (45.2 per cent) and other adults who require support (19.3 per cent). The three blocks are calculated in different ways but all rely on population estimates and deprivation factors, several of which are open to challenge in terms of their relevance to what local authorities need to spend on their personal social services.

As a system, it is open to two major criticisms. First, the overall sums are completely inadequate to meet the objectives for the personal social services being set by the Department of Health. Second, many believe the SSA variations between local authorities cannot be justified. Harding points out that Greenwich's allocation under the Children's Social Index formula is £43 per child, compared to £171 in Lewisham and £242 in Wandsworth. In other words, as Harding points out:

> The calculations used for the weightings have markedly different effects on different authorities – areas with apparently similar populations and social conditions end up with very different financial allocations. (p. 13)

Harding suggests a number of reasons why this might occur, including dependence on an out-of-date 1981 census (presumably a problem that has been remedied) and the omission of key factors such as data on disability prevalence.

The net result is that most local authorities are overspending their SSA for the personal social services. As the charge capping of local government expenditure is tightened, local authorities are forced either to 'steal' money from other services, cut expenditure on the personal social services, or attempt to generate income through the introduction and/or expansion of charges for services. This has not created an easy financial climate within which to introduce the community care reforms, a situation exacerbated by uncertainties over the funding charges for residential and nursing home care introduced from 1 April 1993 onwards. It was decided that there would be no change in funding arrangements affecting existing residents, and that the new system would only affect new applicants. The amount of money available for distribution to local authorities in 1993–4 and the two financial years thereafter did not become known until October 1992. This meant that the first community care plans were expected to outline a strategic direction for services in a situation where local government finance was in turmoil and where information about 'new monies' was not available.

The delay in clarifying the situation was caused by two factors. First, there were arguments between the Treasury and the Department of Health about how much money could be afforded. Second, there were arguments about the criteria for distributing the money to individual local authorities. Should the allocation reflect existing expenditure on provision by the Department of Social Security or should it be based upon an assessment of need related to the SSA formula? A high emphasis upon the former suffered from the fact that a key argument for change was that the old system created incentives to enter institutional care unnecessarily, and so provision did not reflect need. A high emphasis upon the latter risked provoking a collapse of the private residential and nursing home market in some areas, and involved more money flowing to Labour-controlled metropolitan authorities than to Conservative shire counties.

The third area of pressure concerns policy *change overload*, and in particular the fact that the implementation of the community care reforms under the NHS and Community Care Act 1990 was preceded by a complete overhaul of child care law under the Children Act 1989. The aim was to create a uniform and coherent framework for public and private welfare law including the basis on which the state can intervene to protect children as well as the powers and duties of local authorities in respect of family support and preventative action. Not only have the changes required of local authorities been enormous but the philosophy and approach of the child care changes are in marked contrast to those of the community care reforms, as explained by Alaszewski and Manthorpe (1990):

> In some ways the 1989 Children Act and the Community Care White Paper build upon and reinforce different traditions within social services and social work. The Children Act is based on the professional child care tradition and places emphasis on the social workers' role in protecting children, acting as advocates and participating in legal proceedings. The community care proposals are more related to the traditions of the old Welfare Departments, with an emphasis on the social workers' role in allocating limited resources and administering services. (p. 246)

Thus the change overload has been generated by more than the simple volume of legislative change. It has been exacerbated by the contrasting approaches of these two key pieces of legislation.

This links into the final area of pressure, namely the extent of *organisational uncertainty*. The government has insisted that there is no intention to generate two separate local authority departments, namely a child care department and a community care department (Hallett, 1991), but the two pieces of legislation have encouraged local authorities to consider the need for major restructuring with an emphasis upon moving away from generic social services teams dealing with all clients in a locality to the development of more specialist teams. On top of this, local authorities have been considering whether to reorganise so as to reflect a purchaser–provider split in their community care activities. Personal social services departments have experienced regular reorganisations (Challis, 1990) and this seems to be an increasing rather than decreasing tendency as a result of the pressures outlined above. The Audit Commission (1992) described local authorities as facing 'a cascade of change', with the clear implication that they risked being swept away if the timing of change was not carefully thought through. In July 1992, the government established a community care support force to help local authorities, health authorities and other agencies implement the required changes. An early conclusion of the support force was that many social services authorities were in a state of organisational chaos as a result of half completed or recently completed major restructuring of social services departments. Osborne and Rees (1992) in their study of six social services departments found that four had revised their organisational structure and one was about to because of the emphasis placed by central government on the purchaser–provider split.

Finally, social services authorities face in the mid-1990s the prospect of organisational change on an even greater level, given that a review of local government boundaries is taking place with a view to abolishing those units which are seen as unnatural entities (for example, newer counties such as Avon and Humberside) and extending the number of single-tier arrangements whereby all local authority services are provided by a single unit of administration.

This section has underlined the extent of the problems and pressures faced by social services authorities in developing their lead agency rôle and in implementing the community care reforms. The rest of this chapter considers implementation progress despite this difficult climate of uncertainty. This is tackled by first looking at care management and then going on to consider whether local authorities are developing a mixed economy of social care and/or internal purchaser–provider splits. The chapter concludes by considering the implementation of the new funding regime for community care.

Care management

The first major implementation issue to be addressed in this chapter is the amount of progress that has been achieved in developing new needs-led assessment and care management systems. The White Paper stressed that a primary objective of the community care reforms was 'to make proper assessment of need and good case management the cornerstone of high quality care' (Department of Health, 1989a) while the subsequent policy guidance devoted a whole chapter to this issue (Department of Health, 1990).

The policy guidance outlined the three stages of a proper care management system, namely:

1. assessment of the circumstances of the user, including any support required by carers;
2. negotiation of a care package in agreement with users, carers and relevant agencies, designed to meet identified need within available resources;
3. implementation and monitoring of the agreed package, together with a review of outcomes and any necessary revision of services provided.

The implied critique of past provision, as explained in earlier chapters, was that the practice under previous systems involved slotting people into a limited number of inflexible and traditional services which often did not meet their needs or which were organised to meet the requirements of service providers rather than service users and their carers. The policy guidance argued that the new system of needs-driven assessment and care management could overcome these major weaknesses in existing practice and achieve no less than six major objectives:

1. ensuring that the resources available (including resources trans-ferred from social security) are used in the most effective way to meet individual care needs;
2. restoring and maintaining independence by enabling people to live in the community wherever possible;
3. working to prevent or to minimise the effects of disability and illness in people of all ages;
4. treating those who need services with respect and providing equal opportunities for all;
5. promoting individual choice and self-determination, and building on existing strengths and care resources; and

6. promoting partnership between users, carers and service providers
    in all sectors, together with organisations of and for each group
    (Department of Health, 1990, p. 23).

The policy guidance was soon followed by further government reports
offering advice on the details of establishing care management systems
(for example, Department of Health/Social Services Inspectorate,
1991a).

So far, it might appear that care management is like 'mum's apple
pie', an uncontroversial positive development for users, carers and professionals alike. Later in this section we will outline the hesitant
progress that local authorities are making towards implementing care
management strategies, but, to understand some of the reasons for this,
we need to understand the background and some of the disputes which
exist about the way care management should be organised, whom it
should be aimed at and what it might be able to achieve.

There is widespread agreement that case management (or care
management as it is now called) has its roots in North America
(Beardshaw and Towell, 1990; Fisher, 1990–91). Care management
emerged as an approach for steering people through a multiplicity of
health and social care agencies. The care manager tended not to be a
direct service provider but rather was a broker or advocate who mediated
on behalf of the client between service-providing agencies and more
informal care givers such as family members, friends and community
groups. Fisher argues that numerous care management schemes identified
major gaps in the availability of long-term care services for elderly
people. One of the consequences was that they attracted government
funds to stimulate appropriate services, thus developing important financial control responsibilities in potential conflict with their advocacy rôle.
However, the Department of Health were influenced less by this North
American experience, and more by the way it was taken up and applied in
the UK as a result of their own 'care in the community' initiative. More
specifically, the department were impressed by the positive research
findings of the Personal Social Services Research Unit at the University
of Kent in their evaluation of care management pilot projects in Thanet
(Kent) and Gateshead. (Challis and Davies, 1986; Davies and Challis,
1986; Challis *et al.*, 1988). Both were aimed at frail elderly people at risk
of entering residential or nursing home care. Hudson (1993) provides a
very clear description of the basis of the Thanet scheme:

Social workers with considerable experience of work with elderly people and with smaller caseloads than usual were given access to a decentralised budget. The money could be spent on a variety of services not normally available through the social services system but the social workers (in effect acting as care managers) were required to cost the packages of care which they organised. Although there was freedom to construct the packages of care considered to be most appropriate to the needs of clients and carers, this had to be within the overall constraint of two-thirds of the cost of a place in a residential home. A particular feature of the care packages was the inter-weaving of informal care (such as relatives who were willing to handle finances) with semi-formal care (such as a helper to visit daily) and the formal statutory services. (p. 4)

Just under 100 frail elderly people were supported through this care management service in Thanet and their experiences were compared to a matched group receiving services in the conventional way from a neighbouring area in Kent. The results were overwhelmingly positive (as they were in the subsequent Gateshead experiments). The probability of death within one year and of admission to long-term care within one year was halved and the probability of continuing to live at home was doubled. Informal carers felt less exploited and more supported, while perceptions of well-being on the part of service users were improved. All of this was achieved at lower cost than if residential care had been supplied as the main option.

However, at least three complications have arisen in interpreting these results in terms of their general implications for the reform of community care in England and Wales. First, queries have been raised about the robustness of the methodology in terms of whether or not too many problematic clients were filtered out from the experimental group. Second, a conclusion that care management has much to offer frail elderly people does not indicate whether or not the same positive effects will occur for all other groups. Third, there has been a great deal of care management experimentation and so there are now several different models on offer rather than just the Kent/Gateshead approach. Each of these issues is considered in turn.

Fisher (1990–91) has pointed out how the research team excluded 110 of the originally identified cases by using criteria such as clients keen to enter care, carers being unwilling to share care and so on. He points out how Challis and Davies (1986, pp. 24–5) mention that ten were excluded because of such factors as chronic anxiety, deafness and dementia, which leads him to conclude:

> In short, it appears that some key practice dilemmas were not included in the work of the TCCS [Thanet Community Care Scheme]. Clients reluctant to stay in their own homes, chronically depressed clients, clients with dementia or hearing disability and carers reluctant to share care are central areas of practice concern and it is legitimate to question whether care management was fully exposed to these circumstances. (p. 217)

A rather different point is that the success of pilot projects is notoriously difficult to replicate, because they tend to involve highly motivated staff being given preferential workloads and extra resources (Means and Smith, 1988). The Thanet experiment is less exposed to this weakness than many pilot schemes, and the results were replicated in Gateshead, but it is still wise to show caution about the ease with which such gains can be spread throughout the country.

The second point is whether or not 'success' with frail elderly people wishing to avoid residential care can be translated into 'success' for a much wider range of elderly people and also to the other main user groups. Indeed, the PSSRU research team have warned repeatedly that this is an approach which can benefit certain types of users in certain types of situations, rather than an approach which should be applied to all users, or even to all users with complex needs. Hence, their justification for screening large numbers of elderly people from their original case samples is almost certainly that they have known all along that care management cannot keep everyone in the community and out of residential care at low cost and within tolerable levels of burden for carers. Therefore, Davies (1992, p. 20) is unapologetic that the Thanet experiment was based on the principle of offering 'case-managed care for selected users', who were essentially people who were 'at high risk of *inappropriate* and *available* admissions to institutions for long-term care' (author's emphasis). Davies complains that Kent Social Services Department abandoned this clear focus after 1987 and tried to develop a much more general approach to care management which was doomed to fail.

The third complication facing local authorities as they consider their care management implementation strategy is that there are different care management models available, not just the Thanet/Gateshead approach. One reason for this is that the DHSS established in 1983 twenty-eight pilot 'care in the community' projects designed to help long-stay hospital residents move to community settings (see Chapter 6). These pilot projects covered people with learning disabilities, mental health problems and physical disabilities as well as people with age related problems. Cambridge (1992) has stressed the enormous variety of service delivery arrangements which have emerged. Table 5.1 provides a typology of the seven main care/case management arrangements in the twenty-eight projects. In terms of the community care reforms, a key dimension of variation was whether the care management pilots were based in social services, in a health setting or within multidisciplinary teams. The Thanet/Gateshead experiments were based within social services departments and aimed at frail elderly people who had been referred to social services. This was a far less obvious model for the twenty-eight pilot projects whose starting point was people living inappropriately in hospital. Second, several of the models chosen stressed the need for the care manager to act as an advocate or broker on behalf of the client. They should not be constrained by the resource dilemmas of the statutory agencies, but rather should be based in independent or semi-independent organisations (see Chapter 6 for further discussion of this issue).

Thus, local authorities find themselves facing considerable uncertainty and disagreement about what care management is and how it might be able to help within the new community care arrangements. Is care management something to be applied to all clients, all clients with complex needs or clients in very specific situations? Should care managers be located inside or outside social services? Are they advocates on behalf of clients, rationers on behalf of social services, or both? Until such issues are resolved, it is difficult to obtain clarity about the core tasks of care management, and how this relates to existing assessment skills associated with social workers, home care organisers, community nurses, occupational therapists and others. In Thanet, care or case management was carried out only by social workers, but much more flexible models emerged in the twenty-eight care in the community pilot projects.

In fairness to central government, there has been some recognition of the complexity of what is being asked for and social services have been reassured that change will need to be spread over several years (Foster and Laming, 1992). The full extent of the implementation challenge has perhaps been best summarised by the Audit Commission's (1992) report on *Community Care: Managing the Cascade of Change*. This report opens by outlining how, under previous systems, the user was expected

Table 5.1 *A typology of case management arrangements in the Care in the
Community Programme*

Type 1 Residential social work arrangements, where key workers were
responsible for day-to-day monitoring, with project leaders, residential
managers or line managers overseeing assessment and case review, or taking
responsibility for securing particular resources. Examples from the programme
included Islington and Greenwich.

Type 2 Sub-area social services case management, where a senior assistant or
care manager for a client group, network or patch held responsibility for most
case management tasks, and co-ordinated inputs from a range of individuals
inside and outside the agency. Examples were Somerset and Calderdale.

Type 3 Peripatetic social services case management, involving senior social
work staff, some with health authority backgrounds. Service managers or co-
ordinators were also usually team members with caseload responsibilities. Such
teams tended to be democratically managed, with accountability to principal or
chief officers in divisions or headquarters. Examples from the programme
included Kidderminster's resettlement team and Maidstone's integration with
Kent's care management structure.

Type 4 Multidisciplinary case management, with joint health and social services
teams, where case managers either retained separate line management or worked
to a joint management committee. Team members had their own caseloads but
also provided specialist inputs. Examples were Bolton and Brent.

Type 5 Multidisciplinary teams, though solely within the health service, taking
in different specialisms, with accountability to the health authority. Liaison and
co-ordination with voluntary organisations and social services departments does
not extend to team membership. The best example from the programme was the
Chichester community rehabilitation team.

Type 6 Quasi-brokerage case management, using mechanisms such as
individualised funding agreements. The Cambridge project is currently
developing such an approach. Loosely linked were some micro-budgeting
arrangements such as those developed by Maidstone and Darlington, and
individualised budgets controlled by users themselves, as in Glossop.

Type 7 Semi-independent case management outside the public sector, with
responsibility for the regular tasks of case management held by support and care
staff employed by a voluntary organisation. Health, or more usually social
services, professionals shared some case management responsibility, gaining
entry via public funding (from dowries, direct grants, top-ups for residential
placements). Examples from the programme were Torbay and Warwick.

Source: Cambridge (1992) p. 513.

to fit in with existing service requirements, and the service received was often more dependent on which agency received the initial request for help rather than on actual needs, even for people in very similar situations. Hoyes, Means and Le Grand (1992, p. 35) found this tendency to be equally strong within departments. Hence, an occupational therapist referral will be assessed as requiring an occupational therapy service while the same person, if referred to home care, might be defined as requiring a home help. However, the simple decision to place user and carer needs first sparks off a cascade of change, as illustrated by Figure 5.1. The central point about this figure is not only the scale of change required, but also the order in which the changes may have to be tackled. Key strategic decisions have to be made about how to stimulate a mixed economy of care, whether or not to develop an internal split within social services between purchases and providers, and these decisions then have to be underpinned by new and appropriate financial, structural and procedural arrangements. Social services authorities also need to develop new assessment systems and forms which are needs-driven and which are acceptable to a wide range of agencies. Decisions have to be made about who will be a priority for services in the light of likely resource levels. And thought will have to be given to how wide a range of staff within and outside social services might perform the rôle of care manager. All this has to be tackled before a needs led assessment and care management system can be put into operation. As the Audit Commission (1992) explains, 'a process of change has been set in motion which will turn organisations upside-down' (p. 19).

Under these circumstances, it is perhaps not surprising that most authorities have made only limited progress so far in the establishment of needs led assessment and care management systems. Allen, Dalley and Leat (1992) reviewed implementation progress on behalf of the Association of Directors of Social Services in twelve authorities. Overall, they found authorities pursuing a cautious approach with an emphasis upon clarifying assessment structures and eligibility criteria before any attempt to implement fully fledged care management systems. There were fears from social services that 'increased consumer awareness and choice implicit in increased assessment would open up a Pandora's Box full of dissatisfied customers' (para. 11.2) especially given the great uncertainties about future resource levels. There was little agreement about who should be the care manager, who should hold the budget, and whether there should be a clear separation between assessment and the subsequent management of the care package.

Figure 5.1   *The cascade of change*

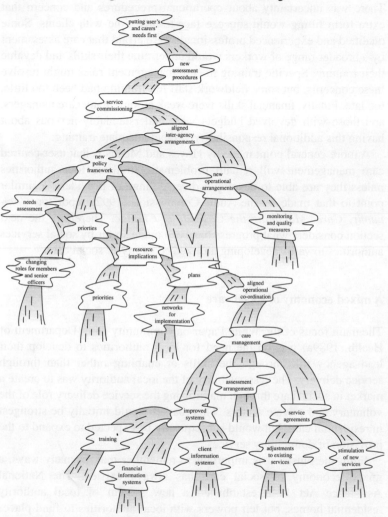

Source: Derived from Audit Commission (1992) p. 38.

Hoyes and Means (1993c) found rather more progress but many of the same problems in their four cases studies, with the cautious optimism of managers contrasting with the pessimism of many field-level staff. Feelings of ill-preparedness or impending chaos were expressed by some of those who were, or will be, performing care management tasks. There was uncertainty about operational procedures and concern that extra form filling would squeeze face-to-face time with clients. Some qualified and experienced professionals were afraid that care assessment by a broader range of workers would undermine their skills and devalue their training. Specific training in care management rôles might resolve these concerns, but some fieldwork staff felt training had been too little, too late. Finally, financial skills were weak among many care managers, and those with devolved budgets were understandably nervous about having this additional responsibility without adequate training.

A more general point made by Hoyes and Means is that user-centred care management will remain problematic in these four authorities unless they are able to develop a diverse range of providers, a similar point to that made by the Audit Commission (1992) report on *Community Care: Managing the Cascade of Change*. Therefore, the next section considers what progress has been made so far by social services authorities towards developing a mixed economy of social care.

A mixed economy of social care

The main focus of the White Paper on community care (Department of Health, 1989a) was on the need for local authorities to develop their lead agency rôle through the skills of enabling rather than through service delivery. The responsibility of the local authority was to create a market in social care through maximising the service delivery rôle of the voluntary and private sectors. This market would initially be strongest in residential care, but would subsequently be expected to expand to the provision of domiciliary services.

From the outset, it is important to remember that, in many ways, a mixed economy of social care has always existed. The National Assistance Act 1948 established a new system of local authority residential homes, but left powers with local authorities to fund places in residential homes run by the independent sector, while it allocated the primary role in the development of domiciliary services to voluntary organisations (see Chapter 2). Although the reasons for this are complex, one key factor was a desire to develop a postwar role for organisations like the W(R)VS, the British Red Cross Society and NOPWC (now Age Concern) which had all developed extensive welfare services during the Second World War (Means and Smith, 1985). However, local authorities became frustrated at the failure of voluntary organisations to develop coherent authority-wide provision for services such as meals-on-wheels, day care and visiting/counselling schemes. This created what one commentator called 'a wind of discontent in the town halls' (Slack, 1960). Chapter 2 described how this was a factor in the gradual extension of local authority powers to provide such services. However, the rôle of the independent sector was never completely squeezed in terms of these traditional services for elderly and physically disabled people, while large voluntary organisations such as MENCAP and MIND began to emerge as service providers for other groups, usually with the aid of grants from the local authority or through joint finance monies. Finally, Chapter 3 illustrated how the social security system funded a major growth of private sector residential and nursing home care in the 1980s.

Table 5.2 illustrates not only the extent of social services funding of non-statutory organisations in the late 1980s, but also the great

Table 5.2 *Local authority social services department funding of non-statutory organisations as percentage of total expenditure, 1988–9[1]*

Authority type and statistics[5]	General contributions to vol. orgs.			Contracts with private vol. orgs.		
	ELD[2] %[5]	MH/LD[3] %[5]	All[4] %[5]	ELD[2] %[5]	MH/LD[3] %[5]	All[4] %[5]
Inner London mean	2.6	1.1	3.2	7.1	27.2	8.0
Outer London mean	0.6	1.0	1.1	5.0	16.9	7.1
Metropolitan district mean	0.3	0.7	1.1	1.4	4.1	3.0
Shire County mean	0.8	1.5	1.4	2.8	10.0	3.8
All authorities mean	0.8	1.1	1.4	3.2	11.2	4.6

Notes
1. Allocations expressed as percentages of relevant total client group expenditure.
2. Services for elderly people.
3. Services for people with mental health problems or learning disabilities.
4. All PSS services.
5. The percentage given is the mean for the local authorities in the category.

Source: from Knapp *et al.* (1993) p. 8.

variation in the extent of that funding between different local authorities. Thus, social services departments have faced very different starting points with regard to the further developments of a mixed economy of social care within their areas. However, it is this development which is at the heart of their enabling responsibilities, as stressed by the White Paper on community care. Wistow *et al.* (1992) have argued that enabling is a many sided concept which can be defined as personal development (maximising individual potential), as community development (mobilisation and support of community-based resources) or as market development (social services need to create a market in social care and then regulate that market through contracts and service agreements).

It is clear that the White Paper on community care was committed to this third approach to enabling, which represents a major cultural shift for both local authorities and voluntary sector organisations. It is therefore important to consider what are the main prerequisites for enabling markets to work in social care. Both Hoyes and Le Grand (1991) and Hoyes and Means (1993a) argue that the rôle of the local authority in the successful introduction of a market-led pattern of services must not be underestimated. It is at least as important that the authority be prepared to generate supply as to purchase services, and the way in which authorities choose to award contracts may in itself have a profound effect upon the local market structure. The existing market structure varies enormously between areas. The uneven distribution of private and voluntary residential homes, with a concentration in seaside resorts, has been graphically demonstrated (Audit Commission, 1986a). The independent market in domiciliary services is far less developed, with few large suppliers and many small ones; local authorities have little experience of contracting out in this field, although, if future services are to be based on individual packages of care for people in their own homes, these are likely to assume greater importance (Booth and Phillips, 1990). The White Paper recognised these potential supply problems, stating that one of its key objectives was 'to promote the development of a flourishing independent sector alongside good quality public services'. Moreover, social services departments are expected to make clear,

> where such providers are not currently available, how they propose to stimulate such activity. In particular, they should consider how they will encourage diversification into the non-residential sector. (Department of Health, 1989a, p. 23)

However, stimulating new and diversified markets may not be easy. The voluntary sector has expressed fears about losing autonomy and flexibility, and about compromising its advocacy and campaigning rôles; smaller groups in particular may not feel up to the demands of bidding for and fulfilling contracts (Gutch, 1989; Taylor, 1992). The government recognises the need for authorities to continue to provide core grant funding to voluntary organisations to underpin administrative infrastructure and development work, but it is questionable whether social services authorities will choose to spend their limited resources on this rather than the purchase of particular services. Diversification from residential provision may appear to be a logical step for many suppliers, especially if demand is shrinking. However, it may not necessarily be a straightforward move for small, or even larger, organisations whose experience is limited to providing care in an institutional setting.

If a local authority is to stimulate a market, it will need to do more than contract out its residential care. Interventions required on the supply side include help with business development grants; subsidies and credit for start-up and working capital; training; and licensing and regulation. On the demand side, care managers need to operate more as brokers and advisers, rather than as agents making all the decisions. There is clearly a lot of scope here for authorities to promote or block market developments and the Social Services Inspectorate may well have a crucial rôle to play in assessing individual authorities' efforts as set out in their community care plans.

In addition to local authorities' abilities to stimulate alternative provision, they will also have scope for manipulating the market by the way in which they use suppliers. For conventional markets to operate efficiently, perfect competition requires that there should be neither a monopoly (one or few suppliers) nor a monopsony (one or few purchasers). It is likely that in some areas, for some services, the social services department will be the only purchaser. Whilst this may make it easier for the authority to dictate terms, it may also deter potential suppliers from entering a market where they will be dependent on a single buyer. On the other hand, if an authority, for the sake of administrative convenience or economy, chooses to enter into block contracts with one or two suppliers, they risk squeezing out other smaller suppliers and will find themselves faced with a monopoly and in a very weak position. Authorities will need to consider to what extent they are able and wish to guard against these situations by, for example, operating care management systems which devolve responsibility and resources to many purchasers, and by encouraging many suppliers by undertaking the interventionist strategies such as those described above.

Several studies have examined the attitudes of senior managers and members towards the move to a system of service delivery which relies more and more upon the contracting out of social care services to independent providers. One of the earliest studies was by Hoyes and Means (1991, 1993b) who carried out a small number of interviews in two shire counties in the period June to November 1990, to ascertain attitudes to the community care reforms. In both case studies, respondents saw the need for a further contracting out of services and they expected this process to gather pace over the next five years. But others emphasised their belief in the quality of many local authority services. Doubts were expressed about the existence of alternative domiciliary providers, and anxieties were outlined about the cost and feasibility of regulating a system of social care based on a multitude of small providers. Similar views have been found in a number of other studies (Allen, Dalley and Leat, 1992; Hoyes, Means and Le Grand, 1992; Hoyes *et al.*, 1993; Osborne and Rees, 1992) which have found in local authorities a desire to move towards a needs-led system through the development of a mixed economy of social care at odds with a pride in existing local authority services and sometimes a deep suspicion, especially from Labour members, of the private sector.

The most detailed study of these issues is an investigation into the implementation of the community care reforms in twenty-four local authorities which was funded by the Department of Health (Hardy, 1992; Wistow *et al.*, 1992). This research has highlighted not only the wide range of mixed economy options available to social services authorities (see Table 5.3) but also the wide diversity of attitudes to the ten options identified in the research report:

> While it would be wrong to generalize too freely, there were some clear and largely predictable rankings in attitudes towards these options. Thus most Labour authorities preferred d to e, and strongly preferred e to f. Indeed, option f was a non-starter in some author-ities. If the possibility was mentioned, they also ruled out j and were often unhappy about h. To take another example, most Conservative authorities supported option g, expressed some practical but not ideo-logical reservations about h, and usually liked the idea of e and f in principle even though elected members had some difficulty support-ing the sale of facilities in their own wards. Option c hardly ever

received support from either officers or members, and it was too early for local authorities to make any judgements about the viability of option j. These are gross generalizations, and only rarely were two authorities alike. Indeed, one of the strong conclusions to emerge from our study was that generalizations along party political lines are often hard to sustain. (Wistow *et al.*, 1992, p. 30)

Not only did attitudes to the options in Table 5.3 vary widely, but implementation strategies were being pursued with some caution in terms of

Table 5.3   *A simple catalogue of potential alternative modes of provision of community care*

---

a. Continuing local authority provision as it is currently organised, with no planned changes to the management, funding or regulation of activities.

b. Continuing local authority provision with reorganisation of the SSD along the lines of a purchaser/provider split of some kind and to some degree.

c. Management or staff buy-outs of some local authority services.

d. Floating off some services to a not-for-profit trust which allows the local authority to retain some degree of control, though with eligibility for DSS payments.

e. Selling off services, perhaps at a nominal price, to voluntary organisations (new or already working in the authority) which act independently of the authority, except for any service agreements or contracts.

f. Selling off services to private (for-profit) agencies (new or already with a presence in the authority) which act independently of the authority, except for any service agreements or contracts.

g. Encouraging (or perhaps simply not stopping) voluntary or not-for-profit organisations setting up new services.

h. Encouraging (or perhaps simply not stopping) private (for-profit) agencies setting up new services.

i. Considering health authorities as potential providers for some social care services, such as residential care for elderly people or people with mental health problems.

j. Bringing NHS trusts into the supply picture.

Source: Wistow *et al.* (1992) p. 30.

developing internal purchaser – provider splits, tendering out services and stimulating markets in social care. The main reasons given for this were those factors outlined at the beginning of this chapter, namely resource uncertainties and the implementation of the Children Act. But the slow development was also explained in terms of pride in existing provision and the difficulties being faced in developing alternative suppliers. Hardy (1992) outlined a number of factors at work in the twenty-four authorities he and his colleagues studied:

1. There is a perceived paucity of alternative suppliers in domiciliary and day care.
2. Some potential alternative suppliers are reluctant to alter their rules.
3. Many alternative suppliers are underdeveloped in terms of management capacity and experience.
4. There is a paucity of volunteers.

The end result is caution in the vast majority of the twenty-four case studies in which a selective approach to the diversification of supply is adopted involving a preference in most authorities for working with voluntary and not-for-profit agencies. However, at the time of the fieldwork, four authorities had still not clarified their view about contracting out, two were 'conscientious objectors', and three were 'proven enthusiasts', determined to implement their policies rapidly.

This picture is confirmed by other studies such as those by Hoyes *et al.* (1993) and Common and Flynn (1992). The latter argue that a more developed market in social care could be created over time if social services purchasers pursue appropriate strategies:

> By providing sufficient cash, offering contracts which give a degree of continuity, encouraging suppliers to come forward and developing a simple contracting process, the market can be stimulated. Conversely, parsimony, short-term contracts and a hostile and complicated purchasing arrangement will discourage existing and potential suppliers. (p. 36)

However, they warn that, even where markets are beginning to emerge, they are not offering more choice to service users and carers. The twelve contracts studied in depth offered little or no more choice to users than had previous arrangements, since access remained controlled by professionals, the contracted-out service was often a replacement for a previous 'in-house' service and it was often the only service on offer.

Lart and Means (1992a) have considered the implications for existing user and carer groups of local authorities wishing to contract out service provision further. They looked at thirty-two such groups in Devon, Hammersmith and Fulham, Oxfordshire and St Helens. The groups varied from an access group to a local MENCAP branch, and from a pensioners' social club to a body positive group. Some of the groups were willing and able to take on a clear service provider rôle on the basis of grants or service agreements with statutory agencies. This meant extending their existing provision or developing new services, but even they were concerned at the dangers inherent in such developments. For example, the Hammersmith and Fulham branch of the Alzheimer's Disease Society ran a day centre, but they were concerned that its setting-up and maintenance had drained energy away from developing more general support activities for branch members. Other groups were even more wary of developing direct services other than advice and information gathering. Such groups saw collective advocacy as central and this was a rôle likely to be compromised by service provider responsibilities. Examples of such groups were the Oxfordshire Council of Disabled People, with 140 full members and twenty-two affiliated groups, and the Living Options Working Party, which co-ordinated organisations of, and for, disabled people, in the area covered by Exeter Health Authority.

However, many of the groups were of a more traditional self-help variety, where people who shared a disability or social problem came together for mutual support and information. A good example of this type of organisation was the St Helens branch of the Multiple Sclerosis Society, which had nearly 80 disabled members and provided a social club, outings, a newsletter, support for members during a crisis, and grants and aids. Such groups were not necessarily happy to develop a clear advocacy rôle, although most would probably gain from closer links with the broader disability movement. They often provided services, but these were not usually of a type easy to cost into an individual care package. And these services were often preventive in focus and hence not necessarily aimed at their most dependent or 'at risk' members. Their contribution to local community care provision needs to be recognised and supported, but this may be difficult in a value-for-money culture with resource constraints.

Purchaser–provider splits

The previous section outlined the slow and rather tortuous progress being made towards developing markets in social care. However, it has also been noted that many social services authorities would explain this in terms of a preoccupation with issues of internal restructuring. Does this imply that social services authorities are implementing purchaser–provider splits within their own departments as a starting point for generating markets in social care?

It should be remembered that the importance of developing purchaser–provider splits within social services departments was emphasised in the White Paper on community care (Department of Health, 1989a) and in the subsequent policy guidance (Department of Health, 1990). The White Paper pointed out that contracting out services would require:

> ... an improvement in information gathering systems and a more vigorous approach to management which is likely to require a clear distinction to be made between the purchasing and providing functions within a local authority. (Department of Health, 1989a, p. 23)

The subsequent policy guidance went even further by stating:

> In practical terms in developing the enabling rôle authorities will need to distinguish between aspects of work in SSDs concerned with
>
> * the assessment of individuals' needs, the arrangement and purchase of services to meet them
>   and
> * direct service provision. It will be important that this distinction is reflected within the SSD's management structure at both the 'macro' level (involving plans to meet strategic priorities as a whole) and at the 'micro' level (where services are being arranged for individuals). (Department of Health, 1990, pp. 37–8)

Hoyes and Means (1993b) have argued that the purpose of this proposed split was twofold. First, it would ensure equality of treatment for alternative suppliers and the authorities' own services in terms of the identification of service costs. Second, it would increase the fairness of consumer choice, since the care manager would feel distanced from in-house provision and hence under no pressure to recommend their take-up in preference to those services available from alternative suppliers.

The Department of Health subsequently commissioned the consultants, Price Waterhouse, to produce a report which offered advice on options and implementation strategies. This report identified three different approaches to developing a purchaser–provider split (Price Waterhouse/Department of Health, 1991). These were:

1. Separation of purchaser/commissioner and provider functions at strategic level only. Here the split is very much at the macro level with headquarters staff contracting with area offices to provide assessment, care management and direct services, within a block contract. The contract would be at a high level of generality even though targets might be set for unit prices and activity levels. The report felt that this was only a transitional option since it did not fully meet the policy objectives.
2. Separation of purchaser/commissioner and provider functions at senior management team level. In this approach, the Director of Social Services would be the only post combining both purchaser/ commissioner and provider functions. Assistant directors would head separate hierarchies including fieldwork teams (on the purchaser side) and establishments (on the provider side). Purchasers would agree which services were to be supplied by providers to individual clients so that service agreements or contracts would be at the micro level.
3. Separation of purchaser/commissioner and provider functions at the local level. This model involves a series of separate purchaser/ commissioner and provider teams operating under a combined management structure at the area level, an approach likely to appeal to those authorities which have already undergone considerable decentralisation of budgets and decision making. Care management teams would take new referrals, assess need and put together packages of care, taking account of resource limitations. They would purchase appropriate care packages from in-house providers or independent suppliers.

The report recognised that all three models posed major implementation challenges and that all three models had major strengths and weaknesses. For example, the first model minimises disruption but fails to separate assessment from provision. The second model achieves a much clearer separation but the purchasers are very centralised and there is a danger of managerial duplication. Model three is potentially the most responsive to local needs, yet is highly complex, placing high demands on middle managers and on information systems.

How have local authorities responded to this challenge? The twenty-four authorities studied by Wistow *et al.* (1992) from April 1990 to May 1992 had made little progress on clarifying their position in relation to the purchaser–provider split:

> Only two had already achieved some degree of split, and another had conducted a small pilot project. Of the others, one had no intention of such a reorganization, and seven were not intending to introduce such a split unless forced. (Two were hoping for a Labour government before April 1993, when full implementation of the 1990 Act is required, but councils run by each of the main political parties were represented among the reluctant. Most saw the split as an inevitable fact of life, but, faced with so many other pressures, welcomed the delay.) The other sample authorities expressed intentions which ranged from a cautious 'possibly, but slowly' approach, to a definite commitment to a split whose details had yet to be agreed ... Directors of social services were almost universally more enthusiastic than their political masters about splitting the purchasing and providing functions. (p. 31)

Of the four authorities studied by Hoyes *et al.* (1993) only one (Devon) had made an early decision about where in the department's structure to make a clear purchaser–provider separation, and had an existing financial system which enabled devolution of budgets to purchasers at care management level. In terms of the Price Waterhouse/Department of Health (1991) framework, Devon is pursuing a model three purchaser–provider split. They tackled this by establishing pilot projects in spring 1991 in order to draw lessons from them, before subsequently implementing the purchaser-provider split across the county. However, in the other three authorities:

> ... purchasing, or commissioning as most respondents in these authorities preferred, was to remain a central activity with care managers calling off services from block contracts, or using a limited amount of money for spot purchases. (p. 30)

They argued that imaginative packages of care tailored to individual needs and preferences could well be easier for care managers with devolved budgets to develop than those restricted to pre-set menus, assuming it was possible to generate a sufficiently wide range of providers. However, Hoyes *et al.* (1993) recognised that the adequacy of budgets was equally crucial, a point repeatedly stressed to them by the user and carer groups interviewed. This brings us to the final section of this chapter, which examines the development of a new funding regime for community care.

New funding regime for community care?

Chapter 3 referred to the new funding arrangements for residential and nursing home care. The commentary on financial uncertainty at the beginning of this chapter summarised the arguments about how to decide on the overall amount of money to be transferred from the social security budget and how this should be divided up between individual local authorities. However, it must be remembered that the intention of introducing these changes was not only to influence institutional care, but also to ensure that stay-at-home options were explored and developed even for very dependent people, where appropriate. In other words, local authorities were not expected to spend all of the transferred money on institutional care.

Local authorities did not hear about their allocations from the social security budget until autumn 1992, when a memorandum (Department of Health, 1992) indicated the overall size of the social security transfer for the next three years (see Table 5.4). The memorandum explained that the government had decided that 50 per cent of the social security

Table 5.4 *Social security transfer money to local authorities, 1993–6*
(figures rounded to nearest million)

	Cumulative amount	Annual increase
1993–4	399	399
1994–5	1 050	651
1995–6	1 568	518

transfer money should be allocated according to existing Department of Social Security (DSS) expenditure on institutional care and the remaining 50 per cent according to a standard spending assessment (SSA)-based formula. It was argued that this meant that the new system would not 'threaten the viability of both existing and future care arrangements of residents in homes in some parts of the country' (p. 5). However, the memorandum also announced the allocation of a further £140 million to help with the transitional costs of implementing the later stages of the community care reforms. This money would be 100 per cent related to the SSA formula and so the short-term 'protection' of existing independent providers of institutional care could be combined with the long-term objectives of shifting patterns of provision to reflect patterns of need. This aspiration was to be further enhanced by the fact that the social security transfer monies would also be transferred into an SSA formula over time, and also gradually incorporated into the main SSA settlement under the revenue grant support system. Finally, the memorandum indicated that 75 per cent of the overall grant to each local authority should be spent on paying for care provided by the independent sector.

Will this new funding regime for community care work? This book is being written at too early a point for it to be possible to make a clear judgement. On the positive side, many local authorities were delighted that the argument for substantial transitional money in addition to social security transfer money had been won. But the allocations to individual local authorities still showed marked variations, with some authorities appearing to have far more room for manoeuvre than others. The journal *Community Care* has compared the positions of Newcastle, Hammersmith and Fulham and East Sussex (Cervi *et al.*, 1992). Newcastle was allocated £3.4 million but faced the difficulty that it was already spending well over its SSA, leading the Director of Social Services to conclude that £5 million would have to be cut from the social services budget over the next three years. Hammersmith and Fulham received £1.5 million, a low figure reflecting the fact that it has only 80 places in two independent homes, although many local residents had found places outside the borough. The Deputy Director of Social Services was quoted as saying that 250 nursing home places might have to be paid for in 1993–4 at a cost of £2.4 million and that no more than 5 per cent of the allocated (new) monies would be available for developing domiciliary services. In contrast, East Sussex, with 8000 private sector beds, were allocated £13.2 million and the Director was quoted as saying that 'the formula favours places like these' while optimism was also expressed about developing alternatives to residential care.

It is clear that many local authorities are going to struggle to meet the demand for independent institutional care and that they will have only limited capacity to develop innovative domiciliary alternatives. This may, in turn, encourage local authorities to focus narrowly on the management of residential and nursing home care rather than on community care provision more generally. Certainly, this seems to be increasingly the perspective of central government since the following were made a condition of the grant:

1. agreed strategies outlining health and local authority responsibilities for placing people in nursing homes, and the numbers likely to be involved during 1993–4;
2. agreement about how hospital discharge arrangements will be integrated with assessment arrangements. (Department of Health, 1992, p. 6)

Might this not lead to the creation, maintenance or even extension of a conveyor belt system, by which large numbers of very frail elderly people are transferred from hospital care to nursing home and residential care with minimum consideration of their preferences or the feasibility of domiciliary based alternatives?

It is also clear that the new funding regime to underpin the community care reforms is bringing to the fore debates about charging in both residential and domiciliary care as a source of income generation. Not only are authorities such as Newcastle and Hammersmith and Fulham identifying shortfalls from the earmarked monies, but even the 'luckier' authorities such as East Sussex are indicating that they would not be able to meet the full cost of care in the more expensive homes, so that users would be excluded from them unless they could find the difference between the weekly fee of their preferred home and the maximum tariff available from East Sussex. Also, the 'extra' money is initially to be earmarked but is then gradually incorporated into SSA monies, so it is as vulnerable to cutbacks and to the idiosyncracies of the assessment formulae as the rest of the money individual authorities are calculated by the Department of the Environment to need to spend on the personal social services.

The principle of charging residents has long been accepted for residential care (Glennerster, 1992) and the residents of local authority homes have always undergone a strict means test (Means and Smith, 1985). With regard to the new funding regime, the key issue is the extent to which those requiring residential care are allowed to choose 'expensive' homes if they are completely dependent on public subsidy. The critical decision will be based on the principles used by local authorities to decide what is a reasonable cost (Gibbs and Corden, 1991) for residential and nursing home care in their authority, since the draft guidance on choice states that 'the test should be whether the preferred accommodation is more expensive than the authority would usually expect to pay for someone with the same assessed needs as the individual concerned' (Department of Health, 1992, Appendix D).

The principle of charging for domiciliary care has never had the same level of acceptance as for residential care (Glennerster, 1992). However, charging for day and domiciliary services is emerging as a central issue for local authorities in implementing the community care reforms, since it represents a mechanism by which income can be generated. Lart and Means (1992b) have identified the three main positions local authorities can take on charging, namely, a radical review of charging, an incremental growth in charges or a continued commitment to free services. They then examined how their four case study authorities responded to the pressures for increasing charging. They pointed out how a radical review of policy had been undertaken in one of the authorities (Devon) which, if implemented, would involve a shift from the idea of charges as fixed amounts with no necessary relationship to costs. Instead, true costs had been worked out for services and the proposal was that a package, once put together for a user, would be costed as a total. The user would then be assessed financially, to determine the level of subsidy to which they were entitled. The financial assessment would include checking users' eligibility for benefits and maximising their income from such sources. The impact for users would be that, while some would be entitled to a full subsidy and so would receive their package free, others would be asked for a major contribution to costs.

In contrast to this, Oxfordshire had adopted the second position of adopting an incremental growth in charging. A flat rate charge for home care for those not on income support was extended in December 1990 into a home care matrix, based on a series of charging bands related to income. However, there was concern at the fact that the banded charges were per week, irrespective of the level of service received. Charging policies were being reviewed at the time of the fieldwork. The third option was the line taken by Hammersmith and Fulham: to maintain a commitment to free services. However, in the context of tighter resources, this meant that some services might have to be reduced and priority criteria drawn more rigidly. It could also become a factor in any squeeze on grants to the voluntary sector. Hammersmith and Fulham's policy ensured that users did not bear responsibility for paying for care, but with the result that services had to be rationed further and a smaller group of people served. St Helens had tried to maintain a similar commitment to free domiciliary and day services, apart from nominal charges but had been forced into a position of introducing a wide range of charges for borough services because of the deteriorating financial position of the local authority.

Local authorities face a dilemma. The pressure to charge for such services is growing all the time, since the alternative is more tightly rationed services, and a narrower base for provision. At the same time it is easy to exaggerate the capacity of users to pay for their services from their own resources. One possibility is to maximise the income of users by increasing the take-up of state benefits such as the attendance allowance, although Lart and Means (1992b) point out that this is also open to criticism:

> Controversy reigns about whether these benefits are intended to be used in this way and authorities vary in the extent to which they intend to draw on these in assessing users for charges. While it may seem appropriate that authorities provide welfare rights advice to enable users to maximise their income, there is a danger that users become simply a channel for these benefits to flow from central to local government, hardly an empowering experience. (p. 21)

Nevertheless, there appears little doubt that income generation through charging is going to be taken very seriously by the majority of social services authorities in the foreseeable future.

Conclusion

This chapter has looked at the progress so far made by social services as the lead agency in community care to establish care management systems, promote a mixed economy of social care, introduce purchaser–provider splits and implement the new funding regime for residential and nursing home care. The overall message is that social services authorities have approached these tasks with some caution, so that full implementation still has a long way to go. Initial energy has gone on developing community care planning systems and on introducing the new funding changes. Many social services authorities have now reorganised themselves in the light of the reforms so as to develop a purchaser–provider split and to establish care management teams. However, many of these changes are still in the process of bedding down and so their implications for the future purchase of social care services in terms of developing a mixed economy are not yet clear.

In the longer term, the reforms will be judged a success if they make a significant contribution to ensuring the provision of flexible care packages that are perceived as appropriate and high-quality by service users and carers. A good test of this will be the experience of clients from minority ethnic groups. Such individuals should receive services appropriate to their needs, not only when they happen to live in local authorities where a significant proportion of the population is from such groups, but also when they happen to be an isolated household in a largely all-white community.

6 The Health Dimension of Community Care: Towards Collaborative Working?

Chapters 3 and 5 focused on the implications for social services authorities of the community care changes outlined in the 1989 White Paper (Department of Health, 1989a). This chapter takes a different perspective by considering its implications for the health dimension of community care. Will the clear identification of social services as the lead agency for all the main service users reduce tension with health care agencies? What are the key issues, such as hospital discharge arrangements into private residential and nursing home care, which could continue to cause trouble? What are the main obstacles to effective working together between health and social care agencies in the 1990s?

The health care and community care reforms

One of the more intriguing features of *Working for Patients*, the White Paper on the future of the National Health Service (Department of Health, 1989b) was the lack of any comment on the implications of this debate for the future of community care. Not only did community care not feature in the NHS White Paper but nursing too lacked prominence. Nothing was said about the community nursing of frail older people, those with learning or other disabilities, or those with mental health problems, except that a nurse with experience of community care should be one of the four professional members of the redesignated Family Practitioner Committee which was given the role of overseeing primary health care services (now called the Family Health Services Authority).

The central thrust of the NHS White Paper, as explained in Chapter 3, was in the creation of internal or quasi-markets which would generate efficiency and be responsive to the consumer. The creation of such a market required the separating out of 'the provision of hospital and community health services, entailing the ownership of health care institutions and the employment of direct care staff' from 'the purchase (or commissioning) of care, that is, the allocation of funds to providing institutions so as to ensure the needs of a population are met' (Harrison, Hunter and Pollitt, 1990, p. 169). The NHS changes are highly complex and have been discussed in detail elsewhere (see for example, Ham, 1992). For our purposes, it is important to examine some of the main changes suggested by the White Paper and subsequently incorporated into the National Health Service and Community Care Act 1990. First, not only did each district health authority have to establish a central purchasing function and numerous provider units, but individual provider institutions (or whole units) were given the power to apply to the Secretary of State for Health for 'self-governing' or 'trust' status. With regard to GPs, the larger group practices were allowed to become fund holders and operate their own budgets, with unspent allocations remaining within the practice.

One consequence of all this has been a period of considerable upheaval as new health care structures have been created and health care staff have been redesignated within these systems. This created major difficulties for social services authorities as the lead agents in community care, since such disruption made it very difficult to establish a coherent dialogue with health care managers about the proposed community care changes. This is important since, despite the neglect of community care within the NHS White Paper, the community care White Paper placed a major emphasis upon the continuing central importance of health care and health care professionals, in terms of assessment, service delivery and strategic planning.

Caring for People (Department of Health, 1989a) allocated a whole chapter to outlining the rôles and responsibilities of the health service within the proposed new system of community care provision. This was justified on the following grounds:

> Community care is about the health as well as the social needs of the population. Health care, in its broadest sense, is an essential component of the range of services which may be needed to help people to continue to live in their own homes for as long as possible. (p. 33)

More specifically, with regard to assessment, it was explained that health care professionals would continue to have a major role to play even though the co-ordination of multidisciplinary assessment was to be the responsibility of social services.

The health care professionals involved in such assessments would sometimes be hospital-based, as with psychogeriatricians when an elderly person with dementia was the focus. However, they were more likely to be primary health care staff. For example, the White Paper recognised that the GP was in regular contact with most people with community care needs so that close liaison between GPs and social services staff would be essential for referral and assessment purposes. Community nursing staff such as health visitors, district nurses and community psychiatric nurses were seen by the White Paper as equally crucial in assessment procedures, the development of care arrangements and the provision of care once a package of services had been designed. However, this encouragement was counterbalanced by a warning that expensive nursing skills should not be wasted on non-specialist tasks which could easily be done by others.

The White Paper recognised that not everyone with health and social care needs could remain in their own homes even with high levels of support. Some would require continuous health care and it was claimed that this would remain the responsibility of health authorities. However, this statement ignored the increasing reliance of the NHS upon private nursing homes as a means of releasing acute hospital beds and closing long-stay beds. The funding of these places for those on low incomes was primarily a social security rather than a NHS responsibility and, of course, the White Paper proposed a shift of responsibility from social security to social services in the future. This is a likely source of tension between health and social services which is considered in detail later in this chapter.

The White Paper placed a high emphasis upon community care planning as the mechanism for setting out the strategic direction of individual social service authorities, and again the rôle of health authorities and other health agencies was underscored. It was stressed that social services authorities would be expected to liaise with and consult health authorities and family health services authorities, among others, in the production of plans, while health authorities were told that they

> will be expected to prepare plans setting out their community care
> policies and the arrangements they propose for securing community
> services and community care. It will be for health authorities to
> decide whether these plans would best form part of their overall plans
> or should be produced separately as a joint exercise with the relevant

local authorities. But their key contents and resource assumptions will need to be shared and agreed with the social services authority. (p. 43)

It was left to individual social services authorities and health authorities to decide if the old systems of joint planning provided a helpful or unhelpful structure for tackling these new planning tasks.

Finally, the White Paper on community care had a considerable amount to say about the future funding and provision of services for people with mental health problems. It pointed out that the policy of successive governments since the publication of the White Paper on *Better Services for the Mentally Ill* (Department of Health and Social Security, 1975) had been the development of locally based rather than hospital-based provision. However, it was admitted that 'there are legitimate concerns that in some places hospital beds have been closed before better, alternative facilities are fully in place' while it was also admitted 'some reports also suggest that, at times, patients have been discharged without adequate planning to meet their needs in the community' (Department of Health, 1989a, pp. 55–6).

Three main proposals were made for addressing these problems. First, health authorities were told that continuous health care must be available to all discharged patients, which would require individual care programmes to be agreed by both health and social services. Second, health authorities were reminded that money from the sale of mental illness and mental handicap hospitals could be used to provide capital to develop new facilities in the community, although the dilemma that these facilities were needed before the hospital could be closed, and hence sold, was recognised. Third, a new system of funding additional local authority social care services for people with mental health problems was announced. The White Paper estimated that about 3 per cent of social service authorities' total expenditure was spent on services specifically for those with mental health problems. Hence, a new earmarked grant was to be made available to fund just this type of development, and this was to be organised in a way which was sure to guarantee a key role for health interests:

In order to encourage the joint planning of services, and proper collaboration in relation to care programmes, the Government will make this grant payable through Regional Health Authorities as the agents of the Secretary of State for Health, on the basis of plans for

the development of social care agreed between social services authorities and the matching district health authorities. (p. 57)

This could be seen as an effective strategy of enforced collaboration, but
to many social services authorities it must have seemed a very perverse
way of offering support to their new rôle as the lead agency in the development of services for people with mental health problems. Did it make
sense to create a new grant which required the lead agency to meet the
requirements of a secondary partner before monies could be released
from central government?

This section has illustrated the extent to which the White Paper on
community care proposed a system of provision dependent on collaborative working between social care and health care staff at both the
strategic and operational levels. The importance of collaboration was
recognised by the White Paper, which devoted a short chapter to this
issue (pp. 49–52). It argued that the underlying incentives for health and
social services to work closely together had increased. Several reasons
were put forward in support of this. One was the need to link hospital
discharge arrangements under the new funding regime with residential
and nursing home provision. Another was the rather more vague view
that the rôles of health and social services authorities were becoming
more complementary, since the emergence of purchasing functions
meant that they were both trying to achieve the best value for money.
And finally it was suggested that the White Paper had helped to clarify
the respective rôles of the health and social care agencies so that tension
and conflict could be greatly reduced. In some areas the distinction
between health and social care remained blurred, but health and local
authorities would 'need to decide locally about how they share objectives, responsibilities and the funding of different services' (p. 50). Is
collaboration as simple as this to achieve?

Collaborative working: the theory

Any review of the extensive literature on joint working would lead the
reader to conclude that the White Paper on community care was very
optimistic about the prospects for positive collaboration between social
services authorities and health care agencies. As Webb (1991) brutally
explains, 'exhortations to organisations, professionals and other pro-
ducer interests to work together more closely and effectively litter the

policy landscape' yet the reality is 'all too often a jumble of services fractionalised by professional, cultural and organisational boundaries and by tiers of governance' (p. 229).

One key difficulty is that governments have often been happy to extol the virtues of collaborative working without ever bothering to address the very real obstacles which exist from the point of view of the proposed collaborating partners. As Hudson (1987) explains:

> From an agency's viewpoint, collaborative activity raises two main difficulties. First, it loses some of its freedom to act independently when it would prefer to maintain control over its domain and affairs. Second, it must invest scarce resources and energy in developing and maintaining relationships with other organisations when the potential returns on this investment are often unclear and intangible. (p. 175)

As we have argued elsewhere, exhortations to work together are not enough and many agencies seek to avoid joint working unless pressured to do so (Smith *et al.*, 1993, especially Chapter 1; Means, 1993).

Hudson (1987) suggests there are three main strategies available to foster collaborative working despite these problems. These are co-operative strategies (based on mutual agreements), incentive strategies (based on 'bribes' to encourage joint working) and authoritative strategies (agencies or individuals are instructed to work together). In the past, the tendency of government has been to request organisations such as social services authorities and district health authorities to collaborate on various initiatives. The alternative authoritative approach usually suffers from the fact that sanctions are weak and that there are numerous devices available to agencies and individuals by which reluctant partners can subvert or undermine policy initiatives (Dalley, 1991; Lipsky, 1980).

Incentive strategies, however, have considerable potential. The authors of this book were involved with colleagues in the evaluation of a Health Education Authority (HEA)-funded regional alcohol education programme which was met initially by a mixture of indifference and hostility from most of the seven councils on alcohol and the twelve health promotion units covered by the initiative. Nevertheless, these negative beginnings were overcome when the HEA agreed to fund 50 per cent of the salary costs of a network of district co-ordinators to develop local alcohol education strategies (Means *et al.*, 1990). However, these incentives needed to be substantial to overcome a previous history of distrust and hostility.

In general, Conservative governments in the 1980s and early 1990s have been quite astute at learning how to manipulate the behaviour of local authorities in a number of policy areas such as housing (Malpass and Means, 1993). This has often involved a mixture of incentive and authoritative strategies. With regard to collaborative working between health and social services over the resettlement of hospital patients, joint finance initiatives can be seen as an incentive strategy where the incentives were continuously increased yet still failed to overcome the main obstacles to joint working. The new funding regime for residential care and the new mental health specific grant suggest that the government has moved to a more authoritative approach where key monies are withheld if certain collaborative tasks are not completed successfully. The danger of this approach for the government is that it generates resentment rather than goodwill, especially if social services perceive health authorities as exploiting unreasonably the pivotal role allocated to them by central government.

Hudson's work is focused in the main on co-ordination and collaboration between agencies, rather than co-operation on a more day-to-day basis between individual professionals from different agencies. Dalley (1991) provides insights into issues raised by this type of activity through her study of health and social work professionals in Scotland. Her respondents were found to differ in their beliefs and their behaviour along three key dimensions. First, professional ideologies varied over such issues as the role of families in community care and the value of institutional care. Second, these professional differences were underpinned by a set of cultural perceptions about their own profession and that of others which took the form of what Dalley (1991, p. 171) called 'tribal ties'. Hostile views by health care professionals towards social care professionals, and vice versa, had the effect of bolstering group identity and solidarity, although in a way which made co-operative working very difficult. Finally, these professional differences were offset to some extent by the conditioning of everyday action. This meant that field-level staff from different professions and managers from different professions often felt themselves to have more in common with each other than with colleagues from the same profession but in different hierarchical positions. This was because these jobs involved coping with similar types of demand and pressure. Dalley concluded that these conflicting dimensions to joint working on a day-to-day basis made it very difficult to predict how health and social care professionals might respond to the community care reforms.

A further complicating factor is that individuals have the capacity not only to undermine joint working through what is sometimes called 'street level bureaucrat' behaviour (Lipsky, 1980) but also to foster such activity. The policy studies literature indicates that some professionals are adept at encouraging joint working. Such individuals are sometimes referred to as 'reticulists' (Friend *et al.*, 1974) while the Audit Commission (1986a) called them 'champions of change'. They are skilled at mapping policy networks and identifying the key resource holders and fellow enthusiasts, both from their own and from other agencies (Means *et al.*, 1991). They tend to feel comfortable working above their hierarchical position, and they are willing to operate in a way not bounded by narrow organisational self-interest.

It might be expected that members and senior managers in social services authorities would feel increasingly able to support such individuals as they move from being the monopoly providers of services to a more enabling role in which a broad range of organisations are expected to take on service delivery functions. It is widely recognised that the traditional systems of bureaucratic and hierarchical management are no longer appropriate, and that the centre needs to allocate more power and discretion to its periphery and to other locally based organisations (see Chapter 3). However, Smith *et al.* (1993) warn that:

> ... in a period of rapid organisational change for the main statutory 'players' there is a danger that managerial stress and anxiety mean a growing gulf between them and operational staff. The inevitable difficulties and failures of collaboration and co-ordination at the periphery may become characterised by the centre as the inability of operational staff to comprehend the 'wider vision'. Such tensions may be exacerbated when attempts are made to include voluntary sector organisations, users and carers into a strategy of working together to achieve better community care. (p. 7)

Smith *et al.* go on to argue that a developmental philosophy of management is required which would offer field-level staff support on a number of grounds (training, time allocation) to establish collaborative field-level initiatives. Such a philosophy would recognise that senior managers could learn from the experiences of lower level staff and could perceive some 'local failures' as the inevitable outcome of a commitment to innovative collaborative working and that positive lessons could still be learnt from such situations.

All this allows us to address the issue of the preconditions for successful collaborative working at the strategic and operational levels. Despite his pessimistic starting point, Hudson (1987) believes it is possible to draw on organisational theory to outline five key factors which do predispose agencies to collaborate. These are:

1. interorganisational homogeneity (how similar in values and culture are the collaborating agencies?);
2. domain consensus (is there agreement on rôles and responsibilities?);
3. network awareness;
4. organisational exchange (will all the parties gain from working together?);
5. absence of alternative resources.

Subsequent work by Webb (1991) suggests that the existence of trust built up through previous joint activity is a sixth key factor which helps any new collaborative initiative towards a successful outcome.

What are the prospects for effective collaborative working between health and social services when judged against these criteria? To make a judgement about this, it is necessary to explore the long history of distrust between health and social care agencies and how this relates to tension and conflict over their respective domains. It is also necessary to look in detail at certain key issues which are likely to raise difficulties in the future, such as the resettlement of hospital patients, the development of mental health services, community care planning, hospital discharge and future relationships with primary health care teams.

Who should lead? Historical perspectives

Within the confines of this chapter, it is possible to give only a glimpse of the ongoing debate about who should take the lead co-ordinating role in community care. Prior to the late 1970s, the central rôle of health care professionals with regard to people with learning disabilities and mental health problems was rarely questioned. However, the debate over lead agency rôles for elderly and physically disabled people goes back much further. Certainly, by the mid-1960s, Titmuss was able to say:

In all this discussion at the present time of who is responsible for what, the family doctor is being cast for the role of co-ordinator, mobilizer, director, stage manager and leader of community care ... Others, however, are seeing the medical officer of health performing this role partly on the grounds that the family doctor is too busy and is trained as a clinician and medical diagnostician. Still others propose that the chief welfare officer and a family welfare service should assume some or most of these responsibilities. (1968, p. 100)

In other words, should such services be led by health care professionals or social care professionals? Medical officers of health were responsible for local authority health departments, and hence were left with the residue of local authority health functions after the removal of hospitals from local government responsibility under the National Health Service Act 1946. Consequently, they had the prestige of being medically qualified but the problem of overseeing a declining empire (Means and Smith, 1985). Several medical officers of health attempted to counter-balance this by arguing that residential care and domiciliary services under the National Assistance Act 1948 should be under their control rather than that of a chief welfare officer who was not medically qualified. For example, Irvine (1950), Medical Officer of Health for Dewsbury, argued for combined health and welfare departments on the grounds that 'the transference of old people from a home to a hostel, from a hostel to hospital, and vice versa can be most readily effected when the decisions lie with medical men [*sic*] who understand the medical basis of the case' (p. 74).

Although the Guillebaud Report (1956) on the costs of the National Health Service supported the idea of combined health and welfare departments, the authority and prestige of medical officers of health continued to decline. Attention began to switch to the general practitioners as the potential leaders of community health and welfare services. This debate was sparked off by concern about the administrative separation of the GP from community-based health provision such as district nursing, midwifery and health visiting, all of which remained the responsibility of medical officers of health and local authorities until the 1974 health care reforms. The Gillie Report (1963) on the field of work of the family doctor argued that the family doctor was:

... the one member of the profession who can best mobilise and co-ordinate the health and welfare services in the interests of the individual in the community and of the community in relation to the individual. (p. 9)

The achievement of this was seen as requiring teamwork between the GP and the preventive health and welfare services of the local authority. The GP needed to be trained into how best to use such staff 'as his [*sic*] ancillary staff in the home' (p. 38). However, the report was worried that the concept of family doctor as the clinical leader of the domiciliary team would remain a platitude unless field-level staff such as district nurses were attached to individual GP practices. So long as this occurred, there would be no need to introduce unified control for the two divisions of the NHS concerned, namely GP services and local authority health services.

Many disagreed. Titmuss (1968, p. 100) pointed out 'there is as yet little evidence that in his [*sic*] day-to-day medical work the family doctor is moving, or wishes to move, in this direction' since consultation rates with elderly people had fallen since 1948. The Royal Commission on Local Government in Greater London (Herbert Report, 1960) agreed that the GP should be the clinical head of the domiciliary team but that it was 'the day-to-day work of the district nurse, health visitor and home help, the ancillary services such as laundry and chiropody, and the voluntary services such as meals on wheels that makes it possible for so many old people to remain in their own homes' (p. 158). The Royal Commission felt the GP could neither provide these services nor co-ordinate their delivery. Such services required an 'administrative head' within the local authority to ensure the availability of these services and their overall co-ordination. In other words, they needed co-ordination by a welfare rather than a medical professional. Against this, others felt the only sensible arrangement was to combine general practitioner and local authority health services. Such a 'community health authority' could become 'the friendly rival of the hospital' (Brockington, 1963, p. 1145).

These arguments were about who should be the clinical and administrative leaders of what in those days was referred to as the domiciliary care team. The eventual restructuring of these services in the early 1970s was based on assumptions about the distinction between health care services (GP, health visitor, district nurse and so on) and social care services (social worker, home help and so on). The National Health Services Reorganisation Act 1973 was an attempt to tackle some of the perceived ineffectiveness associated with the NHS structure created by the 1946 Act. Brown (1979, p. 6) claimed the local authority health services were seen as 'a rag-bag of functions' that needed to be integrated into the hospital and general practitioner services. The 1973 Act was a mechanism by which 'the local authority services were nationalised and brought under the same management as hospital services' (p. 22). District nurses and health visitors were no longer to work in a local authority department but were rather to be responsible to a district nursing officer who would be a member of the district management team of the newly formed district health authority. It was the district nursing officer who would have primary responsibility for the allocation of district nursing and health visitor staff; this might or might not involve their location in GP practices. The post of medical officer of health was abolished. Each district management team instead included a community physician whose task was to assess needs and evaluate service provision within the community.

With regard to local authority services, the leadership rôle fell to the Director of Social Services and social services departments from 1 April 1971. As seen in Chapter 2, the early 1970s saw a major extension of the powers of local authorities to provide services and support for elderly people and for other people with disabilities. Local authority welfare departments had become increasingly interested in employing those with social work skills to help in deciding how to prioritise elderly people wishing to enter residential care and they had begun to argue that such skills could help in preventing elderly people even entering such care, especially if backed up by appropriate domiciliary support such as home care and day care. As early as the late 1960s, Brown (1972) felt 'many welfare departments were finding a growing affinity with children's departments, for example, rather than with health' (p. 51). Their subsequent coming together into social services departments should therefore not surprise us.

The logic of the eventual split between health and social care services through the two Acts was clearly explained by Lord Balniel, in a debate on the Local Authority Social Services Bill:

> It is a demarcation based on primary skill. It is a demarcation so that on one side there should be services which are primarily medical in content and, on the other side, the services which are primarily social in content. I do not think one can try to separate services along the lines of .... some being for children and some being for the elderly. It is the primary skill which is the only conceivable logical line of demarcation in this field. (Quoted in Means and Smith, 1985, p. 338)

Yet this view and the actual reforms had at least two major weaknesses. First, they increased rather than decreased the complexity of service delivery. District nursing was no longer a local authority responsibility yet it remained separate from the administration of GP services despite the creation of family practitioner committees under the 1973 Act. How was all this to be co-ordinated effectively from the point of view of service users? This remained unresolved in 1973 and it remains unresolved over twenty years later. Second, the demarcation line between health care and social care has always been disputed territory, both in terms of institutional provision and of domiciliary services. The reforms of the early 1970s did not resolve the debate.

What is health care? What is social care?

With regard to institutional care, a key debate has always been over the meaning of the term 'in need of care and attention' within the National Assistance Act 1948. Godlove and Mann (1980) have argued that the authors of the 1948 Act did not envisage residential homes 'as being adequate for people suffering from incontinence, serious loss of mobility, or abnormal senile dementia'. These were health problems requiring placement in a hospital or nursing home. Yet an important aspect of the history of welfare services since 1948 has been the shift of definition of 'care and attention' to include those suffering from these illnesses and medical conditions (Means, 1986).

The early debate on this issue was sparked off by two factors. First, the 1950s saw shortages of residential accommodation, caused by capital restrictions on the building of new homes. Second, the same period saw concerns about the high cost of hospital provision within the newly created National Health Service. A number of questions began to be asked. Were expensive hospital beds being blocked by the lack of residential accommodation, or were local authorities being swamped by residents in need of constant nursing care? Was there a group not catered for in the existing legislation so that they were 'stranded in the no man's land between the Regional Hospital Board and the local welfare department – not ill enough for one, not well enough for the other'? (Huws Jones, 1952, p. 22). Was there a need for a national system of rest homes or halfway homes that catered for this special group?

As early as 1953, the Minister of Health (Iain Macleod) described this whole area 'as perhaps the most baffling problem in the whole of the National Health Service' (quoted in Means, 1986, p. 94). This problem was considered in depth by both the Guillebaud Report (1956) into the costs of the National Health Service and the Boucher Report (1957) on services available to 'the chronic sick and elderly'. Both dismissed the idea of halfway houses as an approach which would generate yet more confusion about the respective roles of health care and social care institutions. The better plan was to expand local authority residential care in a form which would enable such homes to cope with the needs of those labelled as 'infirm' rather than 'sick'. This approach was supported by the government, which attempted to specify the responsibilities of local authorities and hospital boards with regard to frail and sick elderly people. Ministry of Health Circular 14/57 stated that local welfare authorities were responsible not only for 'active elderly people' in need of residential care but also for:

1. care of the otherwise active resident in a welfare home during minor illness which may well involve a short period in bed;
2. care of the infirm (including the senile) who may need help in dressing, toilet and so on, and may need to live on the ground floor because they cannot manage stairs, and may spend part of the day in bed (or longer periods in bad weather);
3. care of those elderly persons in a welfare home who have to take to bed and are not expected to live more than a few weeks (or exceptionally months).

Hospital authorities were given their own list of responsibilities by this circular. These included the chronic bedfast, the convalescent sick and the senile confused. At first glance, 'the partly sick and partly well' were no longer in no man's land. They would increasingly be directed to local authority residential accommodation even though this was meant to be a form of social rather than health care provision.

However, Circular 14/57 was only a working guide and was riddled with problems of interpretation. As one of us has asked previously:

> Could one always decide if a bedfast resident would die in three months or three years? How clear cut was the distinction between the senile and the senile confused? At what point did spending part of the day in bed justify a resident being labelled as bedfast and thus requiring admittance to a hospital? How could one know if removal to a hospital was inhumane? (Means, 1986, p. 96)

It seems likely that the reality of the situation was that both hospitals and local authorities remained keen each to persuade the other to accept responsibility for as many cases as possible.

In other words, the circular could be used as a bargaining tool by the professionals involved in specific cases, but it did not by itself point to whether a person should end up in a hospital bed or a residential home. One feature of bargaining is that both sides may need to make concessions. More specifically, a 'swap' system developed (Davies, 1979) by which a hospital would refuse to accept a referral from a residential home unless that home (or another in the local authority) agreed to accept a patient from the geriatric unit. Elderly people had few rights in this situation and many were placed in specific types of institutional care, according to the balance of power of the various health and social care professionals involved in their care. Later circulars made further attempts to clarify responsibilities, but by the early 1980s the actual placement of elderly people in different types of institutional care still bore little relationship to any 'objective' assessment of their material and social needs (Wade, Sawyer and Bell, 1983).

Debates about the health and social care divide with regard to community health and welfare services have perhaps been less fierce but they have been no less important. The health and social care reforms of the early 1970s suggested means by which a service could be defined either as a community health service, and hence part of the NHS, or as a community welfare or domiciliary service which was the responsibility of the social services authority. Hence district nursing became split from home care in terms of the responsible authority. This left unresolved who should have the power to co-ordinate a coherent package of services from both sides of this divide on behalf of the client. Several studies have underlined the lack of co-ordination which continues to exist from the perspective of the service user (Allen *et al.*, 1992). Others have argued that there are major overlaps in the work carried out by many of these community health and welfare professionals (Clarke, 1984). Such overlaps are particularly evident between district nurses and home care staff, especially as the home care service has changed from being a cleaning/domestic service to a personal care service. This generates ludicrous attempts at the local level to distinguish between whether a user needs a bath for medical or for social reasons, since the former is the responsibility of a district nurse or aide while the latter is the responsibility of a home help or assistant. Clarke's solution was to call for combined health and welfare departments as in Ireland.

Hospital rundown and the politics of care in the community

The last two sections have underlined the lack of domain consensus about the respective rôles of health care and social care agencies, as well as the history of rivalry over resources. The more recent history of hospital rundown for people with learning disabilities and mental health problems has raised similar issues, including whether all parties will gain from the switch from hospital to community-based services. Indeed, this switch has queried the very legitimacy of the work of some health care professionals. This section illustrates the importance of addressing this situation through adequate staff development and retraining programmes.

Chapter 3 outlined the emergence of joint planning and the 'care in the community' initiative as part of the strategy to run down long-stay hospitals by transferring patients to accommodation and services within the community. It was the failure of health and social services authorities to collaborate effectively on this issue which was highlighted by *Making a Reality of Community Care* (Audit Commission, 1986a), which in turn led to the Griffiths Report (1988) and the White Paper on community care (Department of Health, 1989a). Some of the reasons for the slowness of hospital rundown were outlined in earlier chapters. In terms of Hudson's (1987) preconditions for successful collaboration, it is not difficult to see why so many problems emerged. Several studies have emphasised the complexity of the process of running down hospitals and developing alternative facilities (Booth *et al.*, 1990; Renshaw *et al.*, 1988; Tomlinson, 1991). This process has placed enormous time costs upon participating managers. There is also evidence of health service managers having become frustrated by the need for social services managers to refer back to their members before important decisions can be confirmed, and hence there has been a lack of what Hudson would call organisational homogeneity.

However, the challenge of joint working goes much deeper than just the struggles of senior managers to find the time for meetings and to remain sympathetic to each other. This is well illustrated by the evaluation of the twenty-eight demonstration projects set up by the 'care in the community' initiative (see Chapter 5). These projects were intended to support the transfer of about 900 people from long-stay institutions into the community. The issue of recruitment and training of staff to the projects became a very central concern, once the characteristics of the rôles and tasks became clear. In brief, the job of project workers was very demanding, requiring the ability to (i) address frustrations, tension and challenging behaviour, (ii) overcome the stresses of shift working, and (iii) negotiate difficulties with colleagues. In many particulars, the work was very different from that experienced in, for instance, a hospital. Some project managers recruited staff without health or social care backgrounds in order to avoid the problems thrown up by strong attachment to earlier working experiences. Such recruits needed training to undertake the work they were expected to do. For instance, the Wells Road project in Bristol, which served people with learning difficulties living in the community, trained its staff from scratch, as 'existing training programmes were geared either to nursing staff, working mainly in hospital settings, or to social services staff, working in hostels or homes' (Ward, 1985, p. 102).

Other aspects of a project's training strategy could address the problems of people coming from different professional cultures. For instance, the notion that people have rights and needs, the philosophy of client empowerment, embraced by some social care workers (though by no means all) could clash with the more paternalistic culture of dependency, typically associated with a patient in a hospital. Yet ex-hospital staff previously working in long-stay institutions could well feel that they knew their patients well and should form part of the staffing of a community care project. Union agreements of no compulsory redundancy could also add to the expectation that ex-hospital staff should be redeployed into community projects. The need for a careful staff development strategy, including joint training, particularly whole team training, was high, but was not always recognised. Other work shows that it is very difficult for small resettlement projects run by voluntary organisations to develop coherent staff development and training package from their own resources (Coleman *et al.*, 1990).

The demonstration projects of the 1983 'care in the community' initiative encapsulate many of the issues about the current and future rôle of health care professionals in the delivery of community care services. The issue is centrally one of professional power, not least in respect of the mental health services:

> Psychiatrists in particular have expressed disquiet over the inadequacy of some of the new community services, a view which may be strengthened by a more strategic worry over losing control of the mental health service. (Renshaw *et al.*, 1988, p. 61)

Again:

> the objections and doubts which consultants and nursing staff may hold about a project stem from a mixture of motives. On one side they probably worry about their own future – their own 'territory' and professional identity – while on the other hand they may feel deep concern about whether the community services can cope. (ibid., p. 85)

Thirdly:

> Nurses' reactions stem from a combination of genuine concern – they may assume that project staff are untrained and ignorant – and the perceived threat to their own professional identity. Nurse training schools will also have to move to the community. Disbelief in the reality of the strategic plans can exacerbate feelings of insecurity. (ibid., p. 178)

As seen in earlier chapters, psychiatrists and nurses in the fields of mental health and learning disability have been amongst the health care professionals most affected by the development of community care in the last thirty years. The policy of closure of long-stay institutions built in the Victorian era, following the transfer of acute services to district general hospitals, the introduction of major tranquillisers (but see Goodwin, 1989, pp. 28–31), the struggle to control the costs of the health service accompanied by the belief that non-institutional care would be cheaper than hospital-based care, and the simple view that living in the community must offer a better quality of life than living in an institution, all contributed to the policy of shifting to the provision of care outside hospital.

Yet central government has been very slow to tackle the training and retraining issue for hospital-based staff working with people with mental health problems and learning disabilities even though the need for this was recognised as far back as the ten-year health and welfare plans of the 1960s (Ministry of Health, 1963, 1966). The Jay Report (1979) did explore the future pattern of training required and called for common training for NHS and local authority staff based upon new emerging 'models of care'. Yet its proposals were not pursued and by the mid-1980s the health service unions were campaigning against people being moved out of mental handicap hospitals unless their new community-based accommodation was staffed by qualified nurses (Malin, 1987, p. 15).

Both *Making a Reality of Community Care* (Audit Commission, 1986a) and the Griffiths Report (1988) emphasised that the skills of hospital staff should not be wasted and that major retraining programmes were required to prepare them for transfer to working in the community alongside local authority staff. As the Audit Commission explained:

> The future is not clear to most of the 70 000 people now working in large mental handicap hospitals who will be displaced by their closure. Their skills, experience and dedication will go to waste, unless steps are taken to retrain them for work in the community ... Some may not be able to cope with the changes and challenges involved with the introduction of community care, but given suitable training, many would be ideal. At present, very little is being done and it is hardly surprising that many staff are apprehensive about their personal positions and thus less likely to support new initiatives. (p. 62)

Pockets of good training practice have emerged since 1986, yet overall much more needs to be done. Despite the production of (i) a strategy for community care training by the Social Services Inspectorate of the Department of Health (1990); (ii) a training and development guidance document produced for the Department of Health by Dearden Management Associates (1993); and (iii) training packages from such bodies as the Joint Initiative for Community Care, the London Boroughs Training Committee and NALGO, training issues have not received more than limited priority at the local level. The Social Services Inspectorate also produced a practice guide on a joint approach to training for community care (Department of Health/Social Services Inspectorate, 1991b), but the values of the collaborating professionals in the resettlement process have remained far apart, with little consensus on respective skills, rôles and responsibilities. Is it too much to hope that the transformation of nurse education, through Project 2000, with its emphasis on much less hospital-based training (United Kingdom Central Council, 1987) will help to bring caring professionals closer together? After all, the Audit Commission had in 1986 already put forward the idea of extending the Project 2000 concept of a common foundation programme to all professionals working in the community.

Achieving collaboration – key policy challenges

This section focuses upon key policy challenges faced by social services authorities and health agencies in the 1990s. To be addressed effectively, all require extensive collaboration, yet each contains the potential for the type of dispute and conflict which is so destructive of joint working. One key challenge is the ongoing programme of hospital closure and the parallel development of services in the community. To address some of the problems arising from that policy, the 1989 White Paper, *Caring for People*, outlined a system of earmarked grants for mental health services. This chapter has already queried whether the payment of this grant through health authorities will foster collaboration or resentment from local authorities. In any case, many people perceive this money to be totally inadequate and it will certainly not be enough to tackle the growing problems of homelessness amongst people with mental health problems (see Chapter 7). Local authorities find themselves with growing responsibilities in the area of mental health, yet there is often a totally inadequate infrastructure of services to support these reponsibilities. Will health agencies provide support and encouragement in this difficult situation or will they express scepticism about the competence of local authorities to develop their rôle in this area? A report from the British Medical Association (BMA) (1992) indicated that 'there is concern ... that most local authorities lack the skills and expertise to take on the responsibility for supporting mentally ill people in the community' (p. 30).

A wider spectrum of commentators than just health care professionals have lobbied for a review of the decision that social services should be the lead agency for people with mental health problems. For example, Glennerster, Falkingham and Evandrou (1990) have described the new system of earmarked grants as a muddle, since it would make much more sense for the health authority to play the role of purchaser/lead agent:

> The clearest and most accountable way to organise the funding of psychiatric services would be to make the district health authorities responsible. The NHS could ... buy in facilities and workers from whatever source it wished. Contracts could be set or grants given to organisations like MIND or the local authority. This would be simple and would conform to the principles in the rest of the White Paper. (p. 101)

It would appear that domain consensus remains as far away as ever. However, this pessimistic view does need to be balanced against the incremental growth of good practice on the ground. Successful examples of community mental health and mental handicap teams continue to develop in which social workers, community psychiatric nurses and consultants all make collaborative contributions. However, these examples are a long way from providing a coherent national structure of service provision, and many of the individual teams exhibit tensions about rôles, responsibilities and expertise.

A second challenge is linked to the provision of health and social care services for people with dementia. The British Medical Association (1992) expressed the following concerns:

> There is evidence that patients with mixed physical and mental symptoms tend to be admitted as inpatients to the geriatric hospital service and to be subsequently resettled in nursing homes without psychiatric assessment. The Association considers that there is an urgent need to establish sound communication networks between all agencies concerned with the care of the elderly. These should include the automatic involvement of specialists and the provision of feedback and progress reports to GPs who have referred patients into the care of other sectors. (p. 33)

But will services be able to cope with the growing demand, as the number of elderly people over 80 continues to increase? It has been estimated that twenty out of every 100 elderly people in their 80s suffer from dementia (M. Johnson, 1990). What services are to be provided for them under the new community care arrangements and who will pay for them?

This is an area where medically qualified staff such as psychogeriatricians are likely to play the lead in assessment and proposals about appropriate service responses, yet the financial implications will often fall upon social services budgets. For example, a psychogeriatrician might propose placement in a residential home or nursing home because of doubts about the ability of carers to continue to cope if the individual stays at home. Alternatively, a consultant might insist upon a highly expensive stay at home package in an attempt to avoid entry into an institution. How understanding will the psychogeriatricians be, or should they be, when such options are challenged or rejected by social services on grounds of cost?

In the past, some of the care costs for those entering independent residential and nursing home care have been 'hidden' from the health and social services agencies through the social security budget. This protection has now gone and this brings us to the third challenge. The new system is likely to generate tensions, especially with regard to people entering institutional care via the acute hospital service, whether they suffer from dementia or not. Hospital discharge arrangements for those entering care and for those returning home are now seen as a major issue in the implementation of the community care reforms. The Deputy Chief Executive of the National Health Service Management Executive and the Chief Inspector of the Social Services Inspectorate set local authority and health care agencies eight key tasks for 1992/3 to ensure the smooth implementation of these changes. The third of these was 'ensuring the robustness and mutual acceptability of discharge arrangements' (Foster and Laming, 1992). Subsequently, the handover of social security transfer monies to individual social services authorities became dependent on signing hospital discharge agreements with their health authorities. At one level, this emphasis on improving hospital discharge arrangements should be welcomed. Recent research has pointed to major inadequacies in discharge arrangements for those returning to their own homes. It was found that, of 60 elderly people discharged from hospital back to their homes,

> One in three of the people in the sample said they had not been asked how they would manage at home after their discharge. Two fifths were told about the discharge either the day before or on the day it was due to happen. (Neill and Williams, 1992, p. 74)

However, the policy debate on hospital discharge may be being driven by the necessity to avoid bed blockages in the acute hospital sector, rather than the capability of the care manager to offer options after hospital treatment, ranging from returning home to entry into a nursing home.

Thus the pressure is on local authorities to fund a large number of nursing home beds for each financial year even though the 'knock on' consequence of that is to tie up a considerable amount of community care money in institutional provision. The fourth challenge therefore is the continuing uncertainty about the health and social care divide. Why should local authorities rather than the NHS be asked to fund a nursing service? As Henwood (1992) points out:

Despite the claim that the responsibilities of the NHS are unchanged, nursing home care is apparently now viewed as social care, not health. Is this contradictory, or are we to accept that there is a real distinction between those needing nursing home care for reasons of ill health and those needing it for other reasons? Surely this is playing *Alice in Wonderland* games with words and semantics. (p. 28)

One strong possibility is that health authorities will run down their remaining nursing home and continuing care bed provision. Another is that some local authorities will deny they have a responsibility for some people referred to them from acute hospitals, on the grounds that their needs are essentially those of health care and not social care. Yet health authorities will not wish to begin purchasing all or part of the cost of large numbers entering independent nursing home care since they were able to avoid this responsibility in the past under the social security funding arrangements. Such tensions may generate the very bed blockages in the acute hospital sector which have concerned government for so long.

The boundaries between health and social care continue to shift with people previously perceived as ill now being increasingly defined as having social care needs which are the responsibility of the local authority and not the NHS. Henwood (1992) has a very unflattering, yet almost certainly correct, explanation for this further shift in boundaries. Health care under the NHS has to be free. Social care can be charged for, and increasingly local authorities have to charge the full economic price of care to the better off. The responsibility for funding long-term health and social care is thus being shifted covertly on to users and their families. Social services authorities and health authorities are being left to struggle with the consequences of this shift. These shifting boundaries, and their consequences for future rôles and responsibilities, are also affecting the provision of care packages in the community. Henwood points out that the ageing of the elderly population combined with policies designed to delay entry into residential care has created a new client group which is not clearly the responsibility of either health or social care services. Using words very similar to those of Huws Jones (1952) some forty years previously (see earlier discussion), she refers to them as 'the borderline people, the partly sick and partly well, who are perceived as too sick for residential support and not ill enough for hospital care' (p. 24). Who should pay for their continued maintenance in the community or make the decision about the most appropriate type of institutional provision?

As in the debate about institutional care, there is often a concern about the implications of these operational uncertainties for budgets. In previous work by one of us, a director of social services expressed concern that the local expansion of hip operations, combined with earlier hospital discharge for all operations, was placing major pressures upon his home care budget (Hoyes and Means, 1991). He argued that the district health authority should be making a contribution to the social services budget because of this. However, a unit general manager from the health authority complained about the social services policy of care at home rather than placement in residential care placing enormous pressure upon the district nursing service. She felt that an argument could be made for a contribution to this budget from social services. The situation becomes even more confusing when the dimension of the GP is brought in. In most areas, district nursing services are part of the health authority provider unit structure, although some community service units now have trust status. The GP is part of the separate family health services authority (FHSA) structure, yet GPs, especially if they are budget holders, perceive themselves as commissioning packages of health care for many of their patients. This requires them to purchase community health services, but it may also require the support of social care services from the local social services authority. One possibility is for the GP to be allocated the care manager rôle in such cases, especially if the local authority is satisfied with the appropriateness of the demands being made upon their services.

Effective co-ordination and the building up of trust are crucial to making the reform structures work to the advantage of users. Some are optimistic. For example, the general manager of the then Bradford Family Practitioner Committee claimed:

> GPs will make a major contribution to individual case funding, assessment, care planning and service delivery. The FHSAs themselves will bring ideas and information to joint planning, and a capacity to shape new services ... They will come to the joint planning arena with a unique and increasingly sophisticated computerised database, with politics and ideas, and with influence over key community key actors – the GPs, (D. Martin, 1990, p. 964)

This is rather more than was suggested in the Griffiths Report or the White Paper and David Martin acknowledges the formidable barriers to working together, barriers created by different personal values, professional cultures, life styles, status, operating procedures, organisational roles and systems of accountability. However, steps could be taken, mainly by the FHSAs, 'to increase the chances of getting it right' (p. 965). In Bradford he instances (i) the appointment of two senior GPs to advise the Director of Social Services and the FHSA, and to influence their colleagues; (ii) the establishment of a working group with social services staff and GP organisers to prepare joint training packages; and (iii) a new model of joint working through a project involving practices preparing for the GP funding initiative and the resources of both the social services department and the relevant health authorities. However, the problem is that research suggests that, whilst GPs perceive themselves to be of central importance in the provision of community services, yet they remain very reluctant to become care managers or enmeshed in the details of care management (Leedham and Wistow, 1992).

One possible way out of this impasse is to make community care a funded activity for GPs. Glennerster, Falkingham and Evandrou (1990) have asked whether approved general practices might take on community care powers, at least on an experimental basis:

> Social services departments are not necessarily the only or best placed organisations to co-ordinate a package of services for an elderly person. Health centres or the enhanced budget holding general practices could be good alternatives ... Faced with a competition, local social services departments might be put on their mettle. In some areas general practices might be the most efficient agents to administer services and employ a specialist doctor to combine both the home visits to elderly people that will be required under their new contracts as well as assessments for social care. (p. 94)

Others have gone one step further because of the perceived need to draw community health and welfare services (including GPs, care managers, home care and district nurses) into a simpler and more coherent structure. For example, Henwood *et al.* (1991) have suggested exploring the feasibility of a primary and community care authority based upon FHSAs or, alternatively, the integration of all health and social care purchasing functions within health authorities. In other words, the legitimacy of social services and care managers as the leaders in community care remains in some doubt.

Community care planning and joint commissioning

Is there any hope that the policy dilemmas and difficulties identified in this and earlier chapters can be tackled in a positive collaborative manner by social services authorities and health care agencies? Not all the evidence is bleak in this respect. Chapter 4 was critical of local authorities for their slowness to involve user and carer groups in community care planning. However, research evidence suggests that, in many areas, an excellent dialogue between health and social services has emerged as a result of the community care planning process (Hoyes *et al.*, 1993; Martin and Gaster, 1993), especially where health and social services boundaries are coterminous or nearly so (Hudson, 1992). If nothing else, social services managers and health service managers have developed a greater network awareness, and a greater appreciation of each others' priorities and preoccupations than existed before. The initial disruptions caused by the NHS reforms seem to have been overcome.

Many community care plans have been jointly published by the social services authority, the health authority and the FHSA. And many have tried to achieve domain consensus over rôles and responsibilities. For example, the 1992–3 community care plan from St Helens not only outlines the broad definitions of social care and health care which were agreed by a working group of health and social services managers, but then goes on to apply these to nearly 150 specific tasks. Social care is defined as interventions designed to meet one of the following needs:

1. Practical assistance in daily living, including provision of food, warmth, clothing, environmental support and assistance with personal care such as washing, dressing, bathing and going to the lavatory.
2. Practical advice and help in coping with day-to-day problems and counselling when needed.
3. Specific teaching and guidance in order to acquire new abilities and skills or to reinforce existing ones; these are often included as part of programmes of rehabilitation for people with severe physical or learning disabilities, for people with mental health problems and for young people as part of their preparation for leaving care.
4. Specialised programmes of care assessment, treatment and rehabilitation which aim to produce substantial changes in the individual's

functioning so that they can live more freely, independently and with integrity.

5. Protecting children from risk and using legislative powers only where individuals are at risk of endangering themselves or others.

However, the St Helens plan accepts that social care will often be provided by health care professionals and that activities definable as health care will often be delivered by social care professionals:

> Care in the community is a composite of elements of health and social care delivered to the individual and his/her family and/or carers. Elements of this care will be delivered within a health care model and others within a social care model, neither framework being exclusive in its function by either health and social services personnel. (St Helens Metropolitan Borough Council Personal Services Department, 1992, p. 43)

Table 6.1 provides examples of the way this leads to the allocation of specific tasks to either the social services authority, a local health care agency or both. Of course, the big test of such guidelines is whether they are used by staff on the ground, and if so whether this is done in a constructive or aggressive way.

Some feel that such guidelines are only the start. Collaboration needs to penetrate much deeper than this and the appropriate strategy is for the development of joint commissioning strategies between health and social care agencies. This was one of the options suggested by Henwood *et al.* (1991), and the need for this has also been argued by Knapp *et al.* (1992). This chapter has identified some of the enormous community care challenges faced by health and social care agencies, and pointed to the likelihood of this generating conflict rather than collaboration. Knapp and his colleagues assert that joint commissioning represents a way out of the impasse, since it involves pooling and the flexible use of resources. They go on to argue:

> From a procedural standpoint, joint commissioning improves the prospects of moving to clearer and more consistent eligibility criteria. It should raise mutual awareness, foster co-operation rather than competition, and weaken previous tendencies to pass the buck – to shunt people and costs on to other agencies. For example, joint commissioning of residential and nursing home care would provide the

Table 6.1   *Establishing the responsible authority in the provision of health and social care tasks*

Tasks	Responsible Authority		
	Health care	Both/either	Social care
House care			
Lighting fires/turn on heat			*
Sewing repairs			*
Make/change bed			*
Light cleaning			*
Heavy cleaning			*
Washing floors			*
Cleaning surfaces			*
Empty/clean commode			*
Cleaning windows (internal)			*
Changing curtains			*
Defrosting refrigerator			*
Washing up			*
Motivating customer		*	
Training/teaching customer or carer		*	
Diet and food preparation			
Preparing meal			*
Cooking meal			*
Making drinks			*
Dietary advice	*		
Rehabilitation in relation to above		*	
Motivating client		*	
Teaching/training		*	
Eating/feeding			
Feeding assistance		*	
Artificial feeding	*		
Motivating client		*	
Washing and dressing			
Dressing/undressing/assistance		*	
Washing assistance face/hands		*	
Strip washing		*	
Assisting to shower		*	
Assisting with bathing		*	
Blanket bathing		*	
In setting of severe disability	*		
If replacing carer			
Rehabilitation in respect of the above		*	
Motivating client		*	
Teaching/training client or carer		*	

Source: St Helens Metropolitan Borough Council Personal Services Department (1992) Community Care Plan, 1992–3, Appendix 1.

opportunity to achieve a much more appropriate balance between congregate and community care across the health and social care system as a whole. (p. 29)

Joint commissioning is equally important for those staying at home. They often have highly complex health and social care needs, and joint commissioning appears to offer the best prospect of offering a balanced and coherent response to the needs of such individuals.

Overall, Knapp *et al.* conclude that this is more than a zero sum game since it involves 'the pooling of sovereignty to achieve ends which individual agencies are less likely to secure alone' (p. 30). The authors recognise the obstacles which lie in the way of extensive joint commissioning. Complex procedures of assessment and financial accountability need to be worked out. Local authority members may be resistant and this may frustrate health service managers. Structures in the health service along the lines of purchaser–provider splits have been largely defined by central government and have been fairly consistently applied throughout the country. However, Chapters 3 and 5 illustrated the lack of central government guidance for local authorities over such issues in community care, and hence very different organisational responses have developed. It may be difficult to obtain agreement on the best balance between macro or block purchasing and micro commissioning by field-level care managers. Joint commissioning is much easier to develop where boundaries are coterminous than where they are not. And it is most feasible where health and social care agencies are building upon existing goodwill and trust, rather than in situations of past distrust.

Collaboration: an assessment of progress

What are the prospects for effective collaborative working after 1993 between health and social services? What does the situation look like when judged against the preconditions for success laid down earlier in the chapter? These were interorganisational homogeneity, domain consensus, network awareness, organisational exchange, absence of alternative resources and the existence of trust. Some positive points can be made. Considerable amounts of community care money are now linked to proof of collaboration over issues such as hospital discharge by central government. The criterion of an absence of alternative resources appears to be met. Yet this authoritative strategy by central government of enforced collaboration will backfire if it generates distrust and resentment from social services towards health authorities. In addition, even where it does foster good working relationships between key managers in social services and the purchasing side of the health authority, this tells us nothing about working relationships elsewhere, in areas such as joint working on assessment and care package delivery for individual service users. Here progress may depend more on whether both sides feel they are gaining from taking a collaborative rather than a competitive or defensive stance. In this respect, it was seen that the provision of mental health services, including provision for people with dementia, remains an area fraught with difficulty for those who aspire to a collaborative approach. With regard to network awareness, the NHS reforms did disrupt existing networks, and hence network awareness. However, the process of community care planning has proved to be an excellent opportunity to repair this situation in many areas.

The situation with regard to trust is likely to vary enormously. Some social service authorities and health authorities have managed to build up trust and mutual respect over a long period of time. In other areas, the opposite is true. If trust is at a low ebb between agencies, Webb (1991) warns that any new attempt to work together should be modest, low-risk and easy to achieve. This will maximise the chances of success and hence help to build improved relationships leading to a capacity to tackle larger-scale projects in the future. Yet the requirements of central government with regard to joint working over community care between health care and social care agencies are far from modest from the point of view of those agencies trying to bury a history of conflict and distrust.

It is unclear whether health care and social care agencies are moving towards interorganisational homogeneity. What may be happening overall is the process of conditioning of everyday action described by Dalley (1991) (see earlier discussion). Health service managers and social service managers may be finding that they have more and more in common and the same may be true of a range of professionals working at field level. It may be that one of the great implementation challenges of the future will be the need to tackle the growing gap and disenchantment of field-level staff with their managers, and vice versa. It is also clear that GPs fit into this picture very uneasily. They consider themselves way above care managers and district nurses in terms of status, yet they have neither the time nor the inclination to feed into more strategic debates. This is an area where interorganisational homogeneity remains almost entirely absent.

Finally, domain consensus remains as elusive as ever over the boundaries between health and social care. In the early 1990s, these boundaries are shifting once again, and this is creating an enormous potential for conflict between health and social care professionals at both the strategic and operational levels. Whether the temptation to settle for conflict will be avoided may well depend upon the qualities of managers and field-level staff. 'Champions of change' who have not lost sight of the needs of the user will want to tackle these dilemmas in a collaborative way. Street-level, and office-level, bureaucrats will not.

7 Housing and Community Care

The Griffiths Report (1988) paid little attention to housing issues and merely stated that the responsibilities of housing agencies should be limited to arranging and sometimes managing the 'bricks and mortar' of housing need for community care purposes (p. 15). The report was widely criticised for its failure to address fully housing and housing policy as one of the foundations of community care (Oldman, 1988; Means and Harrison, 1988). However, the White Paper on community care (Department of Health, 1989a) differs considerably from the Griffiths Report in this respect. 'Suitable good quality housing' is seen as essential to social care packages (p. 9) and it is argued that 'social services authorities will need to work closely with housing authorities, housing associations and other providers of housing of all types in developing plans for a full and flexible range of housing' (p. 25).

This chapter focuses on housing issues from the perspective that housing is an essential element of community care. However, the emphasis of the chapter is not solely on the politics of what is usually called 'special needs' housing, but will also include a consideration of much broader issues such as the meaning of home and the impact of general housing policies upon frail elderly and disabled people.

The meaning of home

Community care policy in the United Kingdom is based on the belief that nearly everyone prefers to live in ordinary housing rather than in institutions, because institutions lack the capacity to be a home. This section explores recent research and theoretical thinking on what constitutes a home and goes on to consider the implications of this for the users of community care services.

Gurney and Means (1993) argue that the late 1980s and early 1990s saw a fierce debate within urban sociology about the meaning of home, although it paid little attention to elderly and disabled people. The background to the debate was a belief in the emergence of a new

166

'middle mass' in British society (Pahl, 1984) with shared goals and aspirations, one of which was the desire to be owner-occupiers. Britain had become, as Saunders (1990) put it, *A Nation of Home Owners*. He was keen not only to show how home ownership was a key source of social stratification in British society but also to explore how the meaning of home differed between tenures. Saunders interviewed 522 individuals from 450 households in Burnley, Derby and Slough who were either owner-occupiers or council tenants. Each respondent was asked the following question: 'People often distinguish between "house" and "home". What does the home mean to you?' (p. 390). Saunders found that owner-occupiers identified their house as a home and 'a place where they feel relaxed and where they can surround themselves with familiar and personal possessions' (p. 272). Council tenants, on the other hand, associated 'home' much more with their relationships with family and neighbours. He concluded from this that the great strength of owner-occupation was its capacity to enable people to express themselves and their identity in a private realm which was free from surveillance.

The strength of Saunders' work is that it brought to the fore debates about the meaning of home. However, his work is highly contentious and generated several critiques even prior to the collapse of the housing market in Britain. In terms of our own commmunity care concerns, the critique of Saunders by Gurney (1990, 1991) is especially relevant and insightful. His starting point is to emphasise the complexity of the concept of home which flows from the wealth of experiences which structure the meaning of the word for individuals. As a result, the meanings attached to 'home' cannot adequately be explained by the kind of generalisation about tenure used by Saunders. More specifically, Gurney has argued that the question 'what does your home mean to you?' may have been too complex for interviewers to have written down the full ambiguity of comments from respondents in the three towns survey. Gurney's own postal survey which asked the same question generated a far wider and more complex set of responses than that uncovered by Saunders (Gurney, 1991).

Second, Gurney (1990) emphasises the emotions of home. He recognises that domestic violence, child abuse and elder abuse often occur in the home, yet goes on to argue:

Whilst it is important not to deny the existence or importance of such behaviour, the likely reason for the association of love and affection with the home, rather than the workplace or domestic property own-ership seems to stem from a fact that it is often taken for granted. It is in the home where supportive and loving relationships between kin and non-kin relations most often take place. (p. 29)

This leads Gurney to emphasise that the security of home alluded to by Saunders (1990) comes from something less tangible than control over the home environment through owner-occupation. Third, Gurney argues that the meanings of home are specific to the experiences of certain moments in time and so are constantly changing. For example, he points out that home will hold less positive meanings and significance for a couple in the middle of a relationship breakdown than for a more stable couple, and that perceptions of home will vary over time in response to life cycle changes. He quotes Anthony (1984) as illustrating how recollections of housing histories are closely linked to important personal events or stages in the life cycle (childhood home, first home away from parents, child rearing home, and so on).

What does all this mean for community care? Higgins (1989) has gone so far as to argue that the very concept of community care can be abandoned because 'the real distinction is actually between the institu-tion and home, and services are normally available either in the institu-tion or from home (in the case of day care) and at home (in the case of domiciliary care)' (p. 15). Not only this but institutions and homes differ markedly in terms of their core characteristics, as suggested by Table 7.1. This typology is driven by the physical characteristics of institu-tions compared to ordinary housing and the knock-on consequences of this for living regimes. The key characteristics of home for Higgins include the ability to exercise choice and the importance of familiarity. Does this suggest that owner-occupiers will have a greater sense of home because they have more control over their housing? And does the emphasis on familiarity mean that people develop a sense of home about particular houses and neighbourhoods? Research on the meaning of home to older people throws light on both these issues. Research on elderly people suggests that strong emotions can be expressed about particular houses as homes. In *The Family Life of Old People*, Townsend (1963) wrote:

Home was the old armchair by the hearth, the creaky bedstead, the polished lino with its faded pattern, the sideboard with its picture gallery, and the lavatory with its broken latch reached through the

Table 7.1   *The key characteristics of institutions and home*

Institutions	Home
1. Public space, limitations on privacy	1. Private space, but may be some limitations on privacy
2. Living with strangers, rarely alone	2. May live alone or with relatives or friends, rarely with strangers
3. Staffed by professionals or volunteers	3. Normally no staff living there but they may visit to provide services
4. Formal and lacking in intimacy	4. Informal and intimate
5. Sexual relationships discouraged	5. Sexual relationships (between certain family members) accepted
6. Owned/rented by other agencies	6. Owned/rented by inhabitants
7. Variations in size but may be large (in terms of physical space and numbers living there)	7. Variations in size but usually small
8. Limitations on choice and on personal freedom	8. Ability to exercise choice and considerable degree of freedom
9. Strangeness (of people, place etc)	9. Familiarity (of people, place etc)
10. 'Batch' or communal living	10. Individual arrangements for eating, sleeping, leisure activities which can vary according to time and place

Source: Higgins (1989) p. 15.

rain. It embodied a thousand memories and held promise of a thousand contentments. It was an extension of personality. (p. 38)

Nearly thirty years later, Harrison and Means (1990) looked at a small group of elderly owner-occupiers, the majority of whom had lived in their homes for over twenty years (see also Gurney and Means, 1993). It was perhaps not surprising that 'I've been here so long' was often offered to the researchers as an explanation and sometimes almost as an excuse for not moving, even when the repair and maintenance of the house had become a major problem. The responses to the question 'could you tell me a little about how long you have lived in this house and this neighbourhood?' often illustrated the interweaving of people's life history with their houses. The house, for some, was still 'the place they· had come as a bride', 'their mother's house', 'their husband's family home'. People could recall specific days and dates when important events took place in the house, such as the day they moved in and the day and circumstances of a partner's death. 'Our roots are really in the house' (Mr and Mrs L., 76 and 71 years) and 'I couldn't leave because of his memories' (Mrs P., 85 years) were two reasons offered as to why people wished to stay put.

The house was either symbolically, or for some actually, an indication of the effort they had put into a life together with their partners. Some people talked of the steady way they had kept the house in good repair and in some cases transformed it over the years, adding amenities or shaping the garden. Some expressed pride in what they had achieved, others tolerated the house, like an eccentric relative, not expecting great things from something of such an age. For the people who had spent many years in the house, their accounts gave the impression of it being a fixed spot from which they had observed, with varying degrees of pleasure or anxiety, the changing scene of the street or neighbourhood. The more housebound respondents derived confidence from having a very vivid mental map of their location. While alternative accommodation might offer improved physical living standards, it was easy to imagine the sense of loss and confusion which might arise for these respondents if they moved from their present homes. Their houses were an anchor orienting them in both time and place.

Mrs P. had lived in her house since she was married, at the age of 21 years. At the time of interview, she was 85 years old and her husband had died 19 years previously. The house had been her husband's family house and during their married life he had done a great deal of work on it. Originally it had only a pump outside for water and a toilet at the bottom of the garden. The house, however, had fallen into rather a bad state of repair, as Mrs P. observed:

I know it's old, it's damp and my roof wants doing – it leaks. It's in a mess. I can't afford to pay for it, but I'm not going to leave it … I've always lived in it. They reckoned it was cold and that to live in, but if you've always lived in it, you don't bother, do you? They keep telling me it's old fashioned – but it's an old house. (p. 63)

Harrison and Means claim that inextricably bound up with these more abstract and emotional attachments of elderly people to their home was a bundle of more pragmatic issues. Individuals who had lived in one place for most of their lives tended to have friends, neighbours and quite often family nearby who could offer a variety of support.

One explanation that has been provided for the strength of these positive feelings about the need to 'stay put' is that elderly people perceive house moves in later life in a negative way. Steinfield (1981) has pointed out that, for younger people, moving house often confirms a positive status passage, because moves are often associated with such events as marriage, new employment or increased affluence. In later life, accommodation change is more likely to signify a negative status passage and so many elderly people may be keen to retain their present accommodation to minimise the impact of loss from reduced income, bereavement or increased disability (see also Means, 1987). However, there is a mass of research evidence relating to retirement to the seaside (Karn, 1977), moving to sheltered housing to rent (Butler *et al.*, 1983; Fennell, 1986) and sheltered housing to buy (Williams, 1990) which suggests some elderly people are able to settle in new accommodation, and re-establish a sense of home within their new environment quite quickly. This would suggest that it is possible to transport one's sense of emotional security from one building (home) to another, although it is equally true that some elderly people may have been more used than others to periodic house moves throughout adult life, and hence much less anxious than others when a further move was required in later life (Clapham, Means and Munro, 1993).

Very little research has been carried out on the meaning of home to older people in rented accommodation. Are attachments to particular homes less strong? Certainly, elderly council tenants are often under pressure to move from their house where they brought up their children in order to release family housing to those on the waiting list. Many such tenants have been willing to consider a move to modern prestigious sheltered housing schemes (Means, 1988), but little is known of emotional feelings about leaving the family home. Perhaps a key issue is whether the move is to another home or to an institution. Willcocks, Peace and Kellaher (1987) suggest that strong emotions and attachments to their houses are expressed by elderly people when they feel threatened by a possible move into residential care. They argue that, in the privacy of their own homes, elderly people can conceal their physical disabilities from others who are prone to assume that a disability in one area means incapacity in every aspect of life. It is 'the remaining domain through which they can connect with the wider context' (p. 7) and so 'it can be argued that older people are reluctant to leave homes which may be inconvenient and difficult, for to relinquish home would be to relinquish a hold on a base from which personal power can be generated and reinforced' (p. 8). The main focus of *Private Lives in Public Places* by Willcocks and her colleagues (1987) is on residential life in local authority old people's homes and they conclude that most elderly residents of such homes fail to re-establish a sense of privacy in this kind of residential setting, which thus fails to provide a home in the same way as their previous accommodation.

So far it would appear that not only can the Higgins' (1989) typology of home versus institution be accepted, but that the advantages of the former over the latter as the place to receive care is overwhelming. However, a number of further points need to be made. First, the resettlement process has involved the movement of many service users, especially those with learning disabilities, from institutions where they have lived for many years to new homes and hostels in the community. The justification for this has been the characteristics of their institutions, as summarised by Higgins (1989) and as described in Chapter 2. However, Saunders (1990) did underline that home for some can be as much a matter of networks and relationships (for council tenants) as of privacy (for owner-occupiers). One danger of the resettlement process is that the hospital-based networks and relationships may be shattered but may not be replaced by equivalent networks in new surroundings. The privacy of the new home or hostel may be experienced by some as a prison of loneliness and despair. However, research on those who leave hospitals does not support this gloomy scenario, although it does suggest that stress can be caused by the loss of previous networks and relationships, and by the difficulties of creating new ones (Tomlinson, 1991; Petch, 1992).

Second, it has been argued that residential care does not have to have the negative features associated with the Higgins (1989) typology of institutions. Willcocks, Peace and Kellaher (1987) state that it is possible to transform both the physical structure and management culture of residential homes. Management can develop a philosophy of individual rights, acceptable risks and normalisation for residents, and back this up with changes to the physical structure of residential homes by creating flatlets within homes which 'establish access to and control over personal territory for elderly people' (p. 170). Dalley (1988) has developed a rather different argument by asserting the potential value of collective life styles which she feels can be a source of freedom from the oppressions of the nuclear family rather than inevitably having to involve a regimented life style with no personal space. She points out that collectivist traditions have existed in Britain and America built around shared religious, political and utopian communities. However, as Baldwin and Twigg (1991) point out:

> Dalley's objective in drawing on these three areas is partly to remind us that more collective forms of living are possible, and she clearly succeeds in this. What is less clear, however, is how these understandings derived from other societies and other periods can directly influence our thinking about the ways care for dependent people in contemporary Britain should be organised. (p. 128)

Nevertheless, Dalley's thesis does make us realise that collective forms of living do not have to be heavily institutionalised.

A third issue derives from the increasing range of accommodation which now exists for people with care needs. It is clear that many of them cannot easily be allocated to either the 'institution' category or the 'home' category in the Higgins (1989) typology, although Higgins herself stresses that many care options will contain both home and 'institutional' elements. The Wagner Committee on residential care found it very difficult to agree on a definition of what they were meant to be studying:

> The boundaries of what constitutes residential care are constantly shifting with the emergence of new forms of provision; some of these, such as Very Sheltered Housing, Core and Cluster schemes, and multiple fostering are expressly designed with a view to combining the benefits of what have hitherto been considered separately as 'residential care' and 'care in the community'. (Wagner, 1988 p. 17)

Core and cluster schemes are especially interesting in terms of our focus on the meaning of home, and how this varies from ordinary housing to residential care. Core and cluster schemes have often been developed for people being resettled from long-stay hospitals. The central principle of such schemes is that flexible support arrangements combine with a range of different sorts of housing. The administrative centre is the core and staff based at the centre provide support to people (usually with learning disabilities or mental health problems) in different sorts (clusters) of housing in the local area. The support is peripatetic and so can change in response to the changing needs of the resident. The emphasis is on the separation of home, work and recreation and so no accommodation is provided in the administrative core (Bayliss, 1987). The core and cluster model raises the interesting question of whether some of the housing clusters are home environments while others are institutions. However, research suggests that the extent of independence and privacy available to residents in supported housing may be determined as much by the philosophies of staff as by physical layout (Coleman *et al.*, 1990).

The fourth issue concerns the limitations of ordinary housing for some people. Higgins (1989) herself recognises that some people lack any home because they are homeless while others may perceive their inadequate housing as no more than shelter. For younger physically disabled people, the achievement of independence may require them to leave their parental home and move to separate accommodation. For some, the move from adapted ordinary housing (the parental home) to the status of tenant in a supported housing scheme may coincide with increased rather than decreased independence. With regard to house-bound elderly people, Gavilan (1992) has argued that the home can take on the features of a total institution because dependence upon home care and other services involves a major intrusion of self and space, although she emphasises that a sensible future strategy requires developing the skills of home care staff rather than the relocation of frail elderly people to institutions. There is also growing evidence about the extent to which elder abuse occurs in the family home as well as in institutions (Pritchard, 1992). Nevertheless, the overwhelming evidence is that most people prefer a home which is linked to concepts such as privacy, independence and freedom from surveillance, which are not commonly found in institutions. For example, Tomlinson's research (1991) on resettlement from Claybury and Friern mental health hospitals indicated that many of those resettled in hostels aspired to move to more independent types of accommodation. However, fulfilling such aspirations depends on the availability of appropriate housing which can be turned into a home. The next section therefore looks at prospects for elderly and disabled people within mainstream housing provision.

Mainstream housing and community care

There is increasing criticism of the concept of 'special needs' housing, both in terms of sheltered housing for elderly people and in terms of other kinds of housing with support schemes. The argument is that the heavy emphasis of central government on such schemes deflects attention away from the need to provide affordable, appropriate and flexible housing within mainstream provision (Means, 1987; Wheeler, 1986). As Clapham and Smith (1990) explain, '"special needs" is a selective redefinition of housing disadvantage, which portrays housing problems as discrete and technical (and therefore politically manageable) and provides criteria for discriminating between groups who are more or less deserving of a share in the progressively limited pool of public funds' (p. 204). Second, it has long been recognised that inadequacies within mainstream housing provision lead people to enter residential care and other supported housing schemes (Sinclair, 1988; Oldman, 1990) or to drift into homelessness (Office for Public Management, 1992b). This section therefore looks at mainstream housing provision in terms of availability, affordability, repair and access, and draws out the implications for the users of community care services.

Availability

Whether or not there is a shortage of housing in England and Wales is a more difficult question than it first appears since it requires much more than matching the overall number of units to the overall number of households. To be used by existing or potential households, houses must be affordable, in the right part of the country and of an appropriate design and size, as well as being in good condition. Studies which try to take all these factors into account suggest major housing shortages exist. For example, Niner (1989) estimated that by 2001 an extra 2.2 million to 3 million households will need housing, with the biggest growth in people living alone and among the over-75s. However, less work has been carried out specifically on the housing needs of the main groups covered by the community care legislation. An important exception to this is the report commissioned from the Office for Public Management (1992b) by the National Federation of Housing Associations. From existing data, the report was able to produce estimates for the following groups:

1. People with learning disabilities in long-stay institutions – 2000 to 3000 units per year over the next decade.
2. People with mental health problems in hospitals – 2000 to 3000 units per year over the next decade.
3. Increase of elderly people over 85 – about 3500 new units of supported accommodation required per annum to meet their needs.
4. Changes in funding of residential and nursing home care – between 2700 and 6750 people per year might require alternative housing (numbers vary according to assumptions made).
5. People with mental health problems who are homeless, in temporary accommodation or in prison may require as many as 15 000 units in total.
6. People with learning disabilities living with families – 2000 units per year.

However, a weakness of these estimates is that they fail to clarify how many of these people must have accommodation in supported housing schemes. In other words, how many could manage in mainstream housing if it was affordable and in reasonable repair, or if appropriate personal assistance and support services were brought to owner-occupiers and tenants of that ordinary housing? To what extent are supported housing schemes attempting to compensate for the failures of mainstream housing provision? Our discussion below suggests that this is a major factor. Indeed, there is growing evidence that homelessness from the non-availability of affordable housing is now a major generator of mental and physical ill health (Shanks and Smith, 1992).

Affordability

In terms of affordability, our main focus is on rented housing. This is not to deny that issues of affordability in owner-occupation do not arise, as the growth of repossessions in the 1990s has served to illustrate. However, elderly owner-occupiers tend to have paid off their mortgage by the time of retirement and hence the major issue for them is often house disrepair (see below). In contrast, younger owners of properties do experience mental health problems; younger physically disabled adults who are owner-occupiers get made redundant; and the house-owning parents of people with learning disabilities die. All three of these situations can raise affordability issues in owner-occupation, which is now the dominant housing tenure in England and Wales.

However, issues of the affordability of housing and community care are most visible in terms of rented property. From 1979, the aim of central government has been to stimulate owner-occupation, to break the near monopoly powers of local authorities in the provision of rented housing and to control public expenditure. Malpass (1993) has shown how the initial emphasis was upon council house sales and upon cutbacks in the housing investment programmes of local authorities. However, the Housing Act 1988 and the Local Government and Housing Act 1989 attempted to take this one stage further. Both Acts are highly complex (Malpass and Means, 1993) but in terms of affordability both had the effect of driving up rents significantly in all types of rented accommodation. The aspiration of central government was to allow markets to determine appropriate rent levels, and then to develop means-tested subsidy systems (housing benefit) to support those on lowest incomes. For example, the aim of the 1988 Act is to replace local authorities with housing associations as the main providers of new rented housing. The Act established a new funding regime for housing associations which presets the amount of public subsidy prior to scheme commencement and requires them to raise the remainder from banks and building societies. The inevitable result has been higher rents for new tenancies:

Average rents in new lettings rose from £18.16 in the second quarter 1988 to £32.89 by quarter 2 1991, an increase of 81 per cent. Rents for lettings of newly developed homes (new lets) increased by 104 per cent. In comparison, the RPI increased by 26 per cent. Average rents have therefore risen at three times the rate of general inflation. (Randolph, 1993, p. 45)

The consequence of this has been to make such tenants highly dependent on the housing benefit system. It has deepened the poverty trap for unemployed disabled people who are keen to find employment. It has created great difficulties for those 'not rich, not poor' (Bull and Poole, 1989) elderly people, with small occupational pensions and/or limited capital savings, who have taken a tenancy under the new Act.

The Housing Act 1988 also introduced a further deregulation of rents in the private sector, a further reduction in security of tenure for some kinds of tenancy, and public subsidy for some types of new private renting schemes. None of this has encouraged a major upsurge in the private rented sector (Kemp, 1993) although much published research predates the collapse of the owner-occupied housing market. However, reduced security of tenure for new tenants after 1988 has made those with care needs more vulnerable to eviction and tenancy termination. The higher rents have not always been accepted as payable to those entitled to housing benefit because 'since April 1989 local authorities have had to refer new claims for housing benefit on deregulated tenancies to the rent office to determine whether the rent is above a "reasonable market rent" or the accommodation "over large for the claimant's reasonable needs"' (Kemp, 1993, p. 67). A new financial regime for local authority housing in England and Wales was introduced by the Local Government and Housing Act 1989. This new system is highly complex and has involved the creation of a housing revenue account ring-fenced from the general funds of the local authority. It is a system which has generated some major rent rises, and council rents rose by an average of 30 per cent in England during the first two years of the new system (Malpass, 1993). Again, increased dependency on housing benefit is an inevitable outcome of these trends for low-income people.

In *Paying for Britain's Housing*, Maclennan *et al.* (1990) drew together data collected in late 1988 and early 1989 from six teams who had surveyed households about housing finance issues in different regions. They pointed out that the data showed that almost half of the households in social housing in Britain did not have access to employment income, and this stood in contrast to the sector two decades earlier. They argued that 'this yawning gap in the sources of income has to be at the forefront of any discussion of the housing subsidy system' (p. 36). A high percentage of these people were elderly and disabled people. Thus the option of staying put and the avoidance of institutional care may be heavily dependent upon the affordability of rents in mainstream housing for low-income elderly and disabled renters.

Repair

Another major issue in mainstream housing is disrepair. Housing association property is at present in the best condition overall although Randolph (1993) warns that the new funding regime may be so 'tight' that housing associations may fail to put aside sufficient monies to cover future maintenance and repair costs. Much of the local authority housing stock has long been known to be in a very poor state of repair (Audit Commission, 1986b) and on some estates this is linked to a more general environmental and social collapse (Power, 1987). Overall, many properties in the most deprived estates may be extremely stressful places for disabled and elderly people to live, with the real possibility that this leads to entry into forms of supported housing not required by levels of frailty or disability.

Disrepair is also a major issue for low income, and especially elderly, owner-occupiers (see Mackintosh, Means and Leather, 1990, Chapter 2). The key difficulty experienced is how to maintain property when on low income. The 1986 English House Condition Survey (Department of the Environment, 1988) confirmed previous surveys that older people are disproportionately more likely to experience poor housing conditions. For example, although making up only 10 per cent of households in the 1986 survey, those with a head aged 75 or more occupied almost one third of dwellings lacking basic amenities. Of owner-occupier households with a head over retirement age in 1986, 43 per cent had repair costs of £1000 or more (at 1986 prices), with 10 per cent having costs greater than £5000. As one would expect, the majority of these elderly people were on very low incomes. However, they did have sizeable amounts of equity tied up in their houses. The 1986 English House Condition Survey (EHCS) found that more than 80 per cent of households headed by a person aged between 65 and 74, and nearly 70 per cent of those headed by a person aged 75 or older, had equity of at least £25 000 in 1986. One key question is whether such equity is likely to be used more and more by elderly owner-occupiers to meet their repair costs. We are doubtful about whether this will happen. First, many of the main mechanisms (such as home income plans) for releasing large amounts of equity are complex and offputting to potential consumers. Second, there is no overall policy relating home equity to entitlement to state benefits. For the majority of benefits, home equity is not taken into account at all and government policies towards the expansion of home ownership have stressed the importance of inheritance. There are potentially many other calls on home equity which should be taken into account before it can be assumed that this source could be used on a major scale to finance building works, although it could be argued that investment in the protection of home equity might be considered a priority. Third, it is also clear from the EHCS that there are wide variations in the amount of wealth which elderly households have available. It is those households living in properties in the poorest condition and requiring the most expensive works who are likely to have the least resources. Finally, to borrow against home equity in practice requires that a household has adequate *income* to meet interest charges, or is eligible for Department of Social Security (DSS) help, or has a sufficient margin of equity to permit some or all of any interest charges to be deferred until death. Many households fall outside this group.

The new renovation grant system established through the Local Government and Housing Act 1989 might be expected to help those low-income elderly people in poorly repaired, and perhaps low equity, property. The new system includes a minor works grant for the first time for works costing under £1080, which may be welcomed by many older people on low incomes who wish to undertake work but do not want the disruption of a full renovation grant. These small grants are discretionary and are not offered by all local authorities, but to date they have been the most used element of the new system now their value is generally recognised. For larger mandatory grants under the new system, applicants have to undergo a test of resources (Mackintosh and Leather, 1992) and it is not yet known if the introduction of means testing has discouraged large numbers of potential applicants. In the past, many elderly people have been able to fund their repairs only if they were able to put together a complex funding package which might include an improvement grant, an interest only maturity loan (with the interest paid by the DSS) and perhaps a 'one off' grant from the community care element of the social fund. The new arrangements reduce the likelihood of older people facing these problems, especially if they are entitled to a full grant after the test of resources. However, it is not clear how long this situation will continue because the Department of the Environment has expressed concern in a recent consultation paper about the rising costs of housing renovation (Department of the Environment, 1993). In any case, even in the present system, many elderly people still lack the knowledge, expertise or confidence to organise building work and so they will continue to depend on the availability of specialist advice from organisations such as the Anchor Housing Trust (for Staying Put Projects) and Care and Repair (England) (Leather and Mackintosh, 1992; Harrison and Means, 1990).

Owner-occupation in later life will be a boon to many. With the mortgage paid off, housing costs will drop at a time when weekly income is reduced, thus avoiding a major decline in living standards. For many, there is the prospect of a move from a family home to a smaller property, thus releasing equity to be used in a variety of ways, including meeting future care needs. But others will be trapped in poorly repaired property of limited value with few assets around with which to develop a maintenance and repair strategy in later life. The housing dimension of community care needs to include a strategy for offering support to elderly and disabled people facing these kinds of repair problems.

Access (new build and adaptation)

In discussing issues of access, it is important to distinguish between wheelchair and mobility standard housing. Mobility housing is housing suitable for ambulant disabled people, while wheelchair housing is housing suitable for the permanent accommodation of wheelchair users. The late 1980s saw a decline in new build housing meeting such standards despite the rhetoric of central government about the import-ance of independent living. The Rowe Report (1992) has stressed how this decline cannot possibly reflect a reduced need for such accommoda-tion. It points out that conservative estimates from government suggest that 6.2 million adults or 14.2 per cent of the population have an impair-ment while four million of the 6.2 million experience mobility difficult-ies and 1.1 per cent of the total adult population use wheelchairs. The Rowe Report (1992, p. 14) draws upon previous research to suggest that there might be a shortfall of 330 000 dwellings which are suitable to accommodate wheelchair users.

Earlier, the impact of the Housing Act 1988 and the Local Govern-ment and Housing Act 1989 was discussed in terms of affordability issues. However, these Acts have also had a major influence on the reduction in building housing to mobility and wheelchair standard. The decline in local authority starts reflects the general discouragement and opposition of central government to all new build by local authorities. However, the poor performance of housing associations in recent years with regard to mobility and wheelchair standard housing has a more complex explanation. Morris (1990b) has argued that:

> The new finance system for housing associations is squeezing the small 'special needs' housing associations and threatening their very existence. At the same time, the larger general needs housing associ-ations, and particularly those in the forefront of using private finance, are ignoring the needs of disabled people. (p. 23)

Morris went on to claim that the financial pressures exerted on housing associations by the new mixed funding scheme meant that space stan-dards were declining in most new build property and needed to be reversed. An attempt to do this was made by the Access Committee for England (funded by the Department of Health) which produced a report on building homes for successive generations (Aaronovitch *et al.*, 1992). The starting point was to argue that the accessibility of non-domestic buildings had been improved in recent years by the inclusion of access considerations in planning law, and the introduction of access requirements into building regulations. The same approach now needed to be applied to domestic housing. Three general principles were listed in terms of mobility housing:

1. The approaches and entrances to dwellings should be accessible to disabled people, including wheelchair users.
2. Areas normally used by visitors, such as hall, WC and living rooms, should be accessible to disabled people, including wheelchair users.
3. Dwellings on more than one storey or level should be designed internally for easy movement and be amenable to modification, if necessary, for persons of limited mobility.

The committee went on to specify what the implementation of these principles would mean in terms of essential design criteria (for example, 'wherever possible there should be a level or gently sloped path, with a maximum gradient of 1:20 from the adopted footway to the door of the dwelling' (p. 11)). They concluded that these criteria should be included within building regulations since 'the advantages of access through regulation for developers and designers is the degree of certainty, and the knowledge that they will be universally applied' (p. 8). Aaronovitch *et al.* (1992) claimed that the financial consequences of such changes would not be great, although the impact would be greatest at the lowest end of the housing market.

A complementary approach to using new build schemes to increase mobility and wheelchair access is to emphasise the importance of adaptation to existing properties. The main public subsidy for adaptation work is now through the disabled facilities grant which was established as part of the home improvement regime under the Local Government and Housing Act 1989. It can be applied for by owner-occupiers, private tenants, council tenants and landlords. The grant is mandatory (subject to a means test) if the housing authority considers the work practicable and reasonable, if the social services authority considers the work necessary and appropriate, and if the work covers any of the following areas:

1. Access in and out of the home.
2. Access to the living room, bedroom, kitchen and bathroom.
3. The provision of bathroom and kitchen facilities that can be reached independently.
4. Adapting heating and lighting controls.
5. Improving the heating system.
6. Making provision for the disabled person to help a person who is dependent on their care.

Discretionary grants may be available for work to adapt the home beyond this standard. The housing authority has financial responsibility for the disabled facilities grant but is required to seek the views of the social services department where the applicant is expected by the means test to contribute to the grant and where she/he is unable to do so. In limited circumstances, social services are able to make a 'topping up' contribution.

The disabled facilities grant has been criticised on a number of grounds (Mackintosh and Leather, 1992). Many fear that the means testing element, which covers both the householder and the disabled person, is discouraging some applications. The test applied excludes major outgoings such as mortgage payments which are not taken into account in considering what the applicant can reasonably afford. The quality of coordination between housing and social services varies enormously from area to area with major assessment delays occurring in some localities because of a shortage of occupational therapists. The processing of grants is also slow in some areas, with the suspicion that this is used to ensure that the housing authority does not overspend its grant budget. Harrison and Means (1993) have argued that the disabled facilities grant illustrates 'the tension of how to provide grants as a right within finite local authority budgets' (p. 136). As such, a study of its operation has much to teach us about the way community care provision should operate from April 1993 onwards.

The Wagner Report (1988) on residential care argued that 'nobody … should be expected to change their permanent residence simply in order to obtain the services, including health care, which they need' (p. 22). However, the issue is not just one of the flexibility, or not, of home care and other domiciliary services. Many people enter residential care and other forms of supported housing, not from positive choice, but through the major inadequacies of availability, affordability, repair and access within mainstream housing provision. Community care planning needs to consider these kinds of issues and not just indicate the main gaps in the availability of supported housing.

Supported housing

Following the discussion on mainstream housing adaptations, it is now appropriate to examine supported housing schemes. The most common and well known type of scheme is sheltered housing for elderly people. However, 'sheltered housing' can refer to a wide range of schemes for a wide range of elderly people and is now available through a wide range of tenure arrangements (to buy, rent or own). A government circular in the late 1960s outlined two main types of scheme (Ministry of Housing and Local Government, 1969):

Category 1 consists of purpose built flats or bungalows with a warden, but often with no common room or other facilities for shared use.
Category 2 is usually identified as a scheme with individual bungalows or flats linked by heated internal corridors. A common room, laundry and guest room, and other facilities for shared use, are normally included.

These kinds of schemes were initially provided by local authority housing departments, and over 100 000 units had been made available by the mid-1980s. Housing associations also became involved in scheme development and by 1984, 700 housing associations were providing sheltered accommodation for 70 000 households.

In the last decade, the overall picture has become very complicated, for a number of reasons. First, there has been the development of very sheltered housing schemes (sometimes called Category $2\frac{1}{2}$ schemes) which are aimed at those whose frailty requires greater provision of communal facilities, enabling main meals and more care for the individual occupier to be provided. Second, local authorities have become more imaginative in the creation of sheltered housing schemes. These have included both the use of tower blocks as vertical sheltered housing units and the creation of dispersed schemes amongst scattered bungalows and ground floor maisonette flats through the introduction of alarm systems and mobile wardens. Since sheltered housing is protected from the right to buy, one interpretation of this development is that it represents an attempt to conserve the housing stock as much as to meet the accommodation needs of elderly people. Third, there has been the emergence of sheltered housing schemes either for sale or involving various types of flexible tenure arrangement.

The big debate in sheltered housing has always been the extent to which it should be perceived as a form of housing provision or a form of care provision. Is it an expensive form of housing in which subsidies are offered to a few, a creative way of responding to the housing needs of some or a cheap non-stigmatising alternative to residential care? It is a debate which has seen the emergence of both stalwart defenders and fierce critics of sheltered housing. For example, Heumann and Boldy (1982) argue that sheltered housing represents 'the most humane and successful formula for long-term assisted independent living in use today in western society' (p. 203) while Middleton (1987) claims such housing represents the unjustified provision of 'so much for so few'. At its simplest, the debate has hinged on whether residents need, want or use the services of their warden or not. Research in the early 1980s by Butler, Oldman and Greve (1983) suggested better housing mattered more than the availability of a warden or an alarm system. However, Fennell (1986) found that his sample of tenants in Anchor Housing Association schemes were very appreciative of such facilities and that over 25 per cent had had to summon warden help in an emergency within the previous twelve months.

One explanation for these contrasting findings is that the tenants of sheltered housing schemes are becoming more frail and more disabled, either in terms of their well-being at the time of allocation or as a result of health changes since the allocation. Certainly, the emphasis is now frequently on the capacity of such schemes to provide care, and there is growing interest in the scope for developing sheltered housing as an alternative to residential care. A number of factors may be influencing this. Many local authorities and housing associations are concerned about growing levels of disability within their existing schemes. Many older schemes have shared facilities and may be hard to let; revamping into a very sheltered housing scheme is one possible future strategy (Means, 1988). Sheltered housing is perceived as a preferable alternative to residential care for those unable or unwilling to 'stay put' (Fletcher, 1991) and an alternative in need of rapid expansion, given the ageing of the elderly population (Kirk and Leather, 1991).

The funding arrangements for local authority sheltered housing established through the 1989 Act for local authorities and through the

1988 Act for housing associations are increasing rents rapidly and making the funding of the warden service highly problematic. The housing policies of central government seem hostile, or at least indifferent, to the future of sheltered housing. Yet community care policy repeatedly emphasises its importance, whilst failing to identify how the revenue costs of care and other support services are to be met. However, this is a major issue for all supported housing schemes and not just for sheltered housing.

The wide range of housing with support schemes which now exist has already been noted. In addition to sheltered accommodation, *Housing: The Foundation of Community Care* (Bayliss, 1987) identified the following options and possibilities:

1. *Fully self-contained flats* with bedroom, living room, kitchen, bathroom and WC.
2. *Self-contained bedsitters*, usually a combined bedroom/living room with a separate kitchen and bathroom/WC, although some bedsitters also have the kitchen in the main room.
3. *Shared housing*, which can encompass a variety of arrangements, including: own bedsitter and shared kitchen and bathroom, own bedroom and shared living/dining room, kitchen and bathroom. Some meals may be eaten communally, for example in the evenings and/or at weekends.
4. *Cluster flats*: self-contained flats or bedsitters in a single house. Tenants cater for themselves and essentially live independently, but may share some facilities such as a laundry room. Individual cluster flats may be for one or more people.
5. *Staffed hostels*, which may be short-stay or cater for people on a more permanent basis; they may have shared or single bedrooms. The level of staff support can vary considerably.
6. *Shared living schemes*, where people with learning difficulties or mental health problems share a house with 'able tenants' who offer varying degrees of support. Many of these schemes have been developed in university towns, with students as 'able tenants'.
7. *Residential care homes*, registered under the 1984 Registered Homes Act, often similar in accommodation and style to staffed hostels, but with a greater range of services provided, such as meals.
8. *Crisis or 'asylum' housing* which can be used on a short- or medium-term basis by people undergoing a crisis.

This type of provision is growing. For example, using the definition of a hostel as all shared housing with warden support, Housing Corporation figures show an increase of 13 000 places between 1985 and 1989, which represents an average increase of 8 per cent per year, as compared to an increase of between 2 per cent and 5 per cent for housing association homes in general (quoted in Watson and Cooper, 1992, p. 4).

Until recently much less was known about the geographical spread of such schemes and how this does or does not relate to local needs. However, Watson and Cooper (1992) have surveyed the provision of supported housing by housing associations in the four areas of Leicestershire, Manchester, the London Borough of Southwark and the Hampshire districts of Southampton, Eastleigh, Winchester, New Forest and Test Valley. They identified 385 schemes, involving 60 housing associations and providing accommodation for 3000 to 4000 tenants. Table 7.2 illustrates the wide range of groups catered for.

This survey revealed that the vast bulk of the schemes had developed in recent times and there had been a shift away from the young homeless

Table 7.2 *Number of schemes for each needs group*

Group	No. of schemes	% ranked
Single homeless people	87	23
Young people	70	19
Learning difficulties	62	16
Mental health problems	52	14
Physical disability	26	7
Alcohol problems	19	5
Ex-offenders	15	4
Women in refuge	13	3
Frail elderly	12	3
Single parents	7	2
Multiple disability	6	2
Drug problems	3	1
AIDS/HIV	3	1
Refugees	3	1
Total	378	100

Not stated: 7.

Source: Watson and Cooper (1992) p. 14.

to those with learning disabilities as the dominant type of scheme. Watson and Cooper also found that 21 (or 5 per cent) of the schemes surveyed accommodated specific ethnic groups. In terms of the management of the care and support services, 42 per cent were directly run by housing associations, 45 per cent were managed by voluntary agencies on behalf of the housing association, 8 per cent were the responsibility of statutory agencies and 4 per cent of housing consortia, while only 1 per cent were managed by the tenants themselves.

The research clearly illustrates how scheme focus and design is often driven by the availability of capital and revenue funds rather than by an assessment of local needs and requirements. For example, the rapid growth of schemes for people with learning disabilities reflected the availability of money to develop such schemes because of the government's commitment to close long-stay hospitals. There is a danger that housing associations may chase such money and abandon other groups for whom they had previously tried to provide accommodation. Second, the majority of the older schemes had shared facilities and many were in older housing. However, the newer schemes, and especially those still being developed, were much more likely to have self-contained units but be part of fairly large new build schemes. These trends reflect the changing criteria of the Housing Corporation for the release of capital funds. It is interesting to reflect on whether a self-contained flat in a large new build scheme or a shared facilities flat in an older property comes close to being the type of housing which can best provide a home.

The biggest difficulty faced by supported housing schemes is how to fund from revenue the care and support elements, and the survey demonstrates how this has affected the type of scheme developed. It is often very difficult to disentangle the high housing management revenue costs of such schemes from the revenue costs of providing care support staff. Nevertheless, the revenue 'top up' systems have tried to make this distinction, with first the Department of the Environment and subsequently the Housing Corporation responding to the housing management issue but not the care issue. In terms of housing management costs, revenue support used to be available through the Hostel Deficit Grant, which, to simplify a complicated system, meant schemes could reclaim their revenue deficit on an annual basis from the Department of the Environment. However, 'the rules attached to this funding (for example, a minimum of six residents) had a strong influence on the types of schemes developed' and 'encouraged the tendency to develop supported housing provision in the form of discrete and recognisable "special projects"' (p. 47). It was also becoming more and more expensive from the point of view of central government. This grant was therefore replaced by the Special Needs Management Allowance (SNMA) which is administered by the Housing Corporation. The SNMA is available for self-contained housing as well as shared housing, is paid at a flat rate per unit, and is cash-limited, with a ceiling of 3000 new SNMA funded places per year. However, neither the Hostel Deficit Grant nor the SNMA were intended to fund the revenue costs of the full-time care component required by many schemes. Watson and Cooper (1992) identified two main mechanisms for addressing this issue, namely registration as a residential home or the use of staff employed by health or social service authorities. They pointed out:

> Many of the associations in the study had taken the first route, as indicated by the fact that 21% of the schemes in the sample were registered homes. The proportion of schemes registered ranged from 12% in Manchester to 34% in Southampton and area. There were widely varying attitudes to registration, with some housing association respondents reporting problems to do with institutional design requirements or inflexible rules about staff cover. Some associations indicated that they would not have sought to have schemes registered if there had been alternative ways of securing the finance to meet care costs. (p. 32)

About thirty schemes had taken the second route and made use of staff employed by statutory agencies. These high care schemes are mainly aimed at people with learning disabilities, physically disabled people and to a lesser extent people with mental health problems. These schemes had emerged from either a partnership arrangement with a statutory agency over a particular scheme or from the establishment of a consortium of local statutory and voluntary agencies.

Overall, the picture which emerges from this study is one of expanding yet insecure growth. Watson and Cooper are particularly critical of the lack of coherent revenue support systems for the high care schemes and they express anxiety as to whether the community care reforms will improve or worsen this state of affairs. This underlines the need for co-ordination between social services as the lead agency in community care and housing organisations.

Towards an integrated service?

Chapter 6 looked at obstacles to effective working together between social services and health agencies. Many of the same problems of mistrust and misunderstanding occur when one looks at housing and social services. To begin with, housing professionals and social workers have often expressed antipathy towards each other. In evidence to the 1982 Barclay Committee on the future of social work, the Institute of Housing stated:

> Unfortunately, in many cases the working relationships between housing officers and social workers are not good. ... generally speaking they view each other with considerable scepticism. There is a stereotyped image of the social worker as young and freshly qualified, straight from school via college, without any practical experience, who would be entirely subjective and idealistic about clients and will seek all manner of handouts and special treatment for them, without ever expecting them to stand on their own feet. By contrast, the housing officer might see himself as objective and fair in ordering priorities for the allocation of houses. He would probably employ ... techniques of management which he believes will develop independence and self-respect for the common good. The Institute of Housing Sub-Committee is of the opinion that these prejudices all too often turn out to be true. (Quoted in BASW, 1985).

Much of this antagonism derives from contrasting views about how best from deal with those families open to the label of 'problem family' rather than from tensions over how best to help elderly and disabled people. Nevertheless, collaboration and co-ordination in the area of community care leaves much to be desired. Morris (1990b) contacted the housing and social services departments of twenty-one local authorities in England and Wales for information on the following:

1. their knowledge of the need which existed amongst disabled people in their population;
2. the provision of housing and housing-related services for disabled people in the area;
3. details of policies directed at meeting the housing and housing-related needs of disabled people.

Only three of the twenty-one housing departments had a written policy on meeting the needs of disabled people; the majority had little data on their housing need; only five could provide information on the numbers of wheelchair and mobility properties in their stock; and disabled people were not integrated into mainstream allocation policies. Social services departments had more information on disabled people in their areas but tended to see residential care as the inevitable outcome for many. Six authorities had or were developing independent living strategies, but these had involved little consultation with disabled people or their organisations.

Considerable liaison was taking place between housing and social services on an ad hoc casework basis but not in terms of more strategic developments. Representatives from housing departments were rarely involved in joint care planning teams. Where good practice was being attempted, this was often undermined by the lack of a commitment to joint working:

> In cases where a local authority had started to develop and implement policies aimed at meeting the housing needs of disabled people, the initiatives usually involved *either* the housing department *or* the social services department, rarely both. Thus it was common for housing departments to complain that social services departments were not playing their part in, for example, offering technical advice on adaptations, or in providing personal assistance support within the home. In turn, social service departments often despaired of being able to find suitable accommodation for physically disabled people and complained that housing officers made unwarranted assumptions about the inability of disabled people to live independently. One county social services department, for example, had great difficulty in persuading a District Council housing department to offer accommodation to a single mother who became disabled and who wished to leave hospital to set up home again and look after her daughter. (Morris, 1990b, p. 17)

For Morris a good arrangement would be for both housing and social services to establish planning and monitoring groups with a strong emphasis upon membership from disabled people and their organisations. She explained that 'the focus of planning for the Housing Group would be all aspects of housing for disabled people ... whereas the focus for the Social Services Group would be the wider issues involved in independent living' (p. 25).

A similar situation was uncovered by Arnold and Page (1992a) in their study of the challenges and choices faced by housing agencies in ten large city authorities. They did identify individual schemes which were 'imaginative, domestically-scaled packages of housing and care involving statutory/voluntary agency partnerships, mixed funding, choice, user-involvement and flexibility' (p. 10). However, such projects got off the ground only through the application of enormous time, energy and skill. Many schemes failed to materialise, or were very badly delayed, because of the difficulties of co-ordinating the input of the different agencies:

> In several cases, success depended on clear contractual agreements between as many as four organisations: the local authority supplying the property; a housing association undertaking Housing Association Grant (HAG) funded conversion; a voluntary organisation providing the practical support (funded through the warden cost element claimed by the housing association) and health or social services providing community psychiatric nurse or social work support. (p. 10)

The prospects for achieving all this in many areas were undermined by a lack of trust between housing agencies and social services. The former had been little involved in joint planning and the latter were failing to bring housing departments and housing associations into the centre of community care planning. In other words, community care planning was being dominated by the social services–health agency agenda.

There are grounds for being optimistic that this situation is now improving. Senior managers from both the world of housing (Smith, 1992) and social services (Warner, 1992) have begun to argue the need to place co-ordination between social services and housing agencies much higher up the community care agenda. The joint Circular 10/92 from the Department of the Environment and the Department of Health on *Housing and Community Care* stressed the rôle of housing agencies in community care planning and the need to address housing issues during the assessment of individual clients and argued that the housing strategies of local authorities need to reflect specific issues such as the programme of hospital closures identified in community care plans. It seems likely that the extent to which housing is recognised as a foundation of community care will increase. Housing agencies are likely to become more involved in community care planning in future years. Housing departments and housing associations will make increased efforts to clarify with social services the rôle of sheltered housing, and numerous joint assessment and allocation arrangements will emerge. Social services, housing departments and housing associations will work together to identify the housing needs of disabled people, and will use this in local bids to the Housing Corporation for new 'special needs' housing schemes. Housing associations and their partner agencies will be making great efforts to clarify with social services what are to be the revenue and contractual arrangements which will emerge under the new funding regime for community care (Bennett, 1992).

However, all this will have to be attempted in the context of doubts about the adequacy of social services funding as the lead agency (see Chapter 5), and in a situation where both the Department of the Environment and the Housing Corporation are trying to minimise their own financial contributions (Cooper and Watson, 1992) through such devices as the 3000 unit ceiling on new SNMA places.

Concluding comments

In such an uncertain environment, it is important to conclude by stressing some of the broader housing and community care issues which tend to be underplayed yet which should lie at the centre of the policy debate. First, the core concern of the independent living movement is enabling people, wherever practicable and wherever desired, to live in independent accommodation which is not part of 'special needs' provision. The argument is that personal assistance should be available to disabled people within their independent accommodation (Morris, 1990b; Laurie, 1991; Fiedler, 1988). Co-ordination between housing and social services should ensure that this happens wherever possible.

Second, the dominant tenure in Britain is owner-occupation. A housing and community strategy in a community care plan needs to cover more than existing and proposed future provision of sheltered accommodation and other supported housing schemes. There needs to be a strategy to help elderly and disabled owner-occupiers to deal with disrepair and adaptations. One option is to have a network of specialist 'Care and Repair' and 'Staying Put' services. These independent small agencies perform the following tasks:

Visit people in their home.
Listen to their problems concerning their houses.

Advise on the choices available.

Organise the money where building work is agreed. (The sources of possible finance are varied and often need a good deal of organisation.)

Draw up a schedule of works, help find reliable builders and monitor the work while it is in progress.

In addition the agency must publicise its service and also ensure that it is working closely with organisations and individuals in the area. Key organisations and people include:

Reliable builders.

Local authority home improvement officers.

Social services occupational therapists.

Building society and bank managers.

Voluntary organisations such as Age Concern and Citizens Advice Bureau.

Local charitable trust. (Care and Repair, 1991, p. 1)

The great virtue of these schemes is that they enable elderly and disabled people to talk through their repair and adaptation needs, the implications of which can be worrying in terms of both finance and disruption. Staff can then help to broker in a package of repair or adaptations that is appropriate for the people concerned (Harrison and Means, 1993). A full network of such schemes across a local authority may be an unrealistic aim in many areas. However, even where this is the case, it is very important that every effort is made to co-ordinate the work of grants officers, occupational therapists and other relevant professionals (Leather and Mackintosh, 1992).

Third, strategic discussions between housing managers and social services managers about the need for joint working will only take root within their organisations if field-level staff are encouraged and supported to work together. A training strategy needs to be developed to ensure staff in housing departments and housing associations understand the community care reforms and their resource and priority implications for social services. Equally, social services staff need to be made more aware of the resource constraints and performance priorities of housing agencies. More specifically, care managers must be trained to address housing issues with potential service users and to be aware of the full range of housing options which might be available. For example, how many care managers will be aware that their disabled client in a mainstream housing association property is entitled to con-sideration for a disabled facilities grant as an alternative to seeking a move to more specialist accommodation?

Fourth, although better co-ordination between the professionals is important, it does have real dangers. The agenda can remain driven by their needs rather than by those of the service user. Social services departments are the lead agency in community care, so social services staff need to recognise that housing associations are providers who are pursuing, quite reasonably, their own provider interests. This is why it is so important that Morris (1990b) and others are listened to when they argue for extensive consultation with users and their organisations.

Fifth, the overall need is to move away from a lottery of provision (Fiedler, 1988) to the development of a continuum of housing options and possibilities available throughout the country. Many users or potential users of community care services will still require sheltered accommodation and other types of supported housing schemes. How-ever, the key point which needs to be made about such schemes is that they should cease to be perceived as separate from other housing provision. There is growing recognition that 'special needs' schemes become stigmatising because they deny that impairment and frailty are the norm for many people within any society. The way forward is to expand the quality and range of wheelchair standard housing, mobility standard housing, adapted housing and housing with support schemes. However, large non-specialist housing providers should do this within mainstream allocation and priority systems rather than totally relying on the small specialist association (Laurie, 1991; Morris 1990b).

And finally, our starting point was the meaning of home to disabled and elderly people. No simple answer was found to that complex question. However, it is essential that those responsible for the strategic and operational implementation of the community care reforms ensure that all professionals develop a sensitivity to the needs of all service users to have a home as well as to possess adequate shelter.

8 European Perspectives on Community Care

The forces which have influenced the development of community care policy and practice have not been confined to the UK. The governments of other countries in Western Europe (both inside and outside the European Community) have also had to address the consequences of demographic changes, high levels of unemployment, deep recession and public expenditure pressures on the role of the family in caring, on the costs of institutional care, on the notion of the mixed economy of welfare, on the problems of inter-agency collaboration and on the voice of the service user or carer.

Whilst the pressures on social welfare policies have not recognised national boundaries, the responses of individual West European states have varied, reflecting the differences in welfare traditions and regimes. There are several typologies of European welfare states but the categorisation to be used in this chapter is that employed by Abrahamson (1991a). Four types of welfare state are identified, each reflecting a particular kind of welfare regime. The *rudimentary* welfare state (or Catholic social policy) is associated with Latin Rim countries, such as Spain and Portugal. This tradition emphasises philanthropic solutions to welfare provision by traditional institutions such as the church, family and private charity, with limited public welfare institutions and policies developing alongside. The *residual* welfare state (or liberal social policy) is associated increasingly with the UK. As outlined earlier in this book, this is characterised by rolling back the boundaries of the welfare state, and public services are contracted out to the independent sector. The state is a safety net rather than a primary provider. The *institutional* welfare state (or corporatist social policy in the Bismarckian tradition) is linked in particular to Germany. This tradition puts emphasis on labour market solutions to social issues, such as unemployment, sickness or old age. Those outside the labour market are likely to be dependent on local charity. The *modern* welfare state (or social democratic policy) is associated with Scandinavian countries. This is characterised by wide provision of good quality publicly provided services, with the private and voluntary sectors becoming increasingly involved in the welfare mix.

These four broad categories may in themselves not be robust enough to withstand the societal and economic pressures impinging on Western European countries in the late twentieth century, but they provide a vehicle for examining the core elements of community care in different European countries. The residual model is not, however, considered below, as it is the focus of most of this book. The European perspectives on community care have been drawn from a small number of European countries, principally Greece, Germany and Denmark, representing three different kinds of welfare regime. Some material has also been drawn from Italy, Spain and Portugal. Ireland has been excluded, for good or ill, because its welfare arrangements are seen as part of the Anglo-Saxon tradition. Belgium, the Netherlands and Luxembourg are linked to the corporatist social tradition of Germany and the non-EC Nordic countries are not unlike Denmark. Of the EC countries this leaves France, which has been described as a hybrid between the Bismarckian Anglo-Saxon and the rudimentary welfare regimes of the Latin Rim countries (Walker, 1992, p. 3).

The role of the family in caring

The family still holds a central position in Catholic social policy. In countries like Portugal and Spain the supply of domiciliary and day care is generally inadequate and dependence on care provided by women in the family system is high. Such community care services as are provided are designed to supplement family care enabling dependent people to remain at home. As Anderson (1992) explains: 'In Greece, the Church and voluntary organisations particularly the Greek Red Cross, dominate provision of welfare services. ... This means that the distribution of such services is related to the presence of voluntary agencies and private benefactors rather than to any assessments of need' (p. 77).

Whilst the family may be central to social policy in the rudimentary welfare states, it is less than clear that this is reflected in everyday experience in Latin Rim countries. Potter and Zill (1992) argue that older people regard the informal care from family members as insufficient, as a burden on the carers which can lead to conflict in the household. In countries like Greece and Spain, value systems are changing more rapidly among younger people, creating the danger 'that the traditional informal support networks of the family are

Table 8.1   *'Families are less willing to care for older relatives than they used to be' (older people only)*

	EC12	Greece	Italy	Portugal	Spain	UK	Germany	Denmark
Agree strongly	33.4	36.0	39.4	42.9	45.2	26.4	24.0	32.7
Agree slightly	34.0	35.5	34.6	36.2	34.8	31.8	37.2	26.6
Disagree slightly	18.2	15.1	17.1	12.6	10.5	18.9	24.8	19.4
Disagree strongly	10.4	7.8	5.1	4.9	5.5	18.3	10.2	16.4
Don't know	4.1	5.4	3.8	3.5	4.1	5.3	3.7	4.8

Source: Eurobarometer Survey (1993) p. 29.

breaking down before these countries acquire the prosperity to be able to fund effective formal care services for older people' (pp. 124–5). It is the case that families are perceived by older people to be less willing to care than in the past. Table 8.1 shows the responses to this issue by older people in a survey carried out in the twelve member states of the European Community in April–May 1992, The EC average showed that about two-thirds of older people agreed that families were less willing to care than in the past, whereas the proportion for Greece and Italy was over 70 per cent and for Spain and Portugal approaching 80 per cent.

The family is also expected to play a central role in the institutional welfare state, particularly for those outside the labour market, creating a major responsibility and strain on relatives, where they exist (Evers and Olk, 1991, p. 66). In Germany the provision of public support can be made only after a comprehensive examination of the circumstances of the individual. As stressed by Jamieson (1990a)

In Germany the ideology of family responsibility is stated very explicitly in the principle of subsidiarity which guides social service provision. According to this principle, people are only entitled to publicly provided social care as a last resort, that is, if the family or other voluntary and private sources of care are shown to be absent. (pp. 42–3)

However, one consequence of this is that many adult children in Germany are struggling to mobilise the resources necessary to carry out the tasks assigned to them by the subsidiarity principle.

The modern welfare state (or social democratic social policy) is also under pressure (Daatland, 1992), but here the thrust is to involve the voluntary and private sectors more, rather than require the family to take on the caring role. In Denmark, compared with Southern European countries, older people are less likely to argue that families are less willing to care (see Table 8.1) but the assumption in Denmark is that the family does not provide care. However, children do care about their older relatives; this takes the form of advocacy and pressure on the professionals. The main burden of informal care in Denmark falls upon spouses or partners and Jamieson (1991a) argues that 'perhaps these are the ones who pay the highest price for a welfare system which is geared towards state provided professional solutions to health and social problems' (p. 120).

The place of institutional care

In a number of northern European countries the policy trend since the mid-1970s has been away from institutional provision, particularly for elderly people (Alber, Guillemard and Walker, 1991, p. 37). The prime reason for this policy shift has been cost to the public purse, supported by what were seen as inappropriate admissions of people who could live in (cheaper) non-institutional settings. Another factor has been the preferences of disabled and older people themselves. These preferences were shared by the vast majority of the general public in the European Community who thought that older people should be helped to stay in their own homes. This consensus extended across virtually the whole of the age group and is shared by both sexes (Eurobarometer Survey, 1993, p. 29).

Italy, as a southern European country, has engaged in a policy debate about the need to run down large institutions for frail elderly people, but it is far better known for its radical experiments to close its psychiatric institutions, based on legislation passed in 1978 (Ramon and Giannichedda, 1991). Under this law (known as Law 180) new admissions to psychiatric hospitals were to cease after 31 December 1979 and there were to be no readmissions after 31 December 1980. No new building in the psychiatric sector was to be permitted from the date the law was put into effect (1 May 1978). Community mental health centres were to be established by the regions throughout Italy. 15 psychiatric beds per 150 000 people could be established in the centres or in general hospitals. Compulsory admissions (for only 48 hours in the first instance) had to be based on an order proposed by a psychiatrist, and agreed by the local mayor. It could be renewed for a further seven days if approved by a judge. This law was the product of a range of local experiments in de-institutionalisation in the 1970s and the movement known as Psichiatria Democratica, which involved left-wing political parties, radical psychiatrists and progressive jurists. It will come as no surprise to learn that there have been major implementation difficulties, and revisions of the law began to emerge in the 1980s.

Apart from ideological conflicts in which 'the closure of mental hospitals' meant the removal of administrative control over the residents and not the emptying of the institution, critics have argued that the success of places such as San Giovanni in Trieste have not been replicated in other parts of Italy. Jones and Poletti (1985, 1986) reported lack of adequate community-based services, especially for the elderly mentally ill or those suffering from depression, anxiety states or long-term psychoses, whilst further south, provision was found to be less available and the problems were greater. Research undertaken by Fasolo and Frisanco (1991) ten years after the passing of the 1978 reforms supported the emphasis on the importance of regional variations. They found a 'considerable disparity from one geographical area to another in terms of efficiency of the services and thus in the realisation of the principles established by the reform. The southern regions and the islands, but also large areas in Lazio, the Marche and Abruzzi, tend to show serious shortcomings, services being static and isolated from the social context' (p. 222).

It is not reasonable to class Italy as a rudimentary welfare state (partly because of the enormous regional variation) but Greece is not untypical of such a regime in having only a small minority of elderly people living in residential homes. In the early 1980s there were just under 6000 residents in just over 100 non-profit-making homes (10 per cent in the public sector and the rest in the independent sector), which amounted to about 0.5 per cent of the elderly population in Greece (Ziomas, 1991, p. 68). As outlined in the previous section, care for elderly people in Greece is mainly a family affair. There is concern that changes in Greek society may reduce the availability of family carers, because of fewer children in the family, greater participation of women in the formal labour market, greater geographic mobility of younger people and increasing divorce rates. Some private sector for-profit homes have been established, mainly in and near Athens to respond to demand from more affluent frail elderly people (or their families) and some day centres have been developed on the initiative of the state.

It is anticipated that the cost to the public purse of supporting frail people in non-profit-making residential homes will be such that policies for alternative non-institutional services, such as the open care day centres (see Amira, 1990, p. 73) will be further developed. This financial argument is underpinned by a view that residential care reflects a paternalistic ideology of protection, a logic of dependence and division between age groups (Ziomas, p. 70). Such an outlook accords with the results of the Eurobarometer survey summarised at the beginning of this section, but contrasts with the view from the EC Observatory on Older People that, 'since community services can only complement but not substitute care rendered in the family system, the twin process of a growing number of elderly people who need support and of a shrinking pool of voluntary female carers – who provided the bulk of support in the past – will invariably lead to a growing demand for institutionalised care in specialised geriatric hospitals or in residential homes for older people' (Alber, Guillemard and Walker, 1991, p. 38).

In the institutional welfare state, represented in this section by Germany, the policy trend, fuelled by the need to cut costs, is to increase day care and domiciliary services at the expense of residential services.

One of the major assumptions of various social reformers during the 1970s was that residential institutions, both for young people at risk and for the physically and/or mentally ill, should be avoided in favour of out-patient or counselling approaches, which respected as much as possible the home environment of the client/patient. Such reforms, which were soon applied to hospitals and homes for the elderly as well, initially encountered a good deal of institutional resistance from the residential lobby, but then found increasing support from decidedly non-reform-minded quarters during the years of austerity. (Brauns and Kramer, 1989, p. 144)

Residential care for elderly people is in the main provided by the non-statutory sector and in 1990 amounted to about 5 per cent of the population of the former West Germany (Landwehr and Wolff, 1992, p. 26). This is because the principle of subsidiarity applies not only to the responsibilities of families for their needy members but also to the relationship between statutory and voluntary bodies. Conditional priority is given to voluntary non-profit organisations which wish to provide such social help. Public social assistance bodies are obliged to support the voluntary welfare organisations, such support including financial help (Jarre, 1991).

The financial responsibility of the family to support an elderly relative often means that the parent moves in with the children rather than entering residential care. However, as in Greece and elsewhere, there is concern that the capability of the family to provide care is lessening because of changes in society and the increasing numbers of older people. Alber (1991) has argued that increases in home and day care services need to be accompanied by an increase in the supply of nursing homes and hospices for frail older people, though progress in providing them is slow. It is also reported that about 30 per cent of all beds in acute hospitals are occupied by elderly patients with an average length of stay as high as forty days. The extent of hospital care is related to a shortage of domiciliary and day care services. It has been officially estimated that some 20–30 per cent of hospital patients over the age of 65 are long-term patients who could be better supported through day clinics, rehabilitation centres or nursing homes. The problem is made more acute by the social insurance system in Germany which draws a distinction between sickness (covered by insurance) and general frailty (perceived as a personal risk). Alber explains how this means that 'prolongation of the stay in acute hospitals is the only way to prevent older patients from having to foot the bill for delivery into nursing homes which they can rarely afford' (p. 25). Dieck (1990) points out that this creates a large gap between policy and practice in that 'whilst it is the official goal of social policy to encourage nursing at home and to stop the trend towards institutionalisation, institutions receive full cost-coverage and ambulant services do not' (p. 115).

It is of interest to note that Denmark, with its emphasis on universality, prevention and the protection of living standards, core characteristics of social democratic social policy, has a comparatively high rate of institutional care for older people in the twelve European Community countries – 14.7 per cent of the 75 plus age group (Walker, 1992) – although this is the lowest volume for the four Nordic countries (Daatland, 1992). The principle of universality covers both health and social care (unlike the case of Germany) and is based on citizenship rather than insurance rights. The services are both financed and provided by the public sector, leaving the voluntary sector to provide advocacy and act as pressure groups.

In the 1960s, both domiciliary and residential care services for older people were expanded, and there was no intention to replace institutional care. Rather, the range of services was to relieve families of the caring role and attempt to improve the quality of life for older people. However, in the 1980s there was a growing critique of institutional care, which resulted in major legislative reform in 1987. In brief, the principle underpinning the legislation was that the care available to people should not be linked to the kind of accommodation they were living in.

> There is no longer to be a dichotomy between nursing homes/ residential homes on the one hand, and home care on the other. … In short, the concept of nursing homes has been abolished by law. In practice this means that no new nursing homes can be built. From now on there are only to be elderly dwellings. (Jamieson, 1991a, p. 119)

The point of the reform was that every older person, whatever kind of care he or she needs, has the right to independent housing and care according to his/her needs. Just as the radical mental health legislation in Italy ran into implementation problems, so the impact of these legal changes has been affected by professional resistance, local politics and the economic disruption caused by the recession (Abrahamson, 1991b, p. 56).

The mixed economy of welfare

Evers and Olk (1991, p. 77) point to the useful distinction between the terms 'welfare mix' and 'welfare pluralism'. The former refers to the empirical issue of the proportion of investment in goods and services provided by the state, by the not-for-profit sector, by the private profit-making sector and by the informal sector. In this respect, all welfare states have a mix of this kind, though the proportions may vary and the degree of interaction between the sectors is also likely to differ. The latter term 'welfare pluralism' addresses the issue of the *preferred* mix in the mixed economy of welfare. What are the values that lie behind the recent arguments about the mixed economy of welfare? Chapter 3 outlined how proponents of welfare pluralism were claiming that the perceived predominance of the state sector was unsatisfactory and that the voluntary, commercial and informal sectors should have a greater role. It is now recognised that, in all welfare regimes, the informal sector has played the dominant, albeit often invisible, role. In the *rudimentary* welfare states, the case is being made for increased state support in response to the changes in society affecting the capability of family and local community to provide the level of care taken for granted in the past. In addition, the amount of community-based care is increasing to fill the gap.

In the *modern* welfare state, the argument is for increasing the role of the non-statutory sector, although not necessarily taken as far as the 'compulsory voluntarism' suggested by the Swedish Secretariat for Future Studies who put forward the idea of community care conscription along the lines of military conscription (quoted in N. Johnson, 1987, p. 58). For Denmark, Abrahamson (1991b) argues for what he calls new concepts in social policy which for disabled and elderly people would mean 'they should have the opportunity – to a much greater degree than beforehand – to purchase services on the market (privatization); to be serviced by a neighbourhood activity center (decentralization); and to be encouraged to obtain help from voluntary and self-help institutions (de-professionalization)' (p. 49).

In the corporatist social policy context, the notion of the mixed economy of welfare has been central to the ideology of the *institutional* welfare state, embedded as it is in the principle of subsidiarity in which non-state institutions play a constitutionally independent role, even where there is extensive support from the public sector. However, this traditional role of the voluntary sector is being challenged by both new style, that is radical, non-profit-making and private sector initiatives, which include, for example, the development in Germany of profit-oriented home nursing and of family-type care for frail older people who have no families of their own (Dieck, 1990). In their commentary on new welfare mixes for elderly people in Germany, Evers and Olk (1991, pp. 78–79) argue for

> a changing welfare mix in care services which allows for more pluralism of organisations and concepts on the side of the providers, more individual arrangements on the side of the users, and more specific help and general support for them in making their decisions on both how to share their own contributions and how to use services ... this leaves the state less impact as a provider but more for its

regulative and redistributive role, in order to enable it to balance the new potentials for individual choice and participation with the need of guaranteeing basically equal rights in care and access to the system.

In order to achieve this new kind of mix, new forms of networking and co-ordination are required both of a top-down kind to integrate strategies and a bottom-up kind to facilitate packages of services influenced by user and carer preferences. Collaboration and the roles of the service user and carer are the concern of the next two sections of this chapter.

Collaboration

Alber, Guillemard and Walker (1991) have highlighted the problem of fragmentation of responsibility for providing community care services. They argued that 'there seems to be insufficient co-operation between the nursing and social support staff of the community services supplied by the various associations and the local government social workers, or between nursing, social support and the other personnel within the community services' (p. 40). They pointed to differing systems of finance and administration for health and social care in different countries and concluded that, 'since community care for persons living in private households often requires the co-ordination of services provided by various public and voluntary agencies, whereas residential care provides most services under one common organisational roof, there continues to be an administrative incentive to admit elderly people to residential care' (p. 37).

This problem appears to be less acute in Denmark, where all home care services are organised by the local authority and where the modern welfare state principle of universality implies comprehensive provision based on citizenship rather than incentive rights. However, problems remain over the co-ordination between hospitals and primary health care and social services since 'the separation of the community care budget (the communes) from the hospital budget (the county) hardly provides any financial incentive for the communes to take over patients ready for discharge from hospital as early as possible' (Holstein *et al.*, 1991, p. 60).

The principle of subsidiarity in the context of corporatist social policy requires partnership between the statutory and the non-statutory sectors, but the diversity of local supply, which is intended to offer choice of services to the individual, does not usually promote collaborative endeavour. In Germany, there may be close links between the state and the non-statutory welfare agencies over matters such as finance and the law but the fragmentation of responsibility for service delivery makes effective co-operation to support particular individuals problematic. Alber (1991) complained that 'although the goal of expanding the supply of ambulatory services was successfully promoted, the plurality of religious, secular and public ... agencies and the dominance of professional nurses rather than social workers and volunteers within the services still bring forth serious problems of co-ordination in planning and implementation' (p. 31).

In the rudimentary welfare state of Spain one of the key concerns has been the co-ordination of the public and private sectors in providing personal social services. The role of the public sector increased after the end of the Franco regime but economic difficulties have since led to demands for reductions in public expenditure plus a more flexible, less bureaucratic management style. The outcome has been a very uneven distribution of supply with traditionally provided services not being linked to more recent developments, particularly for specific groups of people (Rossell and Rimbau, 1989, pp. 118–19).

One of the responses to the lack of collaboration because of the variety of providers and funding arrangements has been to attempt to introduce case (or care) management. The UK experience is addressed elsewhere in this book (see Chapter 5) but it is worth noting that one of the main conclusions of a comparative study of innovations in care in the Netherlands, Sweden and England and Wales was the need to invest in the management of care.

> [The] central issue and problem is one of management – the intelligent, consistent, informed organisation of care .... This problem of management exists at two levels: the level of the individual client and the level of the care system as a whole ... It is no accident that case management at the level of the individual client is more developed in the United Kingdom. It is a solution of later resort, typical of systems where resources are in chronically short supply. (Baldock and Evers, 1991, pp. 193, 196)

It was this pressure to make effective use of scarce resources in an ideological context of consumer choice that made the idea of case management as developed in the United States attractive to the British government struggling to pursue a coherent policy and practice on community care. Residual welfare state systems were perhaps influencing each other's liberal social policies, though with increasing pressures on public expenditure in the late 1980s and early 1990s, countries like the Netherlands and France were beginning to undertake case management experiments or at least to debate the means of integrating social care services.

User empowerment

The notion of 'consumer choice' underlies the debate about empowerment in the residual welfare state. The individual consumer can 'exit' by choosing an alternative source of supply rather than attempt to influence that source of supply by 'voice' or engagement in the process of planning, resourcing, managing and delivering services (see Chapter 4). Empowerment is a slippery term, but it does connote more than the provision of information to allow individuals to exercise choice. It is to do with involvement, with active participation, co-decision making or even control. In some circumstances, the difficulties faced by frail individuals require the presence of an advocate. Alber, Guillemard and Walker (1991, p. 42), for instance, suggest in their European Observatory report that there should be an elected ombudsman of frail older people on the administrative boards of community care agencies.

Whilst family and neighbourly care remain central to the support of frail older people in Greece, the government has provided funding for the development of open care day centres (KAPI), which provide health and social care as well as being community centres. They are administered by a council of representatives from the local municipality, local citizens and older people themselves (Amira, 1990) and so in principle older people have a say in the running of the centres. However, the centres tend to cater for the less frail and those who are homebound are not well served through this initiative (Ziomas, 1991, p. 75).

We have addressed the impact of the 1978 policy of closure of mental hospitals in Italy earlier in this chapter. However, it is important to emphasise that the ideological drive behind the reform movement included giving mentally ill people greater control over their own lives. This was clearly happening in the psycho-social centres developed in Trieste to replace the services previously provided in San Giovanni hospital (Jones, 1988, pp. 56–7) but these centres were not addressing the requirements of disturbed adolescents or elderly mentally ill people, and in other parts of the country, particularly in the south, the new approach had not been strongly implemented (Fasolo and Frisanco, 1991). Also, at the end of the 1970s, the National League for the Right to Work of the Handicapped was formed in Italy. As its title implies, its initial primary concern was to change the law on the way disabled people could obtain work, but its overall programme was to promote the complete social integration of disabled people and to expose all practices tending to marginalise disabled people. Although the local groups of the National League comprised in the main disabled people, sympathetic professionals have been eligible to join, though this has been a matter of debate, not least because the Disabled People's International is a body comprised of organisations of disabled people from different countries. The League has been controlled by disabled people but insists on maintaining a dialogue with professionals in order to create non-antagonistic relationships with them. Tudor (1989, p. 53) has argued that Britain 'could do worse than to look to Italy and struggles there, and, within the movement of disabled people, the leadership of the League in confronting the state both in terms of legislative proposals and extra-parliamentary activity'.

Turning to the corporatist social policy of the institutional welfare state, Evers and Olk (1991) have concluded that for elderly people in Germany there was a strong dominance of producers' over consumers' interests and power. However, they have contrasted this with the debate held by organisations of disabled people who have argued that the power of decision making should be turned upside down to create a user-centred culture of care. In addition, the 'exit' rather than 'voice' strategy was introduced for certain categories of very dependent elderly people living in their homes under reforms initiated in 1989 and 1991. 'Since 1991, those in need of extensive or intensive care who live at home can choose either 25 hours of professional care per month, not exceeding the value of DM 750, or DM 400 in cash, usually for care provided by relatives' (p. 73). It is not clear why the cash total should be so much less than the maximum value of professional care that can be secured. This level of difference has taken on greater significance because of the influence of disabled people who are beginning to assert that 'they know best how to use money for help and care services; they therefore opt for a system which is based on attendance allowances granted to the elderly and to people with disabilities in need of care' (p. 81). For frail, older people and others who could face difficulties in deciding between care or cash, and in deciding what to purchase if the cash option is preferred, the development of independent non-profit-making advocacy and advice centres has been an important innovation in Germany.

Finally, an interesting aspect of the role of user groups in Germany is their emphasis on the process of community involvement in order to gain access to powerful bodies.

> The user groups that are established in Germany tend to be concerned with participating in the process of negotiating welfare services locally. Charitable and statutory organisations need to determine both the local needs and the ways in which resources are to be spent to meet them, and it is here that self-help groups participate. This is where the power lies ... many of the most powerful voices and the people with the highest qualifications can be found in this area. ... Access to this ... is therefore the aim of participation. Local committees and local self-help groups know that this is how to get their voices heard. (Cannan, Berry and Lyons, 1992, p. 134)

The debate on empowerment has been muted in modern welfare states like Denmark and Sweden. Because access to both benefits and services is open to all as a citizen's right, most provision is not seen as stigmatising and is not conditional upon insurance contributions. The main role of pensioners' organisations has been to demand the right to negotiate the amount of pensions and to struggle against the exclusion by professionals of, for instance, elderly people from participating in decision making in domiciliary or institutional care (Jamieson, 1990b, p. 13). An attempt to form a Grey Panthers party in Denmark in 1989 came to nothing. 'The reason for the lack of political movement among ... older people might be ascribed to the fact that the existing political parties all give high priority to old age issues. And another explanation might be that the income of ... pensioners has grown more than income in general during the last decade' (Bertelsen and Platz, 1991, para. 5.6).

The institutions of the European Community (Union) and policy

Examination of certain features of community care policy in a selection of Western European countries may throw some light on our domestic concerns in the UK. But the European Community (Union) itself, as a supranational institution, is also not without influence on the policies of the member states. The second part of this chapter therefore examines the impact of European Community policies and practices on community care strategies in the UK. It begins with a brief description of the institutions of the EC and the process of policy making in the Community, and then examines the impact of its policies for older people, for disabled people and for the providers of community care.

In one sentence, the EC policy process can be summarised as 'The Commission proposes; the Council of Ministers disposes.' Needless to say, it is rather more complicated than that. However, the Commission, the civil service or executive arm of the Community, is the body that has the duty to initiate legislation, amongst its other responsibilities. It is not a large bureaucracy, having about 15 000 operational staff in all, of whom 20 per cent are translators and interpreters. It is divided into twenty-three directorates, covering a range of policy areas, such as agriculture, transport, energy, regional policy and the environment. Directorate-General V covers social and employment issues and is therefore the part of the Commission most closely associated with social and community care.

Policy proposals are developed within, and sometimes between, the directorates of the Commission and, usually after much debate, are formally presented to the seventeen Commissioners. Once a policy proposal is approved by the Commissioners by a simple majority vote it is forwarded to the Council of Ministers for consideration. The Council of Ministers is made up of ministers from member state governments, with the actual composition of the Council depending on the subject under discussion. When a proposal arrives from the Commission, it is passed on to the Committee of the Permanent Representatives of the Member States (COREPER). This comprises civil servants from the governments of the twelve member states and one of their key tasks is to take an initial close scrutiny of the proposal forwarded from the Commission.

As well as forwarding proposals to the Council of Ministers, the Commission sends them to the European Parliament. In 1993, the Parliament comprised 518 members from all twelve member states, 81 of them from the UK. Unlike Westminster, the European Parliament does not propose and pass legislation; rather, it examines and debates the proposals and passes opinions. The mechanism for doing this is by consideration in one of the eighteen Committees of the Parliament which broadly reflect the Directorates-General of the Commission. The Committees are in turn supported by a Secretariat, paid officials of the Parliament, who undertake the detailed work. Typically, one MEP from the Committee is nominated as a rapporteur to produce a draft report. When this has been approved by the Committee, it goes to the full Parliament for debate, adoption or rejection. Its opinion is then communicated to the Council of Ministers. The Parliament also has about 50 inter-groups. These comprise interested members of the European Parliament from different political parties who examine particular issues in great detail, including ageing, disabled people and the family.

The opinions of the European Parliament are considered by both COREPER and the secretariat to the Council of Ministers and a common position is adopted either at official level or, in areas of major difficulty, by the appropriate Council of Ministers. For some policy issues the European Parliament gets a second chance to comment on the proposed legislation, but the final decision is that of the Council of Ministers, which formally adopts the legislation. The outcome is published in the *Official Journal of the European Communities*. The legislation can take different forms. A regulation applies directly from the day it comes into force; a directive requires domestic legislation in member states if appropriate legislation does not already exist; decisions usually apply to specific problems rather than to the Community as a whole, and are binding on those to whom they are addressed. Where there is a failure to agree on legislation in the Council of Ministers, a recommendation or an opinion may emerge. These have no legislative force, though they are not necessarily without influence. Some legislative proposals can be adopted by a majority vote (known as qualified majority voting) with voting weighted according to the population of the member state; other legislation requires unanimity.

The formal process of policy making has been described, but the informal processes are just as important. First of all, the Commission officials do not just sit behind their desks in Brussels and think up new legislation. They are lobbied from every quarter, including other Community institutions, such as the Council of Ministers who can ask them to put their minds to a particular issue, or the European Parliament which can issue its own views on subjects as well as pass opinions on draft legislation. The Commission follows the progress of legislation through the system very closely and is in frequent contact with COREPER working groups. Meanwhile, it is lobbied by a wide range of interests. Individual members of the European Parliament may press for meetings with delegations from a particular region or a particular sector of industry. A number of regional and local authorities have opened offices in Brussels to be able to hear about and influence the policy debate at very early stages, even before a directive is initially drafted within the Commission.

As well as regional authorities and industrial interests, voluntary organisations have also developed a lobbying base in Brussels, some focusing on environmental or consumer issues and others on the 'social dimension' of the European Community. Examples include COFACE (Confederation of Family Organisations in the European Community), Eurolink Age, European Women's Lobby and the European Anti-Poverty Network. They have been prominent in pressing for Community recognition of the massive social implications of its agricultural, economic and industrial policies, and for implementation in member states of EC legislation on equal pay and equal opportunities.

Against this backcloth of the main Community institutions, the policy process and the way interest groups have organised to influence legislative outcomes, we can now turn to the impact of EC policies, practices and procedures on community care in the UK.

The impact of EC policies on community care

Much of social policy is seen as a domestic issue for individual member states of the European Community, as the legal base for Community intervention is very restricted. 'Adherence to (the) policy of subsidiarity has made the EC reluctant to override national sovereignty by introducing any radical action in the social field' (Swithinbank, 1991, p. 4). The Commission tends to limit its role to information exchange, supporting innovations and good practice, and co-funding cross-national action research programmes.

The EC focus has in the main been on economic, industrial and trade policies. It does, however, recognise that strategies such as the completion of the internal market, the free movement of goods, services, capital and labour and other measures of economic integration do cause problems for particular regions or particular groups of people. Discriminatory effects are addressed, though perhaps not adequately, by special support for disadvantaged regions and by special measures to help groups such as disabled people, migrant workers and women to secure employment in the open labour market. The following sections look at a range of EC policies affecting older people, disabled people and the providers of community care.

Older people

The Social Charter, adopted by all member states, except the UK, in December 1989 asserted that elderly people, at the time of retirement, should have resources sufficient to provide a decent standard of living, as well as medical and social assistance suited to their needs. Retirement pensions are thus seen as deferred wages, so the quality of life for older people has become a concern of the European Community. A three-year EC programme for older people was launched at a conference in Brussels in September 1991, with the aim of encouraging the transfer between member states of knowledge, ideas and experience on ageing and elderly people. The programme culminated in the designation of 1993 as European Year of Older People and Solidarity between the Generations.

The European Parliament has formed an Intergroup on Ageing, which meets about four times a year and is serviced by the transnational interest group on behalf of older people, Eurolink Age. The Parliament has pressed the Commission to put forward, through the Social Action Programme that followed the acceptance (except by the UK) of the Social Charter, 'specific solutions at Community level' to challenges posed by an ageing population. Citing the Treaty of Rome provision to improve the living conditions of Community citizens, the European Parliament called for a directive on the right to home care and better provision of home help and health care. It had been influenced by the establishment in 1990 of a European Association of Organisations for Home Care and Help at Home. The objectives of this co-ordinating body are (i) to promote home care and assistance in the member states; (ii) to support contacts between home care organisations; (iii) to promote relevant issues at the Community level; and (iv) to promote research in the problems of home care. Membership is open to non-profit home care and home help services which have a roll of more than 50 helpers or employees, and which provide more than a local service (Harvey, 1992, p. 148). There is a growing awareness that the community care implications of completing the single market could be far-reaching. Chapman (1989) argued that the removal of trade barriers in 1992 would create an internal market for social services as well as in industry and commerce. She pointed out that 'some home care organisations are looking at the potential of expanding their services across national boundaries' and 'sources of funding are expected to change as the market for home care opens up' (p. 19).

There are also possible community care implications of international retirement migration, particularly to the coastal areas of Portugal and Spain. Over the years these elderly migrants will grow 'increasingly frail and dependent in a situation where there is little established structure for collaboration in the personal social services field' (Bongers, 1990, p. 58). What is likely to happen?

> When, for example, older people from Northern Europe migrate to the south but then fall ill, will they be flown back to their countries of origin as soon as their personal resources run out, or their demands on personal and health services intensify, in a sort of new law of settlement? Or will Member States develop schemes for charging the country of origin for such care? (Room 1991, p. 4)

Alternatively, might social services agencies combine to establish care services in these retirement areas, or offer consultancy services to the care authorities in these localities?

The European Community has supported important programmes on technological development and their implications for elderly and disabled people. Part of this framework programme consists of pilot projects for the development of rehabilitation technology to help elderly and disabled people. This sub-programme is know by the acronym of TIDE (technology for the socio-economic integration of disabled and elderly people) and a report on prolonging the independence of elderly people was published in 1992 (Cullen and Moran, 1992). Another sub-programme is called ENS (European Nervous System) which is intended to improve the delivery of social services through a European telematics programme. Emphasis is placed on 'the development of local community-based personal social services eg between local authority services and other community agencies, which are responsible for the provision of social services to groups such as the elderly'(quoted in Batty, 1991, p. 11). The European Regional Office of the World Health Organisation expects to participate in the ENS programme as part of its 1990s strategy of healthy ageing in Europe. As well as TIDE and ENS there is the COST programme, which focuses on new technologies for increased autonomy, elderly consumers, social technology for the home, relations between elderly people and the labour market, and the special needs of elderly people with respect to learning, pension systems and social security.

· The plans for the 1993 EC Year of Older People and Solidarity between the Generations covered an enormously wide range of activities. However, the budget for the European Year was less than had been originally expected and Eurolink Age pointed out that all EC expenditure related to older people and ageing issues had to link into the budget and the programme for the European Year in 1993.

> This places a question mark over all information, research, policy development, organisational support, conference and seminar activity, that either existed prior to the Year or has a timeframe and focus that is not the same as that of the Year. It also wipes out the permanent budget line for elderly people in the EC, which has existed since 1984. Eurolink Age now questions whether there will be enough money to allow a proper European Year of elderly people to take place at all. (Batty, 1992, p. 2)

Overall, older people have in recent years received a fair amount of attention from the range of Community institutions and many interest groups, though the cutback in the budget for the European Year was a blow.

Disabled people

The first EC action programme to promote the social integration of disabled people was a response to the 1981 International Year of Disabled People and ran from 1983 to 1987. A Bureau for Action in favour of the Disabled was established in Directorate-General V (Social Affairs) of the Commission. One of the main features of this programme was to create a network of nineteen local projects across the Community, funded 50 per cent from the European Social Fund. There were two in the UK, Lambeth Accord and the West Berkshire Interface project. The former aimed to improve co-ordination of services for disabled people in Lambeth in the areas of education, employment, housing, information, planning, transport and community care/support. This project actively encouraged the involvement of disabled people in the decision making that affected their lives and supported organisations of disabled people. Its prime purpose was to remove all barriers that prevent disabled people having full participation in society. The West Berkshire Interface project focused on training programmes to enable disabled people to obtain jobs in the open labour market.

The second programme aimed at both vocational and social integration and independent living. It was called HELIOS (Handicapped People in the European Community Living Independently in an Open Society) and ran from 1988 to 1991. The programme covered a large number of initiatives and outlined key policy guidelines. General initiatives included (i) further development of HANDYNET, a multi-national, multilingual computerised database of information on disability questions, including a technical aids module, national regulations and statistical data; (ii) a focus on occupational rehabilitation of disabled women; and (iii) encouragement of integration of disabled people in mainstream education.

The HANDYNET system accounted for the major part of the HELIOS budget. Specific activities covered (a) the further development of the network of rehabilitation centres set up as early as 1974; (b) special programmes to promote independent living, particularly in relation to mobility and the provision of home support services; and (c) activity networks of experts to consider integration in schools, vocational training and social integration. Key policy guidelines covered the employment of disabled people, better co-ordination between the various Directorates of the Commission on issues affecting disabled people, exchange schemes for young disabled people and research projects designed to underpin a positive policy for disabled people. The 1989 Social Charter referred in broad terms to measures to facilitate the social and professional integration of disabled people. The UK had fifteen out of a total of 130 local projects participating in the networks, six (out of a total of 50 across the Community) in the rehabilitation centres network, two (out of twenty-one) in the school integration network, three (out of twenty-seven) in the economic integration network and four (out of thirty-two) in the social integration network. The Disabled Living Foundation was appointed as the UK co-ordination centre for the HANDYNET system, which became operational in 1990.

A third programme, called HELIOS II, was published by the Commission in October 1991 and covered the period 1992–6. It was intended to maintain, promote and intensify the activities undertaken in HELIOS I. However, the implementation of the programme was delayed because of disagreement in the European Parliament over the nature of the proposals and HELIOS I was extended to cover 1992. The HELIOS II was eventually announced in the *Official Journal* on 9 March 1993, and sustained the strategies of supporting innovation, exchange of experience and information and transnational co-operation.

In 1990, the European Community formally agreed three new cross-national grant aid initiatives to improve education and training facilities and to provide new employment opportunities. One of these initiatives, called HORIZON, is aimed at people with physical or mental disabilities, those who work with them, and other disadvantaged individuals. As well as focusing on employment issues, including long-term unemployed people or 'women returners' to the labour market becoming carers of older, frail people, the programme covers the adaptation of public infrastructure to improve access and mobility. There is also a proposal from the Commission that public transport should be made more accessible to people with reduced mobility. The draft legislation proposed the adaptation of public vehicles, related buildings and transport organised by employers to help disabled people get to and from work. Clearly any improvements would benefit all disabled travellers, not only those at work. The proposed legislation covers all categories of workers with reduced mobility, including those with motor, physical, sensory or mental handicap.

Providing care in the community

The focus so far has been on various groups in the population likely to be users of community care. EC policies also impinge on the providers of care, as the emphasis on the single market and labour market issues would lead one to expect. The completion of the single market in principle provides opportunities for businesses, voluntary bodies and self-employed individuals from mainland Europe to establish services in the social care field, including community care. It also offers opportunities for statutory, voluntary and private sector community care providers to export their expertise to continental Europe. 'With a market of twelve national governments and thousands of regional and local authorities and independent social care organisations, the potential scope for selling Kent's progressive innovative work in, for example, community care and child protection, is enormous' (Swithinbank, 1991, Appendix 3, 6).

On the labour market side, UK doctors and nurses have since 1977 and 1979, respectively, been able to work in any member state of the EC, provided they have the appropriate language skills and are prepared to undertake some locally based training. This has not led to major cross-boundary migrations, but the implications are clear. Skills shortages in community health services could be overcome by a recruitment campaign in other member states, while health workers unable to find suitable jobs after completing their training in the UK may look for work elsewhere. On a sceptical note, richer member states may attract workers trained in poorer member states, since 'partners may very easily become poachers' (Harris and Lavan, 1992, p. 13). The European Community legislation on the mutual recognition of professional qualifications came into force on 4 January 1991. Rather than looking at each individual profession, a long and laborious process, the position now is that a qualification based on three or more years' study at higher education level (whatever that means) in one member state has to be recognised in all member states. This is not without its problems, not least for social work, since expectations of relevant language skills and training in local procedures remain. It has been reported that small but significant numbers of social workers have moved from France, Germany and the Netherlands to work in the UK (Hill, 1991). Fry (1989) reported that the London Borough of Newham was addressing its problems of shortages of social workers with an active policy of recruiting recently qualified French social workers through good links with a training organisation.

In 1988 the Central Council for Education and Training in Social Work (CCETSW) issued 141 Letters of Comparability to the UK Certificate of Qualification in Social Work, although only seventeen of them related to applicants from EC countries. The policy changed after March 1990, when Letters of Verification began to be issued. The verification does not imply that the qualification is the equivalent of any UK qualification, only that it is a recognised social work qualification in the country of origin. For 1991–2 there were 257 successful letters of application, thirty-one of which came from people in EC member states.

Concern has been expressed in the UK that (i) social work has no formal regulatory body as required by the mutual recognition directive (though the creation of a General Social Services Council – with a register of practitioners – was under consideration in mid-1993); and (ii) the professional qualification does not fit the three-year criterion. However, in June 1992 a second directive on the mutual recognition of qualifications was adopted and has to be implemented by June 1994. This covered post-secondary level diplomas or certificates gained after a period of less than three years and also applied to people without qualifications but with relevant professional experience. UK social workers wanting to work in mainland Europe have been advised to 'keep note of the courses, assessed work and placements they successfully completed during training and they should even gather their course material, reports and references together into a portfolio' (Lyons, 1992, p. iii). As with doctors and nurses, major cross-boundary moves are not anticipated, but there is an over-supply of social workers in some member states and private, voluntary or statutory sector providers of community care in the UK could decide to mount a recruitment campaign, if they were severely understaffed and had the resources to recruit. Recruiters would need to develop some under-standing of the training and professional qualifications in social care, social work and social assistance in other member states of the Community.

Over the years the European Community has also been concerned to develop an equal opportunities programme, with the primary aim of countering discrimination in the labour market, though with a much greater emphasis on sex equality than race equality (see Buckley and Anderson, 1988; Meehan and Whitting, 1989). Legislation has covered equal pay for equal work, equal access to employment and training, equal treatment in pensions and social security schemes and for self-employed women, and prohibition of discrimination at work. One British case, with implications for community care, was the European Court of Justice decision that married women should receive the same payments as other people for caring for severely disabled people. Previously, they had not been eligible.

Many of the European Community's proposals in its current Social Action Programme are uncontroversial, particularly in the field of health and safety at work. However, some of the proposals on working hours or those that affect part-time or temporary workers are being resisted by the UK government. The implications for the delivery of community care are not inconsiderable. The Commission originally proposed in draft legislation on working hours published in July 1990 that there should be a mandatory minimum daily rest period of nine hours, a weekly rest period of 24 hours (conventionally Sunday) and a ban on overtime for night workers. The implications for the caring services in general are substantial, particularly in residential settings, but there could be major consequences for shift or split shift working, not untypical for care in the community. The proposals for part-time and temporary workers are that they should receive the same benefits as full-time workers on a pro rata basis, whether the benefits be for vocational training, access to social security arrangements, holiday entitlements or redundancy payments. Many workers, mainly women, in community care are part-timers, and the consequences of these proposals could have a major impact on staff costs. The proposed legislation could therefore influence the quality and quantity of services delivered.

Finally, the 1977 EC acquired rights directive may well have major implications for the transfer of staff from one employer to another, for instance from a local authority to a trust responsible for the provision of community care. This directive overrules any domestic legislation with which it is in conflict. There is still some uncertainty whether the directive and Britain's Transfer of Undertakings (Protection of Employment) Regulations 1981 (TUPE) apply, for instance, to compulsory competitive tendering, which, it is argued, is likely to cut the terms and conditions of local authority workers. The Commission of the European Communities has initiated proceedings against the UK government for failure to implement the directive properly and the Trade Union Reform and Employment Rights Act 1993 is intended, amongst other purposes, to eliminate discrepancies between the directive and domestic UK law. It has been calculated that a potential liability of £15 000 per employee should be added to each tender when TUPE is likely to apply (see European Information Service, 1993) so the implications are far from trivial. Indeed, at the time of writing, contracting out has ground to a halt in some local authorities.

Concluding comments

The impact of EC policies on community care developments in the UK has been in the main indirect and, where direct, modest. What is unambiguous is the increased investment by the Community in social policy issues in recent years. There is major concern for the 'social integration' of people seen to have special needs. The implications of moves towards the completion of the internal market have highlighted the social responses needed to address likely problems of dislocation. The debate on political union has brought into focus the position of residents, not only of workers in the European Community. External migratory pressures demand a social policy as well as a border control response. The increasing rôle of women in the formal labour market has added considerably to the force of the argument that the European Community is much more than a common market. The European Charter of Fundamental Social Rights refers to older people, people with disabilities and women among its concerns.

This internationalisation of the policy debate may not lead to a high proportion of social (as opposed to economic) legislation being of Community origin, but it will enable campaigners and policy makers in the UK to become more aware and make use of interesting policies, practices and procedures in community care in other countries.

9 Community Care in the 1990s: Achievements, Failures and Challenges for the Future

The community care reforms brought in by the 1990 Act have been far-reaching and the major financial changes associated with them were not introduced until April 1993. In the longer term, the key test of these reforms will be their impact upon the quality and range of services available at the local level, and how this does or does not relate to the emphasis of the reforms upon stimulating a quasi-market or a mixed economy of social care. Even then any apparent policy failure will be open to numerous interpretations:

- the reforms ushered in a system which was no better, and possibly worse, than the previous more bureaucratic systems of resource allocation;
- the reforms were an excellent idea, but they received little under-standing or commitment from social services as the lead agency in community care;
- the missionary zeal of the local authority was undermined by vested professional interests, low quality staff or the service legacy of the last forty years;
- the reforms were undermined through chronic under-funding by central government;
- the full extent of the implementation challenge generated by these reforms was not appreciated and it is still too early to make an assessment of their impact.

These varying interpretations suggest that a consensus is unlikely to emerge about the strengths and weaknesses of the reforms. Writing in mid-1993, it is too early in the implementation process to provide our own definitive assessment of achievements and failures. It is much easier to outline the implementation challenges which lie ahead. Nevertheless, it is possible not only to specify these challenges but also to carry out an audit of progress so far which critically examines some of the assumptions lying behind the reforms.

In search of achievements

It is tempting to argue that this section of our final chapter could be restricted to a single paragraph, on the grounds that there is little or nothing to report. This would be unfair and misleading, despite the enormous weaknesses in community care policy and practice which remain. Perhaps the main achievement of recent years has been that of users and carers who have increasingly organised themselves at both local and national level to campaign for provision which respects them as citizens. Many of these groups remain dismayed at the inadequacy of the professional response to their requirements and demands; their criticisms have been supported by a number of recent research reports which have been highly critical of professional practice, both at the care management level (Morris, 1993; Ellis, 1993) and the strategic planning level (Glendinning and Bewley, 1992). However, it is our view that the emphasis of the reforms upon user involvement and empowerment has legitimised the voice of the user, carer and disability movements in a way that was not the case previously, even though the majority of groups feel very hostile to the market philosophy of the reforms. Hoyes *et al.* (1993), in their study of four contrasting local authorities, concluded:

> On the whole, and given the difficult resource climate and the lack of experience local authorities have in consulting and involving users and carers, we feel that they are taking the challenge seriously and are open to learning how to succeed ... Examples of good practice include: supporting users with learning difficulties on planning groups; purchasing advocacy services; funding transport for people to attend user group meetings; enabling HIV service users to switch to an alternative home care provider; and piloting 'cash for care' through an Independent Living Scheme.

It would, of course, be unwise to get too carried away by these important scattered examples of good practice. Senior managers increasingly appear to have good intentions with regard to users and carers, but the challenge is to turn this systematically into good practice within their organisations. As Stevenson and Parsloe (1993) argue, this requires managers to recognise the capacity for innovative practice within field-level staff and how this can be stifled by the bureaucratic conservatism of the organisations which they run. They argue that the way forward is to design and run an agency-wide development programme with user and carer empowerment as its goal.

A second achievement was touched on in the quotation from Hoyes and her colleagues, namely that most local authorities are able to point to pockets of innovative practice, involving user empowerment and/or experimental forms of collaborative working. Chapter 3 showed how this was true at the time of the Audit Commission (1986a) survey of care in the community where their overall highly negative assessment of progress was tempered by their discovery of small examples of innova-tion, which were usually driven by local champions of change. More recently, a team of staff from SAUS looked at six case studies, designed to illustrate not only the scope for collaborative working, but also how this could be achieved in a way that respected users and carers (Smith *et al.*, 1993). These covered a wide variety of initiatives:

1. Community care planning in Wolverhampton, where attempts had been made to ensure the full involvement of black and minority ethnic groups;
2. Care management within a primary health care setting in East Sussex;
3. A care management pilot in Cheltenham, where the emphasis was upon developing user-controlled self-determination of need;
4. Radnor Care and Repair project, where staff responded to the housing needs of physically disabled clients and elderly owner-occupiers by brokering in services from a wide range of agencies;
5. Newcastle's Mental Health Services Consumer Group, who are committed to ensuring that local users of mental health services have a real say and significant role in the planning, development and monitoring of these services;
6. Neighbourhood centres in Liverpool run in partnership by Liverpool Personal Service Society and small, locally based residents' associations and community organisations.

These studies underlined the exciting achievements which can be developed despite the pressures of time and finance facing the main statutory and voluntary agencies, and despite the real difficulties and dilemmas of collaborative working and user involvement with which these six case studies were having to grapple. However, the question has still to be asked: how typical are such initiatives and what are the prospects for them surviving, yet alone penetrating fully into the mainstream of community care provision? Put another way, will they move from 'the margin to the mainstream'? (Office for Public Management, 1992a).

One area where collaborative working may have become the norm is that of social services managers and health service managers, which has seen improved relationships in many localities, despite the obstacles to collaboration identified in Chapter 6. Community care planning and the new funding regime for residential and nursing home provision have both demanded an improvement in such joint working. Studies by Hoyes *et al.* (1993) and others suggest that this may really be happening, despite the potential sources of tension and conflict which still exist. However, relationships between social services managers and housing managers seem far less well developed (see Chapter 7) while concern also needs to be expressed that improved professional relationships must not become an alternative to, rather than a prerequisite for, good and open relationships with local user and carer groups.

The next achievement to be considered is that social services and the other key agencies have managed to cope with a mass of change and uncertainty without allowing their basic capacity to deliver services to collapse. This has been true, for the most part, even of those local authorities who have had to make major financial cutbacks to overall budgets because of spending restrictions imposed by central government. Staff have proved to be remarkably robust, and the first months after the transfer of social security money on 1 April 1993 have generated few horror stories of systems collapsing or failing to cope. Armageddon does not appear to be upon us, although it will be easier to make this judgement when we have witnessed how local authorities have been able to marshal their money throughout a full financial year in terms of funding people in residential and nursing home care. It is possible that the very solid conservatism of these large bureaucracies offers a degree of protection from collapse in times of great uncertainty, even if it is this very conservatism which is so very difficult to transform into a commitment to user involvement. Certainly, the assessment of progress in reform implementation carried out in Chapter 5 illustrated that the approach of most social services authorities had been very cautious in terms of how far to contract out services and how radically to create a purchaser–provider split. On the negative side, this can be defined as a resistance to change, but on the positive side it can be argued that change has been tackled at a pace with which staff can just about cope.

So far this section has focused on what we considered to be the limited achievements of the early 1990s with regard to community care. However, Chapter 2 explained how policy making and policy implementation are composed of different stakeholder interests, who may have very different views about what represents 'success' and 'failure'. It is therefore important to ask what the situation looks like from the point of view of central government which initiated the changes. If Hudson (1990) was right to argue that the reforms were driven more from a desire to cap the social security budget than from an aspiration to implement the New Right ideology of marketisation, then central government should be well pleased. The practical problems of identifying and implementing a social security transfer formula have been overcome (see Chapter 5). The poisoned chalice of responsibility for funding independent residential and nursing home provision within finite annual budgets has been passed to local authorities with relatively little fuss or opposition. Even if local authorities struggle to make the new system work, the Conservative Government will be in a position to blame incompetent local authorities rather than the impossibility of the task that they have set them.

If the aim of central government was to encourage social services authorities to contract out rapidly the vast majority of their services to the independent sector, then ministers will feel that their achievements have been disappointing at this stage. In this scenario, the future challenge will be how to develop incentives which will ensure that local authorities increasingly do this in the future (see later). In general, central government has taken far less prescriptive powers over social services authorities than they have over the NHS with regard to issues such as the most appropriate way to develop purchaser–provider splits. This may reduce their direct influence, but, in contrast, the Conservative Government is able to shelter behind local authorities when services are reduced and other harsh rationing systems have to be introduced. It is not clear how many senior Conservative politicians see this continued reliance upon local authorities as a weakness which will require further substantial organisational change based upon their removal as the lead agency in community care.

How many problems? How many failures?

If it is too early to make unambiguous announcements about the achievements of the community care reforms, then it could be argued that it must logically be too soon to pronounce on what are the main failures. From such a perspective, the most that could be done would be to identify certain key problems which will form the main implementation challenges of the future. However, we feel that it is possible to identify certain fundamental flaws or failures within the assumptions which lie behind the reforms as well as key problems which need to be addressed in the future.

Ironically, given the radicalism of the reforms, some of the most glaring failures and weaknesses of community care policy and practice in the early 1990s relate to the continuities of assumptions rather than the negative impact of radical change. Perhaps the most obvious of these concerns attitudes to carers (see Chapter 2). The rhetoric of the 1989 White Paper, *Caring for People*, is about supporting carers, but it is clear that the government sees this in terms of supporting them to care and assist others physically, rather than in terms of enabling them to make real choices about whether or not they wish to do this by offering high quality alternatives. Indeed, access to public subsidy for people to live in independent sector residential and nursing homes is now through care managers, and so it can be argued that it has become easier for the state to discourage people from giving up their caring responsibilities. The main sadness of any failure to offer alternatives and choices is that it encourages an element of hostility between user and carer groups because some users feel they have an enforced dependency on carers and some carers feel that their personal assistance roles have not been taken on by choice. We remain as far away as ever from the model outlined by Morris (1991) in which users and carers are offered high quality non-stigmatising alternatives, which are based upon independent living principles.

In fairness to local authorities, several of them are in the process of developing separate systems of assessment for users and carers which do recognise the dilemmas faced by many carers. However, given the resource pressures faced by local authorities, it is difficult to believe that their energy will not go on developing more sophisticated ways of supporting carers to continue caring rather than upon also offering alternatives. The exception is likely to be where the cost of such support at home is seen as greater than the cost of institutional care for the user. Care management schemes will put stress on helping people to make their own decisions, but the emphasis in practice will be the capacity of flexible care packages to support and encourage relatives to continue their caring roles. However, the implementation of such a strategy is not without its dilemmas. These flow from the growing complexity of the modern British family, and the implications of this for future societal assumptions about caring responsibilities. The following is a pen picture of one such 'modern' family:

> Judy is a mature student of 52, married to Michael, a retired airline pilot whose earlier marriage to Jean had broken up. Jean had also remarried. Michael and Jean had had two children. One of them, Christopher, had married a girl called Nicki whose parents had also divorced and remarried. At the young people's wedding there were four parents and four step-parents. (Jerrome, 1990, p. 196)

Such divided and reblended families generate kinship complications, yet they are becoming a common phenomenon as divorce and remarriage rates continue to rise. One in three new marriages is now likely to end in divorce, and one in every three marriages involves remarriage for one partner. Divorce rates amongst elderly people are rising. Increasingly, elderly people are part of families disrupted by divorce and, in particular, a phenomenon is developing of a multiplication of parents. It seems unlikely that birth rates will keep up with the rate of divorce and remarriage, and this raises the question of who will be willing to take on the 'burden' of care for the many frail elderly parents and step-parents generated by the kind of family described by Jerrome.

Morris's vision of real alternatives is also undermined by the failure of central government to address the income situation of disabled people, the majority of whom remain trapped within benefit systems which ensure their continued poverty and hence dependence upon carers and upon social care professionals. Even the more limited goal of making it legal for social services authorities to hand over money to disabled people so that they can put together their own personal assistance packages has not been grasped by central government. Chapter 7 illustrated the failure of central government to tackle the housing dimension of community care in terms of both the availability of affordable and appropriate housing within mainstream provision and of developing innovative housing with support schemes. The one glimmer of hope is that the Department of Health has begun to recognise the importance of the housing component of community care if people are to be supported in the community rather than drift into institutional care. The main implementation task set for social services authorities in 1993–4 was making the new funding arrangements work, but they are told also to make progress on six other tasks, including 'improving collaboration with housing authorities and agencies' (Langlands and Laming, 1993).

The final issue is whether or not the 'Cinderella' tag for the main community care groups and their services has finally been thrown off or whether it remains as entrenched as ever. The Griffiths Report (1988) seemed to herald a new beginning, even if it was one heavily influenced by a market philosophy. However, since then there has been the protracted dithering of central government prior to the publication of the 1989 White Paper, *Caring for People*, because of the emphasis of the Griffiths Report on the role of local authorities. This was followed by the decision to go for a lengthy three-year phased implementation timetable. This has meant that the Children Act 1989 was given priority (Hallett, 1991) with a consequent lack of momentum for the community care changes. Even when the main financial changes took place in April 1993, the concern of government seemed to have shifted away from the stimulation of innovative new approaches to service delivery in the community to the mechanics of managing the new system of funding for residential and nursing home care. It can be argued that this is an inevitable early focus during the initial phases of implementation and that energies will subsequently be directed elsewhere. Yet it is depressing to recognise the tendency over many years for community care debates to become debates about the cost and quality of institutional care (see Chapter 2). Are we drifting back to this situation with local authorities now seeing their 'new' money as money for funding institutional care, when the emphasis of Griffiths was upon the need to shift resources into community-based provision? Despite this criticism, it could be argued that the 'Cinderella' tag is no longer appropriate, because the government is now showing increased interest in this policy area. However, this is surely mainly in terms of worries about the cost of future provision, especially given predictions about the future growth of the 'old old' (Ermisch, 1990) who are known to be high consumers of expensive health and social care. Again, one is struck by the continuity of policy debates traced in Chapters 2 and 3.

Future challenges: future prospects

The final section of this book sets out the main prospects and future challenges faced by community care policy makers and practitioners in the 1990s. If the reforms are successful in their stated aim of minimising the numbers of those in institutional care, then the biggest challenge faced by central government and by local agencies will be to develop community care systems capable of supporting and protecting very vulnerable people in the community within a mixed economy system which also requires extensive collaboration between the main statutory agencies of social services, health and housing. Is it possible to support people with severe dementia in the community without imposing impossible pressures upon relatives? Will large numbers of people with mental health problems drift into homelessness? Will some elderly people and people with learning disabilities become the victims of physical and sexual abuse because of a failure to monitor effectively the quality of care provided? Supporting very vulnerable people to avoid long-term institutional provision will intensify debates about the legal framework, and whether the required balance has been struck between civil liberty and the need for state officials to intervene on behalf of the individual. There is already a fierce debate about whether or not a legal power in the form of a Community Treatment Order should exist to force people with mental health problems to take treatment when living in the community (Bean and Mounser, 1993). A recent Law Commission (1993) report on mentally incapacitated and other vulnerable adults has opened up a further debate about whether social workers require clear powers to insist on entry into households to assess such people when they are deemed to be at risk of abuse (Marchant, 1993). Interest in these socio-legal issues seems certain to intensify in the next few years.

However, they are unlikely to be the main concern of central government which is more likely to be directing its energies into stimulating the role of the independent sector in domiciliary care as well as institutional care. Chapter 5 described how little progress local authorities have so far made in this respect. Central government would clearly like to see this situation change, but they do face certain constraints. The most important of these concerns the need to introduce the new funding regime for residential and nursing home care without creating mass bankruptcies in that sector. Local authorities have been told to spend at least 85 per cent of social security transfer money on the independent sector, but they have also been encouraged to perceive this in the short term as essentially a matter of funding institutional care. In the longer term, however, attention is bound to be directed to home care, day care provision, meals-on-wheels and other domiciliary services, whether or not local authorities need further stimulation to contract such services out, and to offering equal opportunities to the private as well as voluntary sector when this does occur. It is possible the Conservative Government will respond to this challenge by moving towards compulsory competitive tendering for some community care services or it might lay down stronger service agreement guidance which insists on the right of the private sector to compete for service delivery contracts.

The second challenge facing central government concerns the overriding necessity, from their perspective, to control public expenditure. There is going to be much more talk from ministers about the need for all of us to plan for our health and social care needs in old age, and further criticisms of all universal systems of entitlement as inefficient and unfair since they subsidise the rich and take much needed resources away from the poor and the needy. Since a head on attack on the principles of the NHS is a high-risk political manoeuvre, it is more likely that central government will push the funding of those services which are on the health and social care divide further towards social services rather than health, as we have already seen with nursing homes (see Chapter 6). The problem of how to ration such services can then be left to individual social services authorities to struggle with and, unlike the NHS, these authorities will have the option of charging and imposing means tests (Lart and Means, 1992b). The desire to control public expenditure has, of course, enormous consequences for social services authorities and their ability to make a success of their lead agency role. The rest of this section is concerned with the numerous challenges they face in the 1990s. The starting point is to emphasise the continued uncertain prospects of local authorities in terms of their resourcing, their boundaries and their right to provide, as well as purchase, services. The speed of change seems likely to increase rather than decrease in the next few years, with the real possibility of change exhaustion beginning to set in. The public sector borrowing deficit ensures central government's imposing an extremely harsh financial climate upon local authorities which will require many of them to make major savings and to cut back services, irrespective of whether these are directly provided by the authority or supported through grants and service-level agreements with the independent sector. The challenge to staff in some local authorities will be how to initiate the community care changes despite the declining availability of services.

The impact of local government reorganisation will be enormous and over time will see the emergence of many more unitary authorities which will provide both housing and social service functions. In some cases this will involve the abolition of several small district councils whose responsibilities include housing and their replacement by expanding the powers of larger, all-purpose councils, as proposed in Somerset and Derbyshire. In other cases, the existing county will be abolished and its powers, including those as a social services authority, given to a number of all-purpose councils, as proposed for Cleveland and Avon. The disruption this will cause will be enormous and there is the prospect of planning blight undermining attempts to implement the community care changes. Shadow authorities are to exist in Wales as early as April 1994 and the first tranche of English authorities is expected to have shadow arrangements from April 1995. On the positive side, it can be argued that the emergence of more unitary authorities raises the prospects of closer working between housing and social services and probably the emergence of many more combined housing and social services departments, a development actively encouraged by the White Paper on Welsh local government reorganisation (Welsh Office, 1993).

Our own view is that the challenge of the 1990s will be more demanding than the simple organisational fix of bringing two departments together. This is because local government reorganisation is being paralleled by the move to bring in compulsory competitive tendering for the main housing management functions of local authorities. This will take place over the period 1996–8/9, with authorities being divided up into groups. The first group to let contracts will come into being on 1 April 1996. This will create a very clear separation of purchaser and provider functions within housing departments. We feel it will hasten the collapse of the traditional local authority department. Instead, local authorities will begin to develop a key team of purchasing and planning officers who are accountable to the chief executive. Providers will be a mixture of in-house and independent providers; some of them will face the discipline of competitive tendering and some will not. If our judgement is correct, then such a core team of purchasers would begin to look very similar to the small teams of purchasing and commissioning staff associated with health authorities and family health services authorities. Such a development might further improve collaborative working and encourage joint purchasing strategies (especially where boundaries are coterminous with health agencies). However, such macro purchasing strategies across the agencies sits uneasily with the concept of the care manager as the spot purchaser within a purchaser–provider split in social services. Will the pressure be on social services to define care managers as a provider unit concerned with specialist assessment or will they become the equivalent of the GP fund holder with the right to purchase services on behalf of individual clients within a framework set by the centre? Equally important is whether such moves will improve service coherence for users or merely distance the purchaser still further from any real contact or dialogue with user and carer groups. It is too early to make firm predictions about future directions in this respect.

It is possible to predict that the trend in nearly all local authorities will be to place more and more emphasis upon selectivity and the establishment of clear priority groups. The emphasis will be on the development of care management assessment and intensive packages of services for those perceived as being most 'at risk' and those with the highest dependency needs. The emphasis will be on keeping these groups out of institutional care. Those defined as having medium or low levels of risk and/or dependency may find themselves defined as having non-priority need and hence little or no right to a service. The argument for this is that need outstrips resources, hence the necessity for selectivity, and that the provision of low levels of service for vast numbers of service users would do little to improve the welfare of any. However, one is struck by the lack of information about welfare outcomes available to social services managers when tackling these complex issues. It would obviously be nonsense for a social services department to spend all its budget on a single client and it would be absurd equally for every applicant to be given one hour of home care. But between these extremes how should resources be used? There is some evidence that some departments may be going too far down the intensive domiciliary care package road. Davies, Bebbington and Charnley tracked 500 service users from ten local authorities in England and Wales, and found that 'Community services seem to be under-funded, their targeting requires improvement and, in important respects, their marginal (and average productivities) are low' (1990, p. 290). In other words, the welfare outcomes (client morale, carer morale and so on) are often small relative to the cost of the care package. It could be that increased expenditure on those defined as being at medium risk or medium dependency would transform their welfare and slow down their drift into situations where they are on the verge of entry into institutional care. It is going to be very hard for social services departments to tackle such questions unless they develop better instruments for measuring the impact of their services upon clients.

What is certain is that social services authorities in the 1990s will not be able to respond positively to all the legitimate demands placed upon them by users and carers. The equitable management of this difficult situation is one of the major challenges faced by social services. We would argue that they need to have a positive approach to developing strong networks of user and carer groups who should be encouraged to argue on behalf of their constituents. However, we feel it is the responsibility of the statutory agencies to decide on their priorities and to make these as explicit and clear as possible to all concerned. The consequence of the priority approach chosen then needs to be carefully monitored to identify which groups and which individuals are gaining and losing from the chosen arrangements. One danger of a situation where resources are so tight is that hard-pressed officials start to bring in their own prejudices about who are the most deserving of help and then justify such action by reference to the eligibility criteria. For example, sweeping assumptions may be made about the capacity of an extended Asian family to provide all the care needs of a frail elderly relative. Prejudiced views may be directed at some people with HIV and towards some drug misusers, which lead either to a failure to develop certain types of services or to a biased allocation of people to available services. The sheer range of different types of situation covered by the community care sections of the 1990 Act create an enormous challenge to local authorities if all groups are to be treated equitably within the resources made available.

It will be very tempting for social services authorities and other key agencies in the next few years to hide behind their difficulties, blame central government and pretend that little progress can be made in the existing climate. However, some of the changes demanded by users and carers are not expensive to introduce, but rather relate, for example, to the way users and carers are treated by professionals. In October 1992, SAUS held a workshop for users, carers and professionals from the four local authorities studied by Hoyes *et al.* (1993). During this workshop, the qualities required within a user and carer-centred approach to assessment were considered (Took *et al.*, 1993). This led to the creation of the acronym ETCETERA, which covers the qualities of: efficiency, timing, including urgency in times of crisis, courtesy, effectiveness, truthfulness, equality, respect and appropriateness. Major improvements of this kind can be made in the 1990s despite the difficult resource situations which will be faced by social services and other agencies.

This chapter has illustrated the enormous challenges that will be faced by the different professionals and different agencies involved in the assessment and delivery of community care services in the 1990s. Staff will have to cope with enormous change in a difficult financial climate. We are only now beginning to learn about the purchasing and market-making skills which will be required both by senior staff and by care managers, and even less thought has so far been given to the rôle of the providers and the core skills associated with that activity. It is known

Table 9.1 *Community care in the 1990s: key skills*

Management of change skills	Managers need to support field-level staff through enormous cultural and organisational change.
Collaboration skills	The mixed economy of social care remains dependent on collaboration between social services, health agencies, housing agencies, etc. Equally, social services need to learn how to work in partnership with user and carer groups.
Purchasing and market-making skills	For the mixed economy of social care to work, a variety of provision needs to exist and this requires the development of skills in stimulating innovative forms of provision. Once choice exists, the skill of how to purchase potential services on a 'block' or 'spot' basis becomes crucial.
Information and budgetary skills	Devolved budgets relating to purchaser–provider splits and new care management systems require improved information and budgetary skills.
Regulation and quality audit skills	A mixed economy of social care providing services for very vulnerable people requires appropriate staff to have high-level regulation and quality audit skills.
Care management and provider skills	A literature is beginning to emerge on the required assessment skills of the care manager, but equal thought needs to be given to the core skills required of providers in face-to-face service delivery with users and carers.

that a mixed economy system can expose vulnerable people to low quality services and even abuse, and hence it is going to be essential to transform the regulatory and quality audit systems available to social services. And it is becoming evident that a move to a mixed economy has not reduced the need for staff to have the ability to inspire trust and a desire for collaborative working in colleagues from other agencies. All this implies the need for a transformation in the skills base of professionals, as outlined in Table 9.1. It is an intimidating list, especially if Stevenson and Parsloe (1993) are correct in stating that staff development has rarely been accorded the priority it deserves within social services departments. It is therefore encouraging that a recent publication from the Department of Health (1993) on *Training for the Future* seemed to recognise the scale of what is required in the short, medium and longer terms, including the necessity of developing training programmes with other professionals and with users and carers. It is to be hoped that social services authorities will tackle this developmental agenda with energy and enthusiasm, and in a way which ensures that the necessity to increase certain technical skills (such as budgeting and costing) does not obscure the fact that the new systems of community care remain dependent upon the quality of the relationship between professionals and service users.

Conclusion

The comparative perspective offered in Chapter 8 underlined the fact that issues such as the respective responsibilities of the family and the state towards people with health and social care needs are debated in nearly all countries, as is the question of what the state can afford. Chapter 8 also illustrated the wide variations of policy approaches which might be available, but also the extent to which systems based upon service delivery by large welfare bureaucracies were being rejected by all countries. There is no way of returning to the 'golden age' of the early 1970s, when incremental growth through ever-expanding social services departments, housing departments and health authorities seemed the best approach. Continued radical change is inevitable because, as Chapter 3 argued, we have learnt how to harness information technology to the development of new types of organisation and new approaches to management. However, the values which should underlie such innovation are not given, nor is the amount of public

Community Care in the 1990s

subsidy which should be invested in their development. That debate will
continue and creates the space for us to judge the emerging reforms in
terms of whether or not they make a sufficient contribution to enabling
older people and people with physical disabilities, mental health
problems and learning disabilities to remain or become full citizens of
the society in which they live. It is not until that occurs that the
'Cinderella' tag for community care services will have finally been
removed.

Guide to Further Reading

1 Introducing community care

Readers seeking an introduction to the key issues and debates in community care will find the reader edited by Bornat *et al.* (1993) an excellent starting point. The Griffiths Report (1988), the White Paper on community care (Department of Health, 1989a) and the subsequent policy guidance (Department of Health, 1990) are all essential reading. Fishwick (1992) provides a useful guide to the legislation, while Abberley (1991) provides a good discussion of the limitations of the OPCS disability surveys as a way of measuring overall need.

2 From institutions to care in the community: the history of neglect

Some readers may wish to learn more about the general development of the British welfare state as well as the more specific history of community care policy. Fraser (1984), Lowe (1993), Hill (1993), Pierson (1991) and Thane (1982) all provide clear introductions. Detailed service histories can be found in Means and Smith (1985) for elderly people, Topliss (1979) for physical disability, Jones (1972) for mental health and Malin, Race and Jones (1980) for learning disability. Political economy perspectives on service neglect are well covered by Phillipson (1982) and Oliver (1990), while the role of institutions in society is well summarised by Parker (1988). The feminist literature on community care is now extensive but Pascall (1986) and McClean and Groves (1991) provide clear overviews, while Dalley (1988) and Morris (1991) take a more detailed look at feminist explanations for service neglect. Cultural assumptions about disability and ageing are well covered by Oliver (1990) and Wilson (1991).

3 Community care and the restructuring of welfare

Making a Reality of Community Care (Audit Commission, 1986a) outlines the slow progress in resettling people from long-stay hospitals and was the report which sparked off the Griffiths Report (1988) review of community care provision and the subsequent White Paper on community care (Department of Health, 1989a). Baldwin and Parker (1989), Hudson (1990) and Langan (1990) provide detailed critiques of the proposed reforms.

The aim of the chapter is to set the community care reforms within broader debates and trends in welfare provision. Le Grand and Bartlett (1993) outline the quasi-market perspective while Hoggett (1991) provides an introduction to the

238

post-Fordist and public sector management debate. For those wishing to explore welfare change more fully, Johnson (1990), Glennerster (1992), Pierson (1991) and Taylor-Gooby (1991) provide overviews across policy areas.

4 Towards user and carer empowerment?

Lukes (1974) provides the classic discussion of power, while more general reviews of empowerment and community care are to be found in Taylor *et al.* (1992) and Stevenson and Parsloe (1993). Both Oliver (1990) and Morris (1991) provide excellent introductions to the development of the disability movement and its demand for adequate income, personal assistance and independent living based upon the rights of disabled people to be full citizens of society. Taylor *et al.* (1992) look at whether or not all service users and carers have common needs and common interests. The extensive carer literature is well summarised by Finch (1989), Perring *et al.* (1990) and Twigg *et al.* (1990).

Le Grand and Bartlett (1993) discuss 'exit' and quasi-market approaches to empowerment, while Beresford and Croft (1993) provide an excellent guide from a 'voice' perspective. The edited collection by Coote (1992) is a series of essays on the 'rights' perspective on empowerment.

5 Leaders at last: the changing rôle of social services

Arguments about whether or not local authority social services departments should be the lead agency in community care are covered in detail by Means and Smith (1985). The literature on the way local authorities are tackling the new reforms is sparse, although it is likely to expand rapidly in the next few years. Hoyes and Means (1993b), Hoyes *et al.* (1993) and Wistow *et al.* (1992) provide useful insights into the early implementation experiences and Nixon (1993) reflects on the implications for senior managers. Hudson (1993) gives an excellent introduction to care or case management, while Glendinning and Bewley (1992) take a detailed look at community care planning. The weekly journal, *Community Care*, is an excellent guide to what is happening on the ground.

6 The health dimension of community care: towards collaborative working?

This chapter looks at joint working between health and social services. For those wishing to learn more about policy making in the NHS, Ham (1992) is essential reading. The theory of collaborative working and the reasons why it is so problematic to develop are specified clearly by Hudson (1987) and Webb (1991) while Smith *et al.* (1993) describe useful, practical examples of collaborative working in action. One reason why 'working together' has been particularly difficult in this area is that there has always been a debate going on about what is health care and what is social care, an issue addressed in detail by Means and Smith (1985) while the politics of hospital rundown is well covered by Tomlinson (1991). Glennerster *et al.* (1990), Henwood *et al.* (1991), Henwood (1992) and Knapp, Wistow and Jones (1992) all consider future challenges to successful joint working in health and social care. A good recent textbook on multidisciplinary teams and care management has been produced by Øvretveit (1993).

7 Housing and community care

A useful overview of housing policy is provided by Malpass and Murie (1990) and by Malpass and Means (1993). For those interested in the owner occupation debate, Saunders (1990) is essential reading but needs to be balanced against critiques such as that by Gurney (1990). The difference between a 'home' and an 'institution' is outlined by Higgins (1989). Useful discussions of housing and community care can be found in Harrison and Means (1990), Bayliss (1987) and Arnold and Page (1992b). The 'independent living' perspective is covered by Morris (1990b) while Mackintosh, Means and Leather (1990) offer an overview of housing in later life. Clapham and Smith (1990) discuss the dangers of the term 'special needs', while Watson and Cooper (1992) profile the availability of supported housing and discuss issues around its rôle and funding.

8 European perspectives on community care

Key publications on European welfare traditions and regimes include Esping-Andersen (1990), Mishra (1990), Ginsburg (1992), Leibfried (1992) and Castles and Mitchell (1992), and analyses of the welfare state in Europe can be found in Munday (1989), Room (1991), Chamberlayne (1991/92), Baldock (1993), Jones (1993) and in a special issue of the journal *Policy and Politics* on The Europeanisation of Social Welfare (Cochrane and Doogan, 1993). Overviews of care provision for older people in a number of European countries are provided in Jamieson and Illsley (1990) and Jamieson (1991b) and a useful summary of policies and prospects for older people in the European Community has been produced by Walker (1992). The place of social work in Europe is addressed in Hill (1991), Harris and Lavan (1992) and Cannan, Berry and Lyons (1992). The European Community institutions and its process of policy making are described in many publications for students of public administration and government. Among the more readable are Nugent (1989), Nicoll and Salmon (1990), Keohane and Hoffman (1991) and Archer and Butler (1992). The impact of the EC on local government in the UK is described by Bongers (1992) and Roberts, Hart and Thomas (1993); a guide to European voluntary organisations has been compiled by Harvey (1992) and the challenges presented by a changing Europe for the voluntary sector have been addressed by Baine, Benington and Russell (1992).

9 Community care in the 1990s: achievements, failures and challenges for the future

The further reading identified in Chapter 5 is relevant to the issue of progress, problems and future scenarios in community care, as are Ellis (1993), Morris (1993) and Stevenson and Parsloe (1993). Le Grand and Bartlett (1993) set this within broader debates about welfare provision.

References

Aaronovitch, S. *et al.* (1992) *Building Homes for Successive Generations* (London: Access Committee for England).

Abberley, P. (1991) 'The significance of the OPCS disability surveys', pp. 156–76 in M. Oliver (ed.), *Social Work, Disabled People and Disabling Environments* (London: Jessica Kingsley).

Abbott, P. and Sapsford, R. (1987) *Community Care for Mentally Handicapped Children* (Milton Keynes: Open University Press).

Abel-Smith, B. and Titmuss, K. (eds) (1987) *The Philosophy of Welfare: Selected Writings of Richard M. Titmuss* (London: Allen & Unwin).

Abrahamson, P. (1991a) 'Welfare and poverty in the Europe of the 1990s: social progress or social dumping?', *International Journal of Health Services*, vol. 21, no. 2, pp. 237–64.

Abrahamson, P. (1991b) 'Welfare for the elderly in Denmark: from institutionalization to self-reliance', pp. 35–61 in A. Evers and I. Svetlik (eds), *New Welfare Mixes in Care for the Elderly, Vol. 2, Austria, Denmark, Finland, Israel, Netherlands* (Vienna: European Centre for Social Welfare Policy and Research).

Abrams, P. C. (1977) 'Community care: some research problems and priorities', *Policy and Politics*, vol. 6, no. 2, pp. 125–51.

Alaszewski, A. and Manthorpe, J. (1990) 'Literature review: The new right', *British Journal of Social Work*, vol. 20, no. 3, pp. 237–51.

Alber, J. (1991) *The Impact of Public Policies on Older People in the Federal Republic of Germany*, Konstanz, Spring (submission to the EC Observatory on Older People).

Alber, J., Guillemard, A. M. and Walker, A. (1991) *The Impact of Social and Economic Policies on Older People in the European Community: An Initial Overview*, EC Observatory on Older People, First Report, Commission of the European Communities, Directorate General V, Employment, Social Affairs, Industrial Relations, June.

Allen, I., Dalley, G. and Leat, D. (1992) *Monitoring Change in Social Services Departments* (London: Policy Studies Institute for the Association of Directors of Social Services).

Amira, A. (1990) 'Family care in Greece', pp. 72–79 in A. Jamieson and R. Illsley (eds), *Contrasting European Policies for the Care of Older People* (Aldershot: Avebury).

Amulree, Lord (1951) *Adding Life to Years* (London: National Council of Social Service).

Anderson, R. (1992) 'Health and community care', pp. 63–84 in L. Davies (ed.) *The Coming of Age in Europe: Older People in the European Community* (London: Age Concern England (ACE) Books).

Anderson Report (1947) *The Care and Treatment of the Elderly and Infirm* (London: British Medical Association).

242

Anthony, K. (1984) 'Moving experiences: memories of favourite homes', *Environmental Design Research Association (EDRA) 15 Proceedings*, pp. 141–9.

Arber, S. and Ginn, J. (1991) *Gender and Later Life: A Sociological Analysis of Resources and Constraints* (London: Sage).

Archer, C. and Butler, F. (1992) *The European Community: Structure and Process* (London: Pinter Publishers).

Arnold, P. and Page, D. (1992a) 'A caring community', *Housing*, March, pp. 9–13.

Arnold, P. and Page, D. (1992b) *Housing and Community Care* (York: Joseph Rowntree Foundation).

Atkin, K. (1991) 'Community care in a multi-racial society: incorporating the user view', *Policy and Politics*, vol. 19, no. 3, pp. 159–66.

Atkinson, D. (1988) 'Residential care for children and adults with mental handicap', pp. 125–56 in I. Sinclair (ed.), *Residential Care: The Research Reviewed* (London: HMSO).

Audit Commission (1985) *Managing Social Services for the Elderly More Effectively* (London: HMSO).

Audit Commission (1986a) *Making a Reality of Community Care* (London: HMSO).

Audit Commission (1986b) *Managing the Crisis in Council Housing* (London: HMSO).

Audit Commission (1992) *Community Care: Managing the Cascade of Change* (London: HMSO).

Aves, G. (1964) 'The relationship between homes and other forms of care', pp. 11–17 in K. Slack (ed.), *Some Aspects of Residential Care of the Elderly* (London: National Council of Social Service).

Bailey, R. and Brake, M. (1975) *Radical Social Work* (London: Edward Arnold).

Baine, S., Benington, J. and Russell, J. (1992) *Changing Europe: Challenges Facing the Voluntary and Community Sectors in the 1990s* (London: NCVO Publications and Community Development Foundation).

Baldock, J. (1993) 'Patterns of change in the delivery of welfare in Europe' pp. 24–37 in P. Taylor-Gooby and R. Lawson (eds), *Markets and Managers: New Issues in the Delivery of Welfare* (Buckingham: Open University Press).

Baldock, J. and Evers, A. (1991) 'Concluding remarks on the significance of the innovations reviewed – their implications for social change', pp. 186–202 in R. J. Kraan, J. Baldock, B. Davies, A. Evers, L. Johansson, M. Knapen, M. Thorslund and C. Tunissen (eds), *Care for the Elderly: Significant Innovations in Three European Countries* (Boulder, Colorado: Westview Press).

Baldwin, S. and Parker, G. (1989) 'The Griffiths report on community care', pp. 143–65 in M. Brenton and C. Ungerson (eds), *Social Policy Review, 1988–89* (London: Longman).

Baldwin, S. and Twigg, J. (1991) 'Women and community care – reflections on a debate', pp. 117–35 in M. Maclean and D. Groves (eds), *Women's Issues in Social Policy* (London: Routledge).

Barnes, M., Prior, D. and Thomas, N. (1990) 'Social services', pp. 103–53 in N. Deakin and A. Wright (eds), *Consuming Public Services* (London: Routledge).

Baron, S. and Haldane, J. (eds) (1992) *Community, Normality and Difference: Meeting Social Needs* (Aberdeen: Aberdeen University Press).

Barrett, S. and Hill, M. (1984) 'Policy, bargaining and structure in implementation theory: towards an integrated perspective', *Policy and Politics*, vol. 12, no. 3, pp. 219–40.

Barton, R. (1959) *Institutional Neurosis* (Bristol: John Wright and Sons).

BASW (1985) *Housing and Social Work* (Birmingham: British Association of Social Workers).

Batty, M. (1991) 'New technology programme', *Eurolink Age Bulletin*, October.

Batty, M. (1992) 'European Year budget slashed ...,' *Eurolink Age Bulletin*, July.

Baxter, C., Poonia, K., Ward, L. and Nadirshaw, Z. (1990) *Double Discrimination: Issues and Services for People with Learning Difficulties from Black and Ethnic Minority Communities* (London: King's Fund Centre/ Commission for Racial Equality).

Bayliss, E. (1987) *Housing: The Foundation of Community Care* (London: National Federation of Housing Associations and Mind).

Bean, P. and Mounser, P. (1993) *Discharged from Mental Hospitals* (Basingstoke: Macmillan).

Beardshaw, V. and Towell, D. (1990) *Assessment and Case Management: Implications for the Implementation of 'Caring for People'* (London: King's Fund Institute).

Bennett, S. (1992) *Contracts for Care* (London: National Federation of Housing Associations and National Council for Voluntary Organisations).

Beresford, P. and Croft, S. (1993) *Citizen Involvement: A Practical Guide for Change* (Basingstoke: Macmillan).

Bertelsen, O. and Platz, M. (1991) *The Impact of Social and Economic Policies on Older People in Denmark*, Danish National Institute of Social Research, April (submission to the EC Observatory on Older People).

Beveridge Report (1942) *Social Insurance and Allied Services* (London: HMSO).

Biggs, S. (1990/91) 'Consumers, care management and inspection: obscuring social deprivation and need', *Critical Social Policy*, issue 30, pp. 23–8.

Boddy, M. and Fudge, C. (eds) (1984) *Local Socialism? Labour Councils and New Left Alternatives* (London: Macmillan).

Bone, M. and Meltzer, H. (1989) *The Prevalence of Disability Among Children*, OPCS Surveys (London: HMSO).

Bongers, P. (1990) *Local Government and 1992* (Harlow: Longman).

Bongers, P. (1992) *Local Government and the Single European Market* (Harlow: Longman).

Booth, T. and Phillips, D. (1990) *Contracting Arrangements in Domiciliary Care* (Sheffield: Joint Unit for Social Services Research, University of Sheffield and National Council for Domiciliary Care Services).

Booth, T., Simmons, K. and Booth, W. (1990) *Outward Bound: Relocation and Community Care for People with Learning Disabilities* (Buckingham: Open University Press).

Bornat, J., Pereira, C., Pilgrim, D. and Williams, F. (eds) (1993) *Community Care: A Reader* (Basingstoke: Macmillan).

Bosanquet, N. (1978) *A Future for Old Age* (London: Temple Smith).

Bosanquet, N. and Propper, C. (1991) 'Charting the grey economy in the 1990s', *Policy and Politics*, vol. 19, no. 4, pp. 269–82.

Boucher Report (1957) *Survey of Services Available to the Chronic Sick and Elderly 1954–55*, Reports on Public Health and Medical Subjects No. 98 (London: HMSO).

Bowl, R. (1986) 'Social work with old people', pp. 128–45 in C. Phillipson and A. Walker (eds), *Ageing and Social Policy* (Aldershot: Gower).

Bowling, B. (1990) *Elderly People from Ethnic Minorities: A Report on Four Projects* (London: Age Concern/Institute of Gerontology).

Brauns, H-J. and Kramer, D. (1989) 'West Germany – the break up of consensus and the demographic threat', pp. 124–54 in B. Munday (ed.), *The Crisis in Welfare: An International Perspective on Social Services and Social Work* (Hemel Hempstead: Harvester Wheatsheaf).

British Medical Association (1992) *Priorities for Community Care* (London: BMA).

Brockington, R. (1963) 'A Community Health Authority', *Hospital and Social Services Journal*, 20 September, pp. 1145–6.

Brown, M. (1972) 'The Developement of Local Authority Welfare Services from 1948–1965 under Part III of the National Assistance Act 1948', PhD thesis, University of Manchester.

Brown, R. (1979) *Reorganising the National Health Service* (Oxford: Blackwell).

Buckley, M. and Anderson, M. (eds) (1988) *Women, Equality and Europe* (Basingstoke: Macmillan).

Bull, J. and Poole, L. (1989) *Not Rich, Not Poor: Housing Options for Elderly People on Middle Incomes* (London: SHAC and Anchor Housing Trust).

Butler, A., Oldman, C. and Greve, J. (1983) *Sheltered Housing for the Elderly* (London: Allen & Unwin).

Cambridge, P. (1992) 'Case management in community services: organisational responses', *British Journal of Social Work*, vol. 22, no. 5, pp. 495–517.

Campbell, P. (1990) 'Mental health self advocacy', pp. 69–78 in L. Winn (ed.), *Power to the People* (London: King's Fund Centre).

Cannan, C., Berry, L. and Lyons, K. (1992) *Social Work and Europe* (Basingstoke: Macmillan).

Care and Repair (1991) *Improving Matters: A Guide to the Development, Management and Running of Home Improvement Agencies* (Nottingham: Care and Repair).

Castles, F. and Mitchell, D. (1992) 'Identifying welfare state regimes', *Governance*, vol. 5, no. 1, pp. 1–26.

Cervi, B. , Frances. J, Manhart, C. , Neate P. and Sone, K. (1992) 'Facing a trickle or flood', *Community Care*, 5 November, pp. 14–15.

Challis, D. and Davies, B. (1986) *Case Management in Community Care: An Evaluated Experiment in the Home Care of the Elderly* (Aldershot: Gower).

Challis, D., Chessum, R., Chesterman, J., Luckett, R. and Woods, R. (1988) 'Community care for the frail elderly: an urban experiment', *British Journal of Social Work*, vol. 18 (supplement), pp. 13–42.

Challis, L. (1990) *Organising Public Social Services* (London: Longman).

Chamberlayne, P. (1991/92) 'New directions in welfare? France, West Germany, Italy and Britain in the 1980s', *Critical Social Policy*, issue 33 (vol. 11, no. 3), pp. 5–21.

Chapman, K. (1989) 'Trends of home care provision into the 1990s', *Eurolink Age Bulletin*, September.

Chappell, A. (1992) 'Towards a sociological critique of the normalisation principle', *Disability, Handicap and Society*, vol. 7, no. 1, pp. 35–52.

Clapham, D. and Smith, S. (1990) 'Housing policy and "special needs"', *Policy and Politics*, vol. 18, no. 3, pp. 193–206.

Clapham, D., Means, R. and Munro, M. (1993) 'Housing, the life course and older people', pp. 132–48 in S. Arber and M. Evandrou (eds), *Ageing, Independence amd the Life Course* (London: Jessica Kingsley).

Clarke, L. (1984) *Domiciliary Services for the Elderly* (London: Croom Helm).

Clarke, M. and Stewart, J. (1992) 'Empowerment: a theme for the 1990s', *Local Government Studies*, vol. 18, no. 2, pp. 18–26.

Clay, T. (1989) 'The threat to community care', *The Guardian*, 24 July.

Clode, D., Parker, C. and Etherington, S. (eds) (1987) *Towards the Sensitive Bureaucracy* (Aldershot: Gower).

Clough, R. (1990) *Practice, Politics and Power in Social Services Departments* (Aldershot: Avebury).

Cochrane, A. and Doogan, K. (1993) 'The Europeanisation of social welfare', special issue, *Policy and Politics*, vol. 21, no. 2.

Coleman, G., Higgins, J., Smith, R. and Tolan, F. (1990) *Training and Development for Resettlement Staff* (Bristol: School for Advanced Urban Studies).

Common, R. and Flynn, N. (1992) *Contracting for Care* (York: Joseph Rowntree Foundation).

Cooper, R. and Watson, L. (1992) 'Housing and the homely environment', *Housing*, July/August, p.42.

Coote, A. (ed.) (1992) *The Welfare of Citizens: Developing New Social Rights* (London: Institute of Public Policy Research/Rivers Oram Press).

Craig, G. (1992) *Cash or Care: A Question of Choice?* (York: Social Policy Research Unit, University of York).

Cranston, M. (1976) 'Human rights: real and supposed', pp. 133–44 in N. Timms and D. Watson (eds), *Talking about Welfare* (London: Routledge and Kegan Paul).

Crowther, M. (1981) *The Workhouse System, 1834–1929: The History of an English Social Institution* (London: Methuen).

Cullen, K. and Moran, R. (1992) *Technology and the Elderly: The Role of Technology in Prolonging the Independence of the Elderly in the Community Care Context*, FAST Research Report (Luxembourg: Commission of the European Communities).

Daatland, S. O. (1992) 'Ideals lost? Current trends in Scandinavian welfare policies on ageing', *Journal of European Social Policy*, vol. 2, no. 1, pp. 33–42.

Dalley, G. (1988) *Ideologies of Caring – Rethinking Community and Collectivism* (Basingstoke: Macmillan).

Dalley, G. (1991) 'Beliefs and behaviour: professionals and the policy process', *Journal of Ageing Studies*, vol. 5, no. 2, pp. 163–80.

Dant, T., Carley, M., Gearing, B. and Johnson, M. (1987) *Dependency and Old Age: Theoretical Accounts and Practical Understandings*, Care of Elderly People at Home Project Paper No. 3, Open University/Policy Studies Institute.

Davies, B. (1992) 'On breeding the best chameleons', *Generations Review*, vol. 2, no. 2, pp. 18–21.

Davies, B. and Challis, D. (1986) *Matching Needs to Resources* (Aldershot: Gower).

Davies, B., Bebbington, A. and Charnley, H. (1990) *Resources, Needs and Outcomes in Community-Based Care* (Aldershot: Ashgate).

Davies, M. (1979) 'Swapping the old around', *Community Care*, 18 October, pp. 16–17.

de Jasay, A. (1991) *Choice, Contract, Consent: A Restatement of Liberalism* (London: The Institute of Economic Affairs).

Deakin, N. (1987) *The Politics of Welfare* (London: Methuen).

Department of the Environment (1988) *1986 English House Condition Survey* (London: HMSO).

Department of the Environment (1993) *The Future of Private Housing Renewal Programmes* (London: Department of the Environment).

Department of the Environment/Department of Health (1992) *Housing and Community Care*, Circular 10/92 and LAC (92) 12, (London: HMSO).

Department of Health (1989a) *Caring for People: Community Care in the Next Decade and Beyond* (London: HMSO).

Department of Health (1989b) *Working for Patients* (London: HMSO).

Department of Health (1990) *Community Care in the Next Decade and Beyond: Policy Guidance* (London: HMSO).

Department of Health (1992) *Memorandum on the Financing of Community Care Arrangements after April 1992 and on Individual Choice of Residential Accommodation*, 2 October (London: Department of Health).

Department of Health (1993) *Training for the Future* (London: HMSO).

Department of Health and Social Security (1971) *Better Services for the Mentally Handicapped* (London: HMSO).

Department of Health and Social Security (1975) *Better Services for the Mentally Ill* (London: HMSO).

Department of Health and Social Security (1978) *A Happier Old Age* (London: HMSO).

Department of Health and Social Security (1981a) *Care in the Community: A Consultative Document on Moving Resources for Care in England* (London: Department of Health and Social Security).

Department of Health and Social Security (1981b) *Growing Older* (London: HMSO).

Department of Health and Social Security (1983) *Care in the Community and Joint Finance*, Health Circular (83)6 and Local Authority Circular (83)5, March (London: Department of Health and Social Security).

Department of Health/Social Services Inspectorate (1990) *Training for Community Care: A Strategy* (London: Department of Health).

Department of Health/Social Services Inspectorate (1991a) *Care Management and Assessment: Summary of Practice Guidance* (London: HMSO).

Department of Health/Social Services Inspectorate (1991b) *Training for Community Care: A Joint Approach* (London: HMSO).

Dieck, M. (1990) 'Politics for elderly people in the FRG', pp. 95–119 in A. Jamieson and R. Illsley (eds), *Contrasting European Policies for the Care of Older People* (Aldershot: Avebury).

Digby, A. (1978) *Pauper Palaces* (London: Routledge & Kegan Paul).

Disability Manifesto Group (1991) *An Agenda for the 1990s* (London: Disability Manifesto Group).

Doyle, N. and Harding, T. (1992) 'Community care: applying procedural fairness', pp. 69–82 in A. Coote (ed.), *The Welfare of Citizens: Developing New Social Rights* (London: IPPR/Rivers Oram Press).

Edelman, M. (1971) *Politics as Symbolic Action* (Chicago: Markham).

Ellis, K. (1993) *Squaring the Circle: User and Carer Participation* (York: Joseph Rowntree Foundation/London: Community Care).

Emerson, E. (1992) 'What is normalisation?', pp. 1–18 in H. Brown and H. Smith (eds), *Normalisation: A Reader for the Nineties* (London: Tavistock/Routledge).

Ermisch, J. (1990) *Fewer Babies, Longer Lives* (York: Joseph Rowntree Foundation).

Esping-Andersen, G. (1990) *The Three Worlds of Welfare Capitalism* (Oxford: Polity Press).

Eurobarometer Survey (1993) *Age and Attitudes: Main Results from a Eurobarometer Survey* (Brussels: Commission of the European Communities, Directorate-General V, Employment, Industrial Relations and Social Affairs).

European Information Service (1993) *Acquired Rights and TUPE: What's Going On?*, issue no. 141, 12 July, pp. 27–30.

Evers, A. and Olk, T. (1991) 'The mix of care provisions for the frail elderly in the Federal Republic of Germany', pp. 59–100 in A. Evers and I. Svetlik (eds), *New Welfare Mixes in Care for the Elderly, Vol. 3, Canada, France, Germany, Italy, United Kingdom* (Vienna: European Centre for Social Welfare Policy and Research).

Eyden, J. (1965) 'The physically handicapped', pp. 161–74 in D. Marsh (ed.), *An Introduction to the Study of Social Administration* (London: Routledge & Kegan Paul).

Fasolo, E. and Frisanco, R. (1991) 'Mental health care in Italy', *Social Policy and Administration*, vol. 25, no. 3, pp. 218–26.

Fennell, G. (1986) *Anchor's Older People: What Do They Think?* (Oxford: Anchor Housing Association).

Fennell, G., Phillipson, C. and Evers, H. (1988) *The Sociology of Old Age* (Milton Keynes: Open University Press).

Fiedler, B. (1988) *Living Options Lottery* (London: The Prince of Wales' Advisory Group on Disability).

Finch, J. (1984) 'Community care: developing non-sexist alternatives', *Critical Social Policy*, issue no. 9, pp. 6–18.

Finch, J. (1989) *Family Obligations and Social Change* (Cambridge: Polity Press).

Finch, J. and Groves, D. (eds) (1983) *A Labour of Love: Women, Work and Caring* (London: Routledge & Kegan Paul).

Fisher, M. (1990–91) 'Defining the practice content of care management', *Social Work and Social Services Review*, vol. 2, no. 3, pp. 204–30.

Fishwick, C. (1992) *Community Care and Control* (Birmingham: Pepar Publications).

Fletcher, P. (1991) *The Future of Sheltered Housing – Who Cares?: Policy Report* (London: National Federation of Housing Associations and Anchor Housing Association).

Flynn, N. (1989) 'The 'new right' and social policy', *Policy and Politics*, vol. 17, no. 2, pp. 97–110.

Foster, A. and Laming, H. (1992) *Implementing Caring for People*, EL (92)65 and CI (92)30 (London: Department of Health).

Foucault, M. (1967) *Madness and Civilisation* (London: Tavistock).

Fraser, D. (1984) *The Evolution of the Welfare State*, 2nd edn (London: Macmillan).

Friend, J., Power, J. and Yewlett, C. (1974) *Public Planning: the Intercorporate Dimension* (London: Tavistock).

Fry, A. (1989) 'Crossing the channel and the language barrier', *Social Work Today* , 9 November, p. 9.

Gavilan, H. (1992) 'Taking control from the frail', *Guardian*, 17 June.

Gibbins, J. (1988) 'Residential care for mentally ill adults', pp. 157–97 in I. Sinclair (ed.), *Residential Care: The Research Reviewed* (London: HMSO).

Gibbs, I. and Corden, A. (1991) 'The concept of 'reasonableness' in relation to residential care and nursing home charges', *Policy and Politics*, vol. 19, no. 2, pp. 119–30.

Gillie Report (1963) *The Field of Work of the Family Doctor* (London: HMSO).

Ginsburg, N. (1992) *Divisions of Welfare: A Critical Introduction to Comparative Social Policy* (London: Sage).

Glendinning, C. and Bewley, C. (1992) *Involving Disabled People in Community Care Planning – The First Steps* (Manchester: Department of Social Policy and Social Work, University of Manchester).

Glennerster, H. (1992) *Paying for Welfare: The 1990s* (Hemel Hempstead: Harvester Wheatsheaf).

Glennerster, H., Falkingham, J. and Evandrou, M. (1990) 'How much do we care?', *Social Policy and Administration*, vol. 24, no. 2, pp. 93–103.

Godlove, C. and Mann, A. (1980) 'Thirty years of the welfare state: current issues in British social policy for the aged', *Aged Care and Services Review*, vol. 2, no. 1, pp. 1–12.

Goffman, E. (1968) *Asylums: Essays on the Social Situation of Mental Patients and Other Inmates* (Harmondsworth: Penguin).

Goodwin, S. (1989) 'Community care for the mentally ill in England and Wales: myths, assumptions and reality', *Journal of Social Policy*, vol. 18, part 1, pp. 27–52.

Goodwin, S. (1990) *Community Care and the Future of Mental Health Service Provision* (Aldershot: Avebury).

Green, H. (1988) *Informal Carers: General Household Survey, 1985* (London: HMSO).

Griffiths Report (1988) *Community Care: An Agenda for Action* (London: HMSO).

Guillebaud Report (1956) *Committee of Enquiry into the Cost of the National Health Service* (London: HMSO).

Gurney, C. (1990) *The Meaning of Home in the Decade of Owner Occupation*, Working Paper 88 (Bristol: School for Advanced Urban Studies).

Gurney, C. (1991) 'Ontological Security, Home Ownership and the Meaning of Home: A Theoretical and Empirical Critique', paper delivered to a conference on *Beyond a Nation of Home Owners* at Sheffield City Polytechnic, 22 April.

Gurney, C. and Means, R. (1993) 'The meaning of home in later life', pp. 119–31 in S. Arber and M Evandrou (eds), *Ageing, Independence and the Life Course* (London: Jessica Kingsley).

Gutch, R. (1989) 'The contract culture: the challenge for voluntary organisations', *Contracting: In or Out*, No. 2 (London: National Council for Voluntary Organisations).

Haber, C. (1983) *Beyond Sixty-Five: The Dilemma of Old Age in America's Past* (Cambridge: Cambridge University Press).

Hadley, R. and Hatch, S. (1981) *Social Welfare and the Failure of the State: Centralised Social Services and Participatory Alternatives* (London: Allen & Unwin).

Hallett, C. (1991) 'The Children Act 1989 and community care: comparisons and contrasts', *Policy and Politics*, vol. 19, no. 4, pp. 283–91.

Ham, C. (1992 ed), *Health Policy in Britain* (Basingstoke: Macmillan).

Ham, C. and Hill, M. (1993 ed) *The Policy Process in the Modern Capitalist State* (Brighton: Wheatsheaf).

Hambleton, R. (1986) *Rethinking Policy Planning*, SAUS Study No. 2 (Bristol: School for Advanced Urban Studies).

Hambleton, R. and Hoggett, P. (eds) (1984) *The Politics of Decentralisation: Theory and Practice of a Radical Local Government Initiative*, Working Paper No. 46 (Bristol: School for Advanced Urban Studies).

Harding, T. (1992) *Great Expectations – and Spending on Social Services* (London: National Institute for Social Work).

Hardy, B. (1992) 'Hares and tortoises', *Community Care*, 3 September, pp. 22–4.

Harper, S. and Thane, P. (1989) 'The consolidation of 'old age' as a phase of life, 1945–1965', pp. 43–61 in M. Jefferys (ed.), *Growing Old in the Twentieth Century* (London: Routledge).

Harris, A. (1961) *Meals on Wheels for Old People* (London: National Corporation for the Care of Old People).

Harris, R. and Lavan, A. (1992) 'Professional mobility in the new Europe: the case of social work', *Journal of European Social Policy*, vol. 2, no.1, pp. 1–15.

Harrison, F. (1986) *The Young Disabled Adult, the Use of Residential Homes and Hospital Units for the Age Group, 16–64* (London: Royal College of Physicians).

Harrison, L. and Means, R. (1990) *Housing: The Essential Element in Community Care* (London: SHAC and Anchor Housing Trust).

Harrison, L. and Means, R. (1993) 'Brokerage in action?: Radnor care and repair project', pp. 113–37 in R. Smith, L. Gaster, L. Harrison, L. Martin, R. Means and P. Thistlethwaite, *Working Together for Better Community Care*, SAUS Study No. 7 (Bristol: School for Advanced Urban Studies).

Harrison, S., Hunter, D. and Pollitt, C. (1990) *The Dynamics of British Health Policy* (London: Unwin Hyman).

Harvey, B. (1992) *Networking in Europe: A Guide to European Voluntary Organisations* (London: NCVO Publications and Community Development Foundation).

Health Advisory Service (1983) *The Rising Tide: Developing Services for Mental Illness in Old Age* (London: HMSO).

Hencke, D. (1989) 'Why the delay over Griffiths may lead to more concessions', *Social Work Today*, 13 July, p. 9.

Henwood, M. (1992) 'Twilight zone', *Health Services Journal*, 5 November, pp. 28–30.

Henwood, M., Jowell, T. and Wistow, G. (1991) *All Things Come to Those Who Wait?* (London: King's Fund Institute).

Herbert Report (1960) *Royal Commission on Local Government in Greater London 1957–1960* (London: HMSO).

Heumann, L. and Boldy, D. (1982) *Housing for the Elderly* (London: Croom Helm).

Higgins, J. (1989) 'Defining community care: realities and myths', *Social Policy and Administration*, vol. 23, no. 1, pp. 3–16.

Hill, M. (1993) *Understanding Social Policy*, 4th edn (Oxford: Blackwell).

Hill, M. (ed.) (1991) *Social Work and the European Community: The Social Policy and Practice Context*, Research Highlights in Social Work 23 (London: Jessica Kingsley).

Hills, J. (ed.) (1990) *The State of Welfare* (Oxford: Oxford University Press).

Hirschman, A. (1970) *Exit, Voice and Loyalty: Responses to Decline in Firms, Organisations and States* (Harvard: Harvard University Press).

Hoggett, P. (1990) *Modernisation, Political Strategy and the Welfare State: An Organisational Perspective*, DQM Paper No. 2 (Bristol: School for Advanced Urban Studies).

Hoggett, P. (1991) 'The new public sector management', *Policy and Politics*, vol. 19, no. 4, pp. 243–56.

Hoggett, P. (1992) 'The politics of empowerment', *Going Local*, no. 19, pp. 18–19.

Hoggett, P. and Bramley, G. (1989) 'Devolution of local budgets', *Public Money and Management*, vol. 9, no 4, pp. 9–14.

Hoggett, P. and Hambleton, R. (1987) *Decentralisation and Democracy*, Occasional Paper No. 28 (Bristol: School for Advanced Urban Studies).

Holstein, B. E., Due, P., Almind, G. and Holst, E. (1991) 'The home help service in Denmark', pp. 38–62 in A. Jamieson (ed.), *Home Care for Older People in Europe: A Comparison of Policies and Practices* (Oxford: Oxford University Press).

Hoyes, L. and Harrison, L. (1987) 'An ordinary private life', *Community Care*, 12 February, pp. 20–21.

Hoyes, L. and Lart, R. (1992) 'Taking care', *Community Care*, 20 October, pp. 14–15.

Hoyes, L. and Le Grand, J. (1991) *Markets in Social Care Services: A Resource Pack* (Bristol: School for Advanced Urban Studies).

Hoyes, L. and Means, R. (1991) *Implementing the White Paper on Community Care*, DQM Paper No. 4 (Bristol: School for Advanced Urban Studies).

Hoyes, L. and Means, R. (1993a) 'Markets, contracts and social care services: prospects and problems', pp. 287–95 in J. Bornat *et al.* (eds), *Community Care: A Reader* (Basingstoke: Macmillan).

Hoyes, L. and Means, R. (1993b) 'Quasi-markets and the reform of community care', pp. 93–124 in J. Le Grand and W. Bartlett (eds), *Quasi-Markets and Social Policy* (Basingstoke: Macmillan).

Hoyes, L. and Means, R. (1993c) 'Making changes', *Community Care*, 30 May, p. 22.

Hoyes, L., Means, R. and Le Grand, J. (1992) *Made to Measure? Performance Measurement and Community Care*, Occasional Paper 39 (Bristol: School for Advanced Urban Studies).

Hoyes, L., Jeffers, S., Lart, R., Means, R. and Taylor, M. (1993) *User Empowerment and the Reform of Community Care: An Interim Assessment* (Bristol: School for Advanced Urban Studies).

Hudson, B. (1987) 'Collaboration in social welfare: a framework for analysis', *Policy and Politics*, vol. 15, no. 3, pp. 175–82.

Hudson, B. (1990) 'Social policy and the new right – the strange case of the community care White Paper', *Local Government Studies*, vol. 16, no. 6, pp. 15–34.

Hudson, B. (1992) 'All dressed up – but nowhere to go?, *Health Services Journal*, 22 October, pp. 22–4.

Hudson, B. (1993) *The Busy Person's Guide to Care Management* (Sheffield: Joint Unit for Social Services Research, University of Sheffield).

Hunter, D. and Wistow, G. (1987) *Community Care in Britain: Variations on a Theme* (London: King Edward's Hospital Fund).

Huws Jones, R. (1952) 'Old people's welfare – successes and failures', *Social Service Quarterly*, vol. 26, no. 1, pp. 19–22.

Irvine, E. (1950) 'The place of the Health Department in the care of the aged', *The Medical Officer*, 12 August, p. 74.

Jamieson, A. (1990a) 'Care of older people in the European Community', pp. 32–45 in L. Hantrais, S. Mangen and M. O'Brien (eds), *Caring and the Welfare State in the 1990s* Cross-National Research Paper 2 (Birmingham: The Cross-National Research Group, Aston University).

Jamieson, A. (1990b) 'Informal care in Europe' pp. 3–21 in A. Jamieson and R. Illsley (eds), *Contrasting European Policies for the Care of Older People* (Aldershot: Avebury).

Jamieson, A. (1991a) 'Community care for older people', pp. 107–126 in G. Room (ed.), *Towards a European Welfare State?* (Bristol: SAUS Publications).

Jamieson, A. (ed.) (1991b) *Home Care for Older People in Europe: A Comparison of Policies and Practices* (Oxford: Oxford University Press).

Jamieson, A. and Illsley, R. (eds) (1990) *Contrasting European Policies for the Care of Older People* (Aldershot: Avebury).

Jarre, D. (1991) 'Subsidiarity in social services in Germany', *Social Policy and Administration*, vol. 25, no. 3, pp. 211–17.

Jay Report (1979) *Committee of Enquiry into Mental Handicap Nursing and Care* (London: HMSO).

Jerrome, D. (1990) 'Intimate relation', pp. 181–208 in J. Bond and P. Coleman (eds), *Ageing and Society: An Introduction to Social Gerontology* (London: Sage).

Johnson, M. (1990) 'Dependency and interdependency', pp. 209–28, in J. Bond and P. Coleman (eds), *Ageing in Society: An Introduction to Social Gerontology* (London: Sage).

Johnson, N. (1987) *The Welfare State in Transition: The Theory and Practice of Welfare Pluralism* (Brighton: Wheatsheaf).

Johnson, N. (1990) *Reconstructing the Welfare State: A Decade of Change* (Hemel Hempstead: Harvester Wheatsheaf).

Johnson, P. (1987) *Structured Dependency of the Elderly: A Critical Note* (London: Centre for Economic Policy Research).

Jones, C. (ed.) (1993) *New Perspectives on the Welfare State in Europe* (London: Routledge).

Jones, K. (1972) *A History of the Mental Health Services* (London: Routledge & Kegan Paul).

Jones, K. (1988) *Experience in Mental Health: Community Care and Social Policy* (London: Sage Publications).

Jones, K. and Fowles, A. (1984) *Ideas on Institutions* (London: Routledge & Kegan Paul).

Jones, K. and Poletti, A. (1985) 'Understanding the "Italian experience"', *British Journal of Psychiatry*, vol. 146, pp. 341–47.

Jones, K. and Poletti, A. (1986) 'The "Italian experience" reconsidered', *British Journal of Psychiatry*, vol. 148, pp. 144–50.

Karn, V. (1977) *Retiring to the Seaside* (London: Routledge & Kegan Paul).

Kemp, P. (1993) 'Rebuilding the private rented sector', pp. 59–73 in P. Malpass and R. Means (eds), *Implementing Housing Policy* (Milton Keynes: Open University Press).

Keohane, R. and Hoffman, S. (eds.) (1991) *The New European Community: Decisionmaking and Institutional Change* (Oxford: Westview Press).

Kestenbaum, A. (1992) *Cash for Care* (Nottingham: Independent Living Fund).

King's Fund Centre (1980) *An Ordinary Life: Comprehensive Locally-based Residential Services for Mentally Handicapped People*, King's Fund Project Paper No. 24 (London: King's Fund Centre).

Kirk, H. and Leather, P. (1991) *Age File: The Facts* (Oxford: Anchor Housing Trust).

Knapp, M., Wistow, G. and Jones, N. (1992) 'Smart moves', *Health Services Journal*, 29 October, pp. 28–30.

Knapp, M., Wistow, G., Forder, J. and Hardy, B. (1993) *Markets for Social Care: Opportunities, Barriers and Implications*, PSSRU Discussion Paper 919 (Canterbury: Personal Social Services Research Unit, University of Kent).

Laing and Buisson (1992) *Laing's Review of Private Health Care, 1992* (London: Laing and Buisson).

Land, H. (1978) 'Who cares for the family?', *Journal of Social Policy*, vol. 7, no. 3, pp. 257–84.

Landwehr, R. and Wolff R. (1992) 'The Federal Republic of Germany', in B. Munday (ed.), *Social Services in the Member States of the European Community: A Handbook of Information and Data* (Canterbury: European Institute of Social Services, University of Kent).

Langan, M. (1990) 'Community care in the 1990s: the community care White Paper: "Caring for People"', *Critical Social Policy*, issue 29, pp. 58–70.

Langlands, A. and Laming, H. (1993) *Implementing Caring for People*, EL(93)18 and CI(93)12 (London: Department of Health).

Lart, R. and Means, R. (1992a) 'User power', *Community Care*, 15 October, p. 15.

Lart, R. and Means, R. (1992b) 'To charge or not to charge?', *Community Care*, 17–24 December, p.21.

Laurie, L. (ed.) (1991) *Building Our Lives: Housing, Independent Living and Disabled People* (London: Shelter).

Law Commission (1993) *Mentally Incapacitated Adults and Other Vulnerable Adults: Public Law Protection*, Consultation Paper No. 130 (London: HMSO).

Le Grand, J. (1990) *Quasi-markets and Social Policy*, DQM Paper No. 1 (Bristol: School for Advanced Urban Studies).

Le Grand, J. (1992) 'Quasi-markets and community care', paper delivered at the Joseph Rowntree Foundation Symposium on *The Exchange of Experience Across Welfare Sectors*, University of Birmingham, November.

Le Grand, J. and Bartlett, W. (eds) (1993) *Quasi-Markets and Social Policy* (Basingstoke: Macmillan).

Leat, D. (1988) 'Residential care for younger physically disabled adults', pp. 199–239 in I. Sinclair (ed.), *Residential Care: The Research Reviewed*. (London: HMSO).

Leather, P. and Mackintosh, S. (1992) *Maintaining Home Ownership: The Agency Approach* (Coventry: Institute of Housing/Harlow: Longman).

Leedham, I. and Wistow, G. (1992) *Community Care and General Practitioners* (Leeds: Nuffield Institute for Health Services Studies, University of Leeds).

Leibfried, S. (1992) 'Europe's could-be social state: social policy in European integration after 1992', pp. 97–118 in W. J. Adams (ed.), *Singular Europe: Economy and Polity of the European Community after 1992* (Ann Arbor: University of Michigan Press).

Lipsky, M. (1980) *Street Level Bureaucracy* (New York: Russell Sage).

Lloyd, M. (1992) 'Does she boil eggs? Towards a feminist model of disability', *Disability, Handicap and Society*, vol. 7, no. 3, pp. 207–21.

Lonsdale, S. (1990) *Women and Disability: The Experience of Physical Disability Among Women* (Basingstoke: Macmillan).

Lowe, R. (1993) *The Welfare State in Britain Since 1945* (Basingstoke: Macmillan).

Lowther, C. and Williamson, J. (1966) 'Old people and their relatives', *Lancet*, 31 December, p.1460.

Lukes, S. (1974) *Power: A Radical View* (London: Macmillan).

Lyons, K. (1992) 'The mobile profession?', *Inside Community Care*, no. 913, 30 April, pp. ii–iii.

Mackintosh, S. and Leather, P. (1992) (eds) *Home Improvement Under the New Regime*, Occasional Paper 38 (Bristol: School for Advanced Urban Studies).

Mackintosh, S., Means, R. and Leather, P. (1990), *Housing in Later Life*, SAUS Study 4 (Bristol: School for Advanced Urban Studies).

Maclean, M. and Groves, D. (eds) (1991) *Women's Issues in Social Policy* (London: Routledge).

Maclean, U. (1989) *Dependent Territories: The Frail Elderly and Community Care* (London: The Nuffield Provincial Hospitals Trust).

Maclennan, D., Gibb, K. and More, A. (1990) *Paying for Britain's Housing* (York: Joseph Rowntree Foundation)

Macnicol, J. and Blaikie, A. (1989) 'The politics of retirement, 1908–1948', pp. 21–42, in M. Jefferys (ed.), *Growing Old in the Twentieth Century*. (London: Routledge).

Malin, N. (1987), 'Community care: principles and practice', pp. 1–61 in N. Malin (ed.), *Reassessing Community Care* (London: Croom Helm).

Malin, N., Race, D. and Jones, G. (1980) *Services for the Mentally Handicapped in Britain* (London: Croom Helm).

Malpass, P. (1993) 'Housing policy and the housing system since 1979', pp. 23–38 in P. Malpass and R. Means (eds), *Implementing Housing Policy* (Milton Keynes: Open University Press).

Malpass, P. and Means, R. (eds) (1993) *Implementing Housing Policy* (Milton Keynes: Open University Press).

Malpass, P. and Murie, A. (1990 edn) *Housing Policy and Practice* (Basingstoke: Macmillan).

Marchant, C. (1993) 'Out in the cold', *Community Care*, 27 May, pp. 24–5.

Martin, D. (1990), 'Getting it together', *The Health Services Journal*, 28 June, pp. 964–5.

Martin J., White, A. and Meltzer, H. (1989) *Disabled Adults: Services, Transport and Employment*, OPCS Surveys (London: HMSO).

Martin, J., Meltzer, H. and Elliot, D. (1988) *The Prevalence of Disability Among Adults*, OPCS Surveys (London: HMSO).

Martin, L. and Gaster, L. (1993) 'Community care planning in Wolverhampton', pp. 15–52 in R. Smith, L. Gaster, L. Harrison, L. Martin, R. Means and P. Thistlethwaite, *Working Together for Better Community Care* (Bristol: School for Advanced Urban Studies)

Martin, M. (1990) 'The development of residential care for elderly people 1890–1948', unpublished PhD, University of Bristol.

Martin, M. (1992) *The Manufacture and Mass Production of the Chronic Sick: A Historical Perspective*, paper delivered to the Annual Conference of the British Society of Gerontology, University of Kent, 18–20 September.

Matthews, O. (undated) *Housing the Infirm*, published by the author and originally distributed through W. H. Smith and Son.

McEwan, P. and Laverty, S. (1949) *The Chronic Sick and elderly in Hospital* (Bradford: Bradford (B) Hospital Management Committee).

McGrath, M. and Grant, G. (1992) 'Supporting "needs-led" services: implications for planning and management systems', *Journal of Social Policy*, vol. 21, part 1, pp. 71–98.

Meade, K. and Carter, T. (1990) 'Empowering older users: some starting points', pp. 19–28 in L. Winn (ed.), *Power to the People* (London: King's Fund Centre).

Means, R. (1986) 'The development of social services for elderly people: historical perspectives', pp. 87–108 in C. Phillipson and A. Walker (eds), *Ageing and Social Policy: A Critical Assessment* (Aldershot: Gower).

Means, R. (1987) 'Older people in British housing studies', *Housing Studies*, vol. 2, no. 2, pp. 82–98.

Means, R. (1988) 'Council housing, tenure polarisation and older people in two contrasting localities', *Ageing and Society*, vol. 8, part. 4, pp. 395–421.

Means, R. (1991) 'Community care, housing and older people: continuity and change', *Housing Studies*, vol. 6, no. 4, pp. 273–284.

Means, R. (1992) 'From the poor law to the marketplace', pp. 154–64 in C. Grant (ed.), *Built to Last?: Reflections on British Housing Policy* (London: Roof).

256   *References*

Means, R. (1993) 'Perspectives on implementation', pp. 4–22 in P. Malpass and R. Means (eds), *Implementing Housing Policy* (Milton Keynes: Open University Press).

Means, R. and Harrison, L. (1988) *Community Care: Before and After the Griffiths Report* (London: Association of London Authorities).

Means, R. and Harrison, L. (1990) *Housing: The Essential Element in Community Care* (Oxford: Anchor Housing Trust/SHAC).

Means, R. and Smith, R. (1985) *The Development of Welfare Services for Elderly People* (London: Croom Helm).

Means, R. and Smith, R. (1988) 'Implementing a pluralistic approach to evaluation in health education', *Policy and Politics*, vol. 16, no. 1, pp. 17–28.

Means, R., Harrison, L., Jeffers, S. and Smith, R. (1991) 'Coordination, collaboration and health promotion: lessons and issues from an alcohol education programme', *Health Promotion International*, vol. 6, no. 1, pp. 31–40.

Means, R., Smith, R., Harrison, L., Jeffers, S. and Doogan, K. (1990) *Understanding Alcohol: An Evaluation of an Educational Programme* (London: Health Education Authority).

Meehan, E. and Whitting, G. (eds) (1989) 'Gender and public policy: European law and British equal opportunity policies', special issue, *Policy and Politics*, vol. 17, no. 4.

Mental Health Foundation (1993) *Mental Illness: the Facts* (London: Mental Health Foundation).

Middleton, L. (1987) *So Much for So Few: A View of Sheltered Housing* (Liverpool: Liverpool University Press).

Miller, E. and Gwynne, G. (1972) *A Life Apart* (London: Tavistock).

Ministry of Health (1957), *Local Authority Services for the Chronic Sick and Infirm*, Circular 14/57 (London: HMSO).

Ministry of Health (1963) *Health and Welfare: The Development of Community Care* (London: HMSO).

Ministry of Health (1966) *Health and Welfare: The Development of Community Care – Revisions to 1975–76* (London: HMSO).

Ministry of Housing and Local Government (1969) *Housing Standards and Costs: Accommodation Specially Designed for Old People*, Circular 82/69 (London: HMSO).

Mishra, R. (1984) *The Welfare State in Crisis: Social Thought and Social Change* (Brighton: Wheatsheaf).

Mishra, R. (1990) *The Welfare State in Capitalist Society: Policies of Retrenchment and Maintenance in Europe, North America and Australia* (Hemel Hempstead: Harvester Wheatsheaf).

Modood, T. (1991) 'The Indian economic success: a challenge to some race relations assumptions', *Policy and Politics*, vol. 19, no. 3, pp. 171–90.

Moroney, R. (1976) *The Family and the State* (London: Longman).

Morris, C. (1940) 'Public health during the first three months of war', *Social Work* (London) January, pp. 186–96.

Morris, J. (1990a) 'Women and disability', *Social Work Today*, 8 November, p. 22.

Morris, J. (1990b) *Our Homes, Our Rights: Housing, Independent Living and Physically Disabled People* (London: Shelter).

Morris, J. (1991) *Pride Against Prejudice: Transforming Attitudes to Disability* (London: The Women's Press).

Morris, J. (1993) *Community Care or Independent Living* (York: Joseph Rowntree Foundation/London: Community Care).

Morris, P. (1969) *Put Away: A Sociological Study of Institutions for the Mentally Retarded* (London: Routledge & Kegan Paul).

Munday, B. (ed.) (1989) *The Crisis in Welfare: An International Perspective on Social Services and Social Work* (Hemel Hempstead: Harvester Wheatsheaf).

Murphy, E. (1991) *After the Asylums: Community Care for People with Mental Illness* (London: Faber & Faber).

Neill, J. and Williams, J. (1992) *Leaving Hospital: Elderly People and their Discharge to Community Care* (London: HMSO).

Nicoll, W. and Salmon, T. (1990) *Understanding the European Communities* (London: Philip Allan).

Niner, P. (1989) *Housing Needs in the 1990s: An Interim Assessment*, National Housing Forum (London: National Federation of Housing Associations).

Nixon, J. (1993) 'Implementation in the hands of senior managers: community care in Britain', pp. 197–216 in M. Hill (ed.), *New Agendas in the Study of the Policy Process* (Hemel Hempstead: Harvester Wheatsheaf).

Nuffield Provincial Hospitals Trust (1946) *The Hospital Surveys: The Domesday Book of the Hospital Services* (Oxford: Oxford University Press).

Nugent, N. (1989) *The Government and Politics of the European Community* (Basingstoke: Macmillan).

Office for Public Management (1992a) *Initatives in User and Carer Involvement – A Survey of Local Authorities* (London: Office for Public Management).

Office for Public Management (1992b), *Assessment of the Housing Require-ments of People with Special Needs over the Next Decade* (London: National Federation of Housing Associations).

Oldman, C. (1988) 'More than bricks and mortar', *Housing*, June/July, pp. 13–14.

Oldman, C. (1990) *Moving in Old Age* (London: HMSO).

Oldman, C. (1991) *Paying for Care: Personal Sources of Funding Care* (York: Joseph Rowntree Foundation).

Oliver, M. (1990) *The Politics of Disablement* (Basingstoke: Macmillan).

Osborn, A. (1991) *Taking Part in Community Care Planning* (Leeds: Nuffield Institute for Health Services Studies).

Osborne, S. and Rees, L. (1992) 'Managing the transition to community care: an exploratory study of six local authorities in England', *Research, Policy and Planning*, vol. 10, no. 1, pp. 6–9.

Ovretveit, J. (1993) *Co-ordinating Community Care: Multidisciplinary Teams and Care Management* (Buckingham: Open University Press).

Pahl, R. (1984) *Divisions of Labour* (Oxford: Blackwell).

Parker, J. (1965) *Local Health and Welfare Services* (London: Allen & Unwin).

Parker, R. (1988) 'An historical background', pp. 1–38 in I. Sinclair (ed.), *Residential Care: The Research Reviewed* (London: HMSO).

Parker, R. (1990) 'Care and the private sector', pp. 293–361 in I. Sinclair, R. Parker, D. Leat and J. Williams, *The Kaleidoscope of Care* (London: HMSO).

Parton, N. (1983) *The Politics of Child Abuse* (Basingstoke: Macmillan).

Pascall, G. (1986) *Social Policy – A Feminist Analysis* (London: Tavistock).

Peace, S. (1986) 'The forgotten female: social policy and the older women', pp. 61–86 in C. Phillipson and A. Walker (eds), *Ageing and Social Policy: A Critical Assessment* (Aldershot: Gower).

Perring, C., Twigg, J. and Atkin, K. (1990) *Families Caring for People Diagnosed as Mentally Ill: the Literature Reviewed* (London: HMSO).

Petch, A. (1992) *At Home in the Community* (Aldershot: Avebury).

Peters, T. and Waterman, R. (1982) *In Search of Excellence* (New York: Harper & Row).

Phillipson, C. (1982) *Capitalism and the Construction of Old Age* (Basingstoke: Macmillan).

Pierson, C. (1991) *Beyond the Welfare State?* (Oxford: Polity Press).

Plant, R. (1992) 'Citizenship, rights and welfare', pp. 15–30 in A. Coote (ed.), *The Welfare of Citizens: Developing New Social Rights* (London: IPPR/ Rivers Oram Press).

Potter, P. and Zill, G. (1992) 'Older households and their housing situation', pp. 109–131 in L. Davies (ed.), *The Coming of Age in Europe: Older People in the European Community* (London: Age Concern England (ACE) Books).

Power, A. (1987) *Property before People* (London: Allen & Unwin).

Pressman, J. and Wildavsky, A. (1973) *Implementation* (Berkeley: University of California Press).

Price Waterhouse/Department of Health (1991) *Implementing Community Care: Purchaser, Commissioner and Provider Roles* (London: HMSO).

Pritchard, J. (1992) *The Abuse of Elderly People* (London: Jessica Kingsley).

Race, D. (1987) 'Normalisation: theory and practice', pp. 62–79 in N. Malin (ed.), *Reassessing Community Care* (London: Croom Helm).

Ramon, S. (1991) 'Principles and conceptual knowledge', pp. 6–34 in S. Ramon (ed.), *Beyond Community Care: Normalisation and Integration Work* (London: Macmillan).

Ramon, S. and Giannichedda, M. G. (eds.) (1991) *Psychiatry in Transition: The British and Italian Experience*, 2nd edn (London: Pluto Press).

Randolph, B. (1993) 'The re-privatisation of housing associations', pp. 39–58 in P. Malpass and R. Means (eds), *Implementing Housing Policy* (Milton Keynes: Open University Press).

Renshaw, J., Hampson, R., Thomason, C., Darton, R., Judge, K. and Knapp, M. (1988) *Care in the Community: The First Steps* (Aldershot: Gower).

Report of the Mental Deficiency Committee (1929) *Part III – The Adult Defective* (London: HMSO).

Robb, B. (1967) *Sans Everything: A Case to Answer* (London: Nelson).

Roberts, G. (1992) 'Legal aspects of community care', paper delivered to the Law Society Conference on *Community Care: A Challenge to the Legal Profession*, 20 November.

Roberts, N. (1970) *Our Future Selves* (London: Allen & Unwin).

Roberts, P., Hart, T. and Thomas, K. (1993) *Europe: A Handbook for Local Authorities* (Manchester: Centre for Local Economic Strategies).

Roebuck, J. (1979) 'When does old age begin? The evolution of the English definition', *Journal of Social History*, vol. 12, no. 3, pp. 416–428.

Room, G. (1991) 'Towards a European welfare state?', pp. 1–14 in G. Room (ed.), *Towards a European Welfare State?* SAUS Study 6 (Bristol: School for Advanced Urban Studies).

Rossell, T. and Rimbau, C. (1989) 'Spain – social services in the post-Franco democracy' pp. 105–23 in B. Munday (ed.), *The Crisis in Welfare: An International Perspective on Social Services and Social Work* (Hemel Hempstead: Harvester Wheatsheaf).

Rowe Report (1992) *Housing – A Question of Influence* (London: Royal Association for Disability and Rehabilitation).

Rowlings, C. (1981) *Social Work with Elderly People* (London: Allen & Unwin).

Rowntree Report (1980 ed) *Old People: Report of a Survey Committee on the Problems of Ageing and the Care of Old People* (New York: Arno Press).

Rudd, T. (1958) 'Basic problems in the social welfare of the elderly', *The Almoner*, vol. 10, no. 10, pp. 348–9.

Ryan, J. with Thomas, F. (1980) *The Politics of Mental Handicap* (Harmondsworth: Penguin).

St Helens Metropolitan Borough Council Personal Services Department (1992) *Community Care Plan* (St Helens: The Council)

Samson, E. (1944) *Old Age in the New World* (London: Pilot Press).

Saunders, P. (1990) *A Nation of Home Owners* (London: Unwin Hyman).

Scull, A. (1977) *Decarceration: Community Treatment and the Deviant: A Radical View* (Englewood Cliffs: Prentice-Hall).

Scull, A. (1979) *Museums of Madness: The Social Organisation of Insanity in Nineteenth Century England* (London: Allen Lane).

Seebohm Report (1968) *Report of the Committee on Local Authority and Allied Personal Services* (London: HMSO).

Shanas, E., Townsend, P., Wedderburn, D., Friis, H., Milhof, P. and Stehouwer, J. (1968) *Old People in Three Industrialised Societies* (London: Routledge & Kegan Paul).

Shanks, N. and Smith, S. (1992) 'Public policy and the health of homeless people', *Policy and Politics*, vol. 20, no. 1, pp. 35–46.

Sheldon, J. (1948) *The Social Medicine of Old Age* (London: Oxford University Press).

Sinclair, I. (1988) 'Residential care for elderly people', pp. 243–91 in I. Sinclair (ed.), *Residential Care: the Research Reviewed* (London: HMSO).

Slack, K. (1960) *Councils, Committees and Concern for the Old* (London: Codicote Press).

Smith, D. (1992) 'Taking the lead', *Housing*, May, pp. 9–11.

Smith, G. and Cantley, C. (1985) *Assessing Health Care: A Study in Organisational Understanding* (Milton Keynes: Open University Press).

Smith, R., Gaster, L., Harrison, L., Martin, L., Means R. and Thistlethwaite, P. (1993) *Working Together for Better Community Care*, SAUS Study No. 7 (Bristol: School for Advanced Urban Studies).

Social Services Committee (1985) *Second Report: Community Care*, House of Commons Paper 13–1, Session 1984–85 (London: HMSO).

Steinfield, E. (1981) 'The place of old age: the meaning of housing for old people', pp. 198–246 in J. Duncan (ed.), *Housing and Identity: Cross Cultural Perspectives* (London: Croom Helm).

Stevenson, O. and Parsloe, P. (1993) *Community Care and Empowerment* (York: Joseph Rowntree Foundation/London: Community Care).

Sumner, G. and Smith, R. (1969) *Planning Local Authority Services for the Elderly* (London: Allen & Unwin).

Swithinbank. A. (1991) *Audit of the Implications of Greater European Integration for Kent Social Services* (Maidstone: Social Services Department, Kent County Council).

Taylor, M. (1992) 'The changing role of the non profit sector in Britain: moving towards the market', pp. 147–75 in B. Gidron, R. Kramer and L. Salamon (eds), *Government and the Non profit Sector in Comparative Perspective* (San Francisco: Jossey Bass).

Taylor, M., Hoyes, L., Lart, R. and Means, R. (1992) *User Empowerment in Community Care: Unravelling the Issues*, DQM Paper No. 11 (Bristol: School for Advanced Urban Studies).

Taylor-Gooby, P. (1991) *Social Change, Social Welfare and Social Science* (Hemel Hempstead: Harvester Wheatsheaf).

Thane, P. (1982) *Foundations of the Welfare State* (London: Longman).

Thomas, F. (1980) 'Everyday Life on the Ward', pp. 30–46 in J. Ryan with F. Thomas (eds), *The Politics of Mental Handicap* (Harmondsworth: Penguin).

Thompson, A. (1949) 'Problems of ageing and chronic sickness', *British Medical Journal*, 30 July, pp. 250–251.

Titmuss, R. (1968) *Commitment to Welfare* (London: Allen & Unwin).

Titmuss, R. (1971) 'Welfare "rights", law and discretion', *Political Quarterly*, vol. 42, no. 2, pp. 113–32.

Titmuss, R. (1976 edn) *Problems of Social Policy* (London: HMSO).

Tomlinson, D. (1991) *Utopia, Community Care and the Retreat from the Asylums* (Milton Keynes: Open University Press).

Took, M. (1992) *User and Carer Involvement in Care Services* (Southampton: National Schizophrenia Fellowship).

Took, M., Stacey, J., Shackleton, A. and Lart, R. (1993) *Users, Carers and Professionals: Towards a Dialogue in Community Care* (Bristol: School for Advanced Urban Studies).

Topliss, E. (1979) *Provision for the Disabled* (Oxford: Basil Blackwell).

Townsend, P. (1963 edn) *The Family Life of Old People*, Harmondsworth: Penguin.

Townsend, P. (1964 edn) *The Last Refuge: A Survey of Residential Institutions and Homes for the Aged in England and Wales* (London: Routledge & Kegan Paul).

Townsend, P. (1981) 'The structured dependency of the elderly: the creation of social policy in the twentieth century?', *Ageing and Society*, vol. 1, no. 1, pp. 5–28.

Townsend, P. (1986) 'Ageism and social policy', pp. 15–44 in C. Phillipson and A. Walker (eds), *Ageing and Social Policy: A Critical Assessment* (Aldershot: Gower).

Tredgold, A. (1952) *A Textbook on Mental Deficiency (Amentia)*, 8th edn (London: Bailliere, Tindall & Cox).

Tudor, K. (1989) 'The politics of disability in Italy: La Lega per il Diritto al Lavoro degli Handicappati', *Critical Social Policy*, issue 25, pp. 37–55.

Twigg, J., Atkin, K. and Perring, C. (1990) *Carers and Services: A Review of Research* (London: HMSO).

Ungerson, C. (1992) *Payment for Caring – Mapping a Territory*, paper delivered to the Social Policy Association Annual Conference, University of Nottingham, July.

United Kingdom Central Council for Nursing, Midwifery and Health Visiting (1987) *Project 2000: The Final Proposals*, Project Paper 9, February (London: UKCC).

Wade, B., Sawyer, L. and Bell, J. (1983) *Dependency with Dignity: Different Care Provision for the Elderly* (London: Bedford Square Press).

Wagner Report (1988) *Residential Care: A Positive Choice* (London: HMSO).

Walker, A. (1982) 'The meaning and social division of community care, pp. 13–39 in A. Walker (ed.), *Community Care: the Family, the State and Social Policy* (Oxford: Martin Robertson).

Walker, A. (1986) 'Pensions and the production of poverty in old age', pp. 184–216 in C. Phillipson and A. Walker (eds), *Ageing and Social Policy: A Critical Assessment* (Aldershot: Gower).

Walker, A. (1989) 'Community care', pp. 203–24 in M. McCarthy (ed.), *The New Politics of Welfare: An Agenda for the 1990s* (Basingstoke: Macmillan).

Walker, A. (1992) 'Integration, social policy and elderly citizens: towards a European agenda on ageing?', *Generations Review*, vol. 2, no. 4, pp. 2–8.

Ward, L. (1985), 'Training staff for "an ordinary life": experiences in a community service in South Bristol', *British Journal of Mental Subnormality*, vol. XXXII, part 2, no. 61, pp. 94–102.

Warner, N. (1992) 'Housing discontent', *Community Care*, 4 June, pp. 19–21.

Watson, L and Cooper, R. (1992) *Housing with Care* (York: Joseph Rowntree Foundation).

Webb, A. (1991), 'Coordination, a problem in public sector management', *Policy and Politics*, vol. 19, no. 4, pp. 29–42.

Welsh Office (1993) *Local Government in Wales: A Charter for the Future* (Cardiff: HMSO).

Wertheimer, A. (1990) 'Users speak out', *Community Care*, 28 June, pp. 26–27.

Wheeler, R. (1988) 'Housing policy and elderly people', pp. 217–76 in C. Phillipson and A. Walker (eds), *Ageing and Social Policy: A Critical Assessment* (Aldershot: Gower).

Willcocks, D., Peace, S. and Kellaher, L. (1987) *Private Lives in Public Places* (London: Tavistock).

Williams, G. (1990), *The Experience of Housing in Retirement* (Aldershot: Avebury).

Williams, R. (1976) *Keywords* (Glasgow: Fontana).

Wilson, E. (1977) *Women and the Welfare State* (London: Tavistock).

Wilson, G. (1991) 'Models of ageing and their relation to policy formation and service provision', *Policy and Politics*, vol. 19, no. 1, pp. 37–47.

Wistow, G., Knapp, M., Hardy, B. and Allen, C. (1992) 'From providing to enabling: local authorities and the mixed economy of social care', *Public Administration*, vol. 70, no. 1, pp. 25–46.

Wolfensberger, W. and Thomas, S. (1983) *Program Analysis of Service Systems' Implementations of Normalisation Goals (PASSING): A Method of Evaluat-*

ing the Quality of Human Services according to the Principles of Normalisation, Normalisation Criteria and Ratings Manual, 2nd edn (Toronto: National Institute on Mental Retardation).

Working Group on Joint Planning (1985) *Progress in Partnership* (London: Department of Health and Social Security).

Ziomas, D. (1991) *The Elderly in Greece: A Review of their Current Situation with reference to Economic and Social Policies*, Athens, March (submission to the EC Observatory on Older People).

Index